Game-Changing Leadership in Action

Game-Changing Leadership in Action invites school and systems leaders to engage in a personalized professional learning approach to advance the collective pursuit of educational progress. Throughout this practical resource, you're encouraged to reimagine and redesign your schools and districts for long-term sustainability and success. This inquiry-based, transformational leadership approach delves into three key domains – personal, environmental, and institutional – in order to help leaders hone necessary skills and mindsets to tackle today's leadership challenges. The five sets of modules in this practical book provide you with real-life lessons, problem-solving activities, collaboration opportunities, and hands-on exercises that will amplify your impact within your own sphere of influence. You will engage with practical tools and resources to help rewrite the rules of engagement for the students, families, and staff you serve. Your move!

Kim Wallace is an Educational Consultant with over 30 years of experience as a teacher, principal, superintendent, and university administrator.

Also Available from Routledge Eye on Education
(www.routledge.com/eyeoneducation)

*How to Have Difficult Conversations as an Educational Leader:
Self-Reflections and Strategies for Success*
Patty Corum

*The Respected School Leader: Developing your Character Traits
and Transformational Leadership Skills*
Howard J. Bultinck, Lynn H. Bush, Noreen A. Powers

*The International Education Leadership Companion: Lessons
and Best Practices from Expert Leaders*
Lindsay Prendergast, Catarina Song Chen, Colin Brown

*Leadership Teams in America's Best Schools: Improving the
Lives of All Students*
Joseph F. Johnson, Jr., Cynthia L. Uline, Stanley J. Munro, Jr., Francisco Escobedo

*Making Community Schools a Reality: Harnessing Your Power
as a School Leader through Collaboration*
Emily L. Woods

*Wholehearted School Leadership: Rewiring our Schools for
Courage, Justice, Learning, and Connection*
Kathryn Fishman-Weaver

Data Analysis for Continuous School Improvement, 5th Edition
Victoria L. Bernhardt

*Culturally Conscious Decision-Making for School Leaders: A
Toolkit for Creating a More Equitable School Culture*
Shauna McGee

*Teacher Leadership Practice in High-Performing Schools: A
Blueprint for Excellence*
Jeremy D. Visone

Game–Changing Leadership in Action: An Educator's Companion
Kim Wallace

Game-Changing Leadership in Action

An Educator's Companion

Kim Wallace

NEW YORK AND LONDON

Designed cover image: Getty Images

First published 2026
by Routledge
605 Third Avenue, New York, NY 10158

and by Routledge
4 Park Square, Milton Park, Abingdon, Oxon, OX14 4RN

Routledge is an imprint of the Taylor & Francis Group, an informa business

© 2026 Kim Wallace

The right of Kim Wallace to be identified as author of this work has been asserted in accordance with sections 77 and 78 of the Copyright, Designs and Patents Act 1988.

All rights reserved. The purchase of this copyright material confers the right on the purchasing institution to photocopy or download pages which bear the support material icon and a copyright line at the bottom of the page. No other parts of this book may be reprinted or reproduced or utilised in any form or by any electronic, mechanical, or other means, now known or hereafter invented, including photocopying and recording, or in any information storage or retrieval system, without permission in writing from the publishers.

Trademark notice: Product or corporate names may be trademarks or registered trademarks, and are used only for identification and explanation without intent to infringe.

ISBN: 978-1-041-10305-9 (hbk)
ISBN: 978-1-041-10304-2 (pbk)
ISBN: 978-1-003-65441-4 (ebk)

DOI: 10.4324/9781003654414

Access the Support Material: www.routledge.com/9781041103042

Typeset in Warnock Pro
by SPi Technologies India Pvt Ltd (Straive)

To my wife, Marilyn, who unconditionally supports my work as a writer, keeps me humble as a leader, and makes me a much better human being. And to my boon companion, Stella, the best dog of all dogs ever.

Contents

Meet the Author	*ix*
Preface	*x*
Online Support Materials	*xvii*

Introduction   1

Introduction	1
Breaking it Down	6
Engagement Mindsets	9
References	10

▶ Module 1 Exploration of Self   11

Introduction	11
Foundations	13
Branding, Planning & Preparing for Promotion	20
Role Transitions	24
The Six Ps of Promotion	28
Motivators and Activators	36
Module 1 Exercises	39
Conclusion	48
References	49

▶ Module 2 Mobilizing Support   51

Introduction	51
Foundations	53
Team Roles, Functions, and Responsibilities	62
Mobilization	74
Theoretical Paradigms	77
Leadership vs. Management	81
Module 2 Exercises	91
Conclusion	100
References	101

▶ Module 3 Analysis of Setting   104

Introduction	104
Foundations	106

Geographical Locale	111
Universal Design for Learning (UDL) Spaces	140
Module 3 Exercises	145
Conclusion	156
Note	156
References	157

▶ Module 4 Awareness of Surroundings — 160

Introduction	160
Foundations	161
Geographic Locale: Deeper Dive	165
Wide-Angled Lens: Leading in Rural, Urban, and Suburban Schools	171
Place-Based Educational Opportunities	187
Expanded Leading and Learning Partnership with Community	188
Module 4 Exercises	197
Conclusion	208
References	209

▶ Module 5 Leveraging Structures & Navigating Systems — 213

Introduction	213
Foundations	214
Systems Thinking for Schools of the Future	218
Tenacious Tensions	223
Making the Invisible Visible	229
Practices Promoting Inclusion	235
Cultivating Successful Systems	239
Module 5 Exercises	248
Conclusion	255
Notes	256
References	257

Conclusion: Strategies for Sustenance — 261

Introduction	261
Care and Feeding	263
Game–Changing Leadership in Action	269
Concluding Exercises	274
Conclusion	279
References	280

Meet the Author

Born and raised in an educator-filled household, Dr. Kim Wallace started her own career in public education 30 years ago as a high school English and history teacher before becoming a site principal and district office administrator. Her most recent K-12 role was as superintendent of one of the 20 largest school districts in California. In 2020, Kim joined the University of California Berkeley School of Education Leadership Programs division as the Associate Director of the 21st Century California School Leadership Academy (21CSLA) State Center. She also runs her own consulting company, Process Makes Perfect, specializing in real-world solutions for practitioners in the field. Kim consults, writes, and presents internationally on systems change and emerging trends in educational leadership. An award-winning, innovative educator, Kim leverages her abilities in educational administration, program management, and relationship development to optimize institutional effectiveness and deliver remarkable results. Dr. Wallace's first leadership book, *Leading the Launch: A Ten-Stage Process for Successful School District Initiatives*, was published by Solution Tree Press in 2021, followed by *Leading Through an Equity Lens* in 2023. Kim attended the University of California Santa Barbara as a history major, earned her Master's in Education (M.Ed.) at the University of California Los Angeles followed by a Doctorate in Education (Ed.D.) from the University of California Davis.

Preface

Like many people around the globe, I grew up playing games with my family. Though I grew up near the advent of Atari and Nintendo in the late 1970s, we mainly played board games and worked jigsaw puzzles around the kitchen table. *Uno. Monopoly. Chutes and Ladders. Operation. Battleship.* The games cupboard was a treasure trove. At school, even more games awaited. Remember those rainy-day indoor activities that teachers relied on like Heads Up Seven Up and I Spy (with my little eye) when it was too wet to venture outside? In all other conditions, kids played freeze tag, red rover, hopscotch, tetherball, and capture the flag. Just visit any elementary school at recess or lunch time, and you'll still see much of the same. Running, skipping, falling down, picking up, chasing, and jumping. But close your eyes and listen, too. Shrieks, shouts, laughter, squabbles, and other emotional outbursts permeate the air. That's the spirit of play and discovery I'm inviting you to tap into and hold close as you read on.

Gaming has been around as long as people have been alive. Early games were rudimentary by our standards but have entertained denizens for time immemorial. People continue to play versions of cards, dice, and street games invented long ago in places such as India, China, Italy, England, and Persia. Games are powerful instructors. They help us plan ahead, make calculated risks, cooperate and use teamwork, enhance language and communication skills, practice math facts, develop hand-eye coordination, and accept the fact that failure is an essential part of the learning process. Whether you lean toward casual game apps, real-time strategy games, or multiplayer video games or engage in physical athletic interactions on the court or field, the path toward mastery is happening at every turn. You are learning through exploration without even knowing it.

We also play games to simply connect with one another. Games spark joy, promote socialization, and offer shared cognitive amusement. From an abandoned lot to a snowy hill or a grassy field to a neighborhood scavenger hunt, play is not bound to any location other than one's own creative hands and mind. Games help us escape from the troubles of reality, but they often mirror our existence as well. Every day, people big and small engage with allies and opponents and seek to overcome challenges in the pursuit of success. Games teach us lessons, bolster relationships, and generate new capabilities.

The Game Maker for *The New York Times*, Sam Von Ehren, explores all of the above suppositions in an opinion piece called "Why Do People Love Games?" (June 11, 2020):

> Imagine a circle drawn in chalk on a sidewalk. When we are inside the chalk we are "playing" the game. We'll only do what the rules of the game allow. We will try to win. When the game ends, we leave the circle and return to normal. The magic circle is what separates a game from reality. I use the metaphor of a chalk line because the magic circle is not an absolute barrier or even a physical one. We can enter and exit the magic circle freely. We bring our bodies, personalities, and life experiences into the game. We take the memories and experience of the game with us when we leave. The chalk line casts a spell on that space of sidewalk and turns it into a space for playing...When we enter the magic circle, we give ourselves permission to explore, to fail, to lose.
>
> (p. 1)

By engaging in this leadership series, I'm asking you to join me outside of the magic circle. And here's why.

Throughout planet earth, each of us exists as a metaphorical game piece or pawn. As defenseless infants, humans emerge into distinct environments, climates, and zeitgeists; likewise, humans join families of diverse races, religions, cultures, linguistics, and socio-economic statuses. Historically, the birth lottery has had an undeniable impact on one's survival. It has determined individual outcomes for millennia. Life expectancy rates, earning potential, access to health care, socio-economic mobility, job opportunities, and exposure to trauma impact demographics and populations disproportionately, often depending upon where one's life begins. The one game–changer to level the playing field? Educational access and opportunity.

I believe that the greatest power we can harness to elevate both individuals and our society is a laser-focused commitment to a high-quality education for every single one of us, at all ages and life stages. I am also certain that we, as school and systems leaders, already possess the limitless and requisite intellect, talent, drive, passion, and creativity needed to help our institutions better reflect the 21st-century realities within which our students can flourish. What we need to concentrate on is dislodging previous mindsets about what public education is (and has been) as the only way forward and then align our actions to intentions. It is within our scope to rewire the infrastructure, code the conditions, and reframe our system to serve a singular focus: *learning and learners* by creating authentic learning experiences as the vehicle to grow healthy and fulfilled human beings. Many pockets of innovation out there show us that it's possible. So how do we move from pockets to prevalence and from possible to presumable? I submit that we must rewrite the rules of school through game–changing leadership.

We can transform the education system if enough of us decide to. *If enough of us decide to.* It's a numbers game; democracy at its core. Enough. And it's a conscious choice. Decide. Whether we topple it by force, chip away at it, or assist in its erosion, we made this thing, and we have consented and colluded to keeping it alive since the Industrial Revolution. Here's the charge: Calling all Game–changers to unite for the next revolution. It's high time we channeled our consolidated energy to alter the course and character of public education going forward. It won't be easy, but it will be worth it.

▶ THE GAME PLAN

My first two books with Solution Tree Press, *Leading the Launch* (2021) and *Leading Through an Equity Lens* (2023), are practitioner guides that assist leaders in implementing overarching, as well as equity-centered, initiatives into their organizations via a ten-stage field-tested process. Based on my own experiences in diverse TK-12 roles, the books spell out concrete and proven approaches to mitigate initiative overload and maximize educational outcomes. After facilitating workshops all over the country, I've come to grasp that transformation on the personal, environmental, and institutional levels takes more than a ten-step protocol can offer (though it was never intended to). That's why I'm embarking on this third leadership framework, which takes a holistic view of leadership growth and development that attends to the person behind the profession.

Utilizing research, employing professional expertise, and tapping my own personal involvement in this work for nearly three decades, the forthcoming set professional learning modules will help you discover how leadership in action can fortify our pursuit of a quality education for all and (re)invigorate our schools and districts for the long term. Throughout the lessons, you will engage with the three domains of the game–changers framework – inter/personal, environmental, and institutional – to develop skills and mindsets needed to tackle today's most challenging leadership dilemmas. Drawing from a variety of sources, the modules present real-life lessons, problem-solving activities, collaboration opportunities, and hands-on exercises that intend to amplify each leader's impact within their own sphere of influence. You will engage with practical tools and resources to help you rewrite the rules of engagement for the students, families, and staff you serve.

These learning modules are geared toward leaders at all levels and capacities, including certificated and classified administrators and managers who play diverse and contributive roles at the site, district, county/region, state, or national level. The activities are adaptable and applicable to any stage of your leadership development. There is something here for everyone, from aspiring leaders in prep programs to seasoned administrators. Some parts may resonate particularly well at this point in your career, and others may feel right later on. The contents are intended to strengthen your sense of self, expand your circle of supporters, immerse you in your setting and surroundings, and equip you to take charge of your systems and structures. This is game–changing leadership at its core.

As you work your way through this book, you will

1. Actively engage with the game–changers leadership domain topics: self and support; setting and surroundings; and structures and systems.
2. Learn how collective leadership in action can elevate and enhance the lived experiences of students, staff, and families in your community.
3. Discover ways to build a collaborative network of support to sustain momentum, morale, and professional well-being for the long term.
4. Craft plans of action to implement protocols, programs, or policies with integrity.

▶ MODULES OVERVIEW AND COMPONENTS

Game–changers seek to understand themselves in order to efficaciously serve others. Thus, the first of the five sets of professional learning modules begins with the fundamentals: a self-examination of your leadership identity and how you interact with groups and individuals in the organization. In Modules 1 and 2, you'll explore your core beliefs, how others experience your executive style, what drives as well as drains you, and ways to seek out and offer the right kinds of support at the right time.

The second set of modules are context-based and designed to give you tools for analyzing and interpreting influential aspects of your setting and surroundings. You'll engage in activities to expand your perspectives and insights into the school and greater community and responsively meet their needs throughout Modules 3 and 4. Exercises include auditing your campus, interrogating your data, and investigating the assets within your immediate region.

The final module widens the scope to the organizational and institutional constructs you regularly encounter and encourages you to question and scrutinize ways that your current systems and structures may be out of sync with the educational experiences you desire for your students, families, and staff. The lessons in Module 5 offer strategies for initiating programmatic and constitutional changes to the ways your school or district functions, and the emphasis is on humanizing our institutions by elevating diverse voices and maximizing agency.

The concluding chapter wraps up the content from the first five modules – exploration of self, mobilizing support, analysis of setting, awareness of surroundings, leveraging structures, and navigating systems – and presents leaders with a comprehensive view of their role as well as how to sustain momentum for the long run. The book closes with a few final ingredients to add to your personalized recipe for game–changing leadership.

Each module is organized similarly, beginning with a theoretical framework and relevant research that furnishes a foundation for the topic at the center of the learning activities that follow. You will also be presented with practical job-embedded examples, case studies, or scenarios that illustrate how the module's focus may look or feel in a variety of TK-12-serving organizations. Embedded within each module are several action learning exercises to ground you in the material and develop your leadership capacities within each of the three domains of the Game–Changing Leadership in Action framework. Many of the over 30 reproducible resources in the book are also included as downloadable activities for individual or teams and will be marked with a special icon to signify a digitally available version.

While there is a distinct rhyme and reason to the order in which they are organized – beginning from the inside and working your way out – there's no harm done in picking and choosing what you want to focus on at any given time. We'll start with exploration of identity, then situate ourselves in our habitats, and end with maneuvering through our organizations. As a composite, the modules are designed to create coherence, deepen understanding, and spark creativity – all of which make your leadership path forward more sustainable and reinforced at critical junctures in your personal and professional development.

Ready Player One? It's your move!

References

Von Ehren, S. (June 11, 2020). Why Do People Love Games? The Game Maker for The New York Times (Yes! There is a Game Maker) explains. Accessed on April 4, 2025 from https://www.nytimes.com/2020/06/11/style/why-people-love-games.html?smid=url-share

Wallace, K. (2021). *Leading the launch: A ten-stage process for successful district initiatives.* Bloomington, IN: Solution Tree Press.

Wallace, K. (2023). *Leading Through an Equity Lens.* Bloomington, IN: Solution Tree Press.

Online Support Materials

Some of the resources in this book can be accessed online by visiting this book's product page on our website: www.routledge.com/9781041103042 (then follow the links indicating support material, which you can then download directly).

Module 1:	Exploration of Self	11
Exercise 1.1	Assessing Your Self-Efficacy	40
Exercise 1.2	Through the Looking Glass	43
Exercise 1.3	Cultivating Your Brand	45
Exercise 1.4	Transition Planning	47
Module 2:	**Mobilizing Support**	**51**
Exercise 2.1	Leader Belief Questionnaire	92
Exercise 2.2	Teaming Up	94
Exercise 2.3	Mobilizing Leadership	96
Exercise 2.4	Multiplier Effects	97
Module 3:	**Analysis of Setting**	**104**
Exercise 3.3	Climate Checklist	148
Exercise 3.4	Data Equity Walk	149
Exercise 3.5	Cross-Observational Exchange	152
Exercise 3.6	Universal Design Principles Application	154
Module 4:	**Awareness of Surroundings**	**160**
Exercise 4.1	Control, Influence, and Concerns Schematic	198
Exercise 4.2	Nested Layers of Environmental Surroundings	199
Exercise 4.3	Rural, Suburban, and Urban Launching Pads	201
Exercise 4.5	Reciprocal Leading and Learning Partnerships	205
Module 5:	**Leveraging Structures & Navigating Systems**	**213**
Exercise 5.1	Systems Thinking Conditioning	249
Exercise 5.2	Root Cause Analysis Fishbone Diagram	250
Exercise 5.3	Making the Invisible Visible	251
Exercise 5.4	Infrastructure Investigation	252

Conclusion:	**Strategies for Sustenance**	261
Exercise C.1	Roll Call	275
Exercise C.2	Fifteen Fundamentals	276
Exercise C.3	Game–Changing Leadership in Action	277
Exercise C.4	In the Arena	278

Introduction

▶ **INTRODUCTION**

Educators are a special breed. Unlike other adult mammals, people of our ilk remain in school long after it's required. As a profession, we tend to be imbued with the rare quality of wholly investing ourselves in future outcomes with little expectation for personal benefit or gain. We willingly, purposely, and voluntarily nurture the academic, social, emotional, behavioral, and civic growth of thousands of other people's children for years, decades, or throughout lifelong careers. Every day we show up on site to teach, counsel, coach, inspire, instruct, and enlighten our community's children. To the young people under our *in loco parentis* care, we serve as role models, mentors, and guides through an increasingly complex world. The metaphorical game of life is full of twists and turns, chance and opportunity, and skills and mastery – so the pathbreakers, trailblazers, and changemakers among us play an essential role in launching each new generation off onto their own ventures.

Whether you chose educational leadership, or it chose you, thank you for answering the call! Our kids need you. Society does, too. Now more than ever.

Though you may already be a leader in title or not quite yet, it's critical to remember that you are still a student and will remain a teacher throughout your professional advancement. Learning, teaching, and leading naturally go hand in hand. Whether you are a teacher-leader aspiring for your first management position, a rookie administrator in a new role, or a seasoned practitioner at the site or district level, learning the ropes can be tricky (and mastering them, an ongoing endeavor). The study Leader Development Across the Lifespan by Zhengguang Liu et al. (2021) suggests that learning experiences spanning early childhood through adulthood all contribute to one's formation as a leader. They also cite prior research that purports:

> The importance of on-the-job experiences can be reflected by the well-known (but non-validated) 70/20/10 rule: the notion that 70% of leader development comes from on-the-job experiences, 20% from developmental relationships and 10% from formal programs
>
> (Day & Thornton, 2018) (p. 1).

That means 90% of our professional learning is acquired through osmosis, trial and error, and job-embedded mastery. And the opportunities for growth – often earned by making ample mistakes – are in endless supply. Unspoken rules. Power dynamics. Politics and diplomacy. Institutional knowledge. Past practice. Culture and conventions. These are just a few of the intricacies that TK-12 leaders must successfully navigate out on the educational playing field today. Luckily, there is wisdom in experience, and the Game–Changing Leadership framework modules that follow will be your personal coach (and cheerleader) along the way.

Kathy L. Guthrie and Daniel M. Jenkins observe in their 2018 book, *The Role of Leadership Educators*, "*Leaders* are the individuals, with or without formal positions of authority, who work collectively to tackle social problems. *Leadership* is the collaboration of these leaders, interactions between leaders and followers, and the process occurring among and between them" (emphasis added) (p. 5). These are certainly nuanced spaces we lead within. As such, leadership is not a one-size-fits-all prospect, and we need people in our profession who possess and activate their unique and diverse traits, assets, perspectives, backgrounds, and ideas that will collectively contribute to 21st-century learning and working conditions where human beings will thrive.

Leaders come in many forms, figures, and flavors. Claiming the title, much less embracing the role itself, takes a certain level of confidence that may not come naturally to everyone. Terms such as born leader, top dog, head honcho, and big boss don't help either. Traditional imagery tends to paint a narrow picture of what a leader looks, sounds, and acts like. For those of us who don't fit that mold, finding mentors and models can be tough. Luckily, people are stepping up and redefining what it means to lead and smoothing the way for others. As John Storey, Jean Hartley, Jean-Louis Denis, Paul 't Hart, and Dave Ulrich, editors of a 2017 compendium on modern-day leadership state,

> A growing number of works explore the role of everyday informal leaders, the 'ordinary persons' doing extraordinary things. This is the idea of 'learning leadership' through practical action (Antonacopoulou and Bento 2011; Ibarra 2015). The power and pull of this conceptualization are not hard to imagine. It casts leadership in a very different light. It opens up the scope for significant social action; it opens up the potential for almost anyone to 'make a difference' – with potential reverberations across a wide canvas.
>
> (xvii)

The subtitle of this book is purposeful: An Educators' Companion. It could also be called collaborator, confidante, or champion. A companion, however, embodies all of those synonyms and more. A companion travels alongside, sharing stories, listening deeply, and offering counsel. They stick by your side when you stumble, and they celebrate when you triumph. The word educator is intentional as well. Teacher leaders, department- or grade-level chairs, committee facilitators, executive council members, and coaches and specialists alike play critical parts in our school systems. This book is for you, too. Today's principals, directors, managers, supervisors, and superintendents were once in the classroom or counseling office or coaching out on the field as well. Nobody needs to ask for a hall pass to access the modules to come. But you do need to accept the invitation to see yourself as a leader and be willing to change the game of education.

So, what does it mean to be a leader who's also a game–changer? Classic definitions point to game–changer as a noun being: "a newly introduced element or factor that changes an existing situation or activity in a significant way" (Merriam-Webster online dictionary) or that "has a big and important effect on something, usually making the difference between one thing happening and another" (Collins online dictionary) (n.d.). Even Urban Dictionary has a version of the term: "Visionary; someone who looks beyond conventional methods; conceives new strategies, works to transform their industry." In the business world, aptly summarized on Investopedia (May 2, 2023):

> A game-changer is a person who, by the force of their personality, desires to do things differently, and their belief in the change they envision, alters the status quo. The changes that result can affect communities, industries, nations, and the world.
>
> (p. 1)

A variation on the theme is posed by ACSD+ISTE CEO Richard Culatta: "To me, a changemaker is somebody who is not satisfied with the status quo when the status quo is not serving students and educators well – and who is smart enough to know the difference" (Rebora pp. 16–17, *Educational Leadership*, March 2023).

Based on these premises and translated into the educational leadership domain, my take is that game–changing leaders do the following:

- Confront biases and barriers to student and adult learning with the explicit aim of opening up options and opportunities for continued growth.
- Fortify their skills, aptitudes, and talents to promote educational progress.
- Embrace mindsets and foster ways of being (such as inclusion, involvement, and inquiry) that redefine their organizational culture and climate.
- Seek out and listen with compassion to voices that differ from their own, especially those who've been traditionally sidelined in our schools.
- Generate ideas and try out innovations to address problems of practice while verifying that initial outcomes are promising before implementing on a large scale.
- Maintain hope in the face of adversity by collaborating with and supporting their teams and colleagues.

The Game–Changing Leadership in Action framework centers on three domains and two subsets within each domain, as illustrated in Figure I.1.

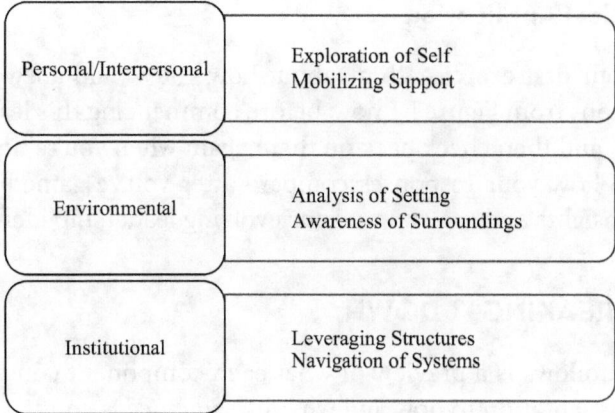

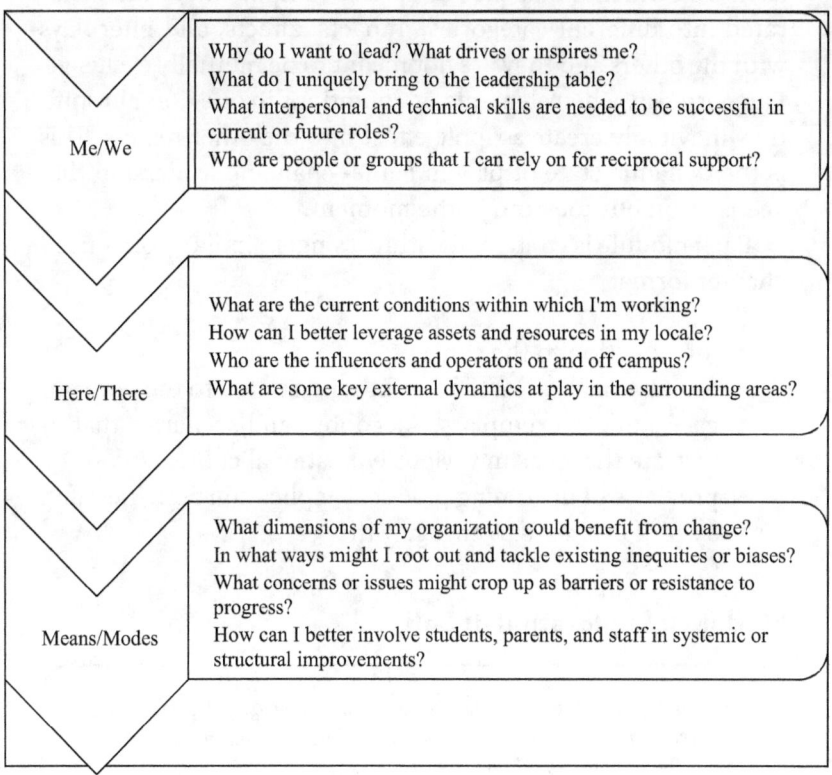

Figure I.1: Game–Changing leadership in action domains and essential questions

Practical Application

For your first exercise, think about how you would answer the questions from Figure I.1 now, before commencing this learning series, and then check back on them again when you're finished to see how your responses compare after you've gained some new insights and grown into your evolving leadership identity.

▶ BREAKING IT DOWN

What follows is a preview of what each component consists of as an orientation to how and why the sequence is configured as such. You will find that each of the five components, while separated into different categories, impacts, affects, and interplays with the others and they are not meant to be mutually exclusive. Furthermore, when elements or conditions in one domain shift, they inevitably create a ripple effect into the other realms. This is the dynamic state of play in game–changing leadership that keeps us on our toes and in the moment.

Each module is contained within a single, similarly organized chapter format:

- introduction to the concept;
- foundational research on subtopics related to the domain;
- case studies, exemplars, anecdotes, and scenarios that illustrate the ideas in various educational contexts;
- previews of upcoming practical application activities; and
- a set of exercises to engage with.

Module 1: Exploration of Self

> *Key Tenet: Leaders are keenly aware of how their personal beliefs, biases, and dispositions influence their behaviors, interactions, and execution of their professional duties and roles.*

In this first learning module, you will explore your natural leadership dispositions, identify areas for professional growth, and (re)connect to what inspires you as an educator. Plus, you'll get a peek behind the hiring curtain to get yourself in great shape for the job hunt process. Discovering your niche, establishing your purpose, and setting an individualized course of action are embedded in the activities in this introductory section of the Game–Changing Leadership in Action framework.

Module 2: Mobilizing Support

> *Key Tenet:* Leaders understand that they cannot hit all targets going it alone and that a collective or team approach enriches their own work as well as that of their colleagues.

Leadership can be lonely, but it doesn't have to be! In this module, you will learn the value of the collective, which emphasizes a shared approach to addressing situational problems of practice. Developing thriving partnerships with other leaders inside and outside of your network is essential to long-term sustainability; therefore, building functional teams and forming supportive relationships are at the heart of these lessons.

Module 3: Analysis of Setting

> *Key Tenet:* Leaders seek to develop a comprehensive view of their campus, site, or physical location with an eye on identifying assets and filling gaps unique to their own circumstances.

Whether you are new to an environment or have been at your site for the long term, it can be a cognitive challenge to separate yourself from your setting (like the metaphoric goldfish unconsciously swimming in its own water). The intent behind this set of activities is for you to investigate your campus or workplace from multiple perspectives and develop tactics to remove issues causing stumbling blocks or malfunctions. Scrutinizing your setting will unlock the potential for true change efforts that will benefit those who work and learn at your site every day.

Module 4: Awareness of Surroundings

> *Key Tenet: Leaders learn the lay of the land in the immediate areas close to their work location and the various synergies at play in the local arena to forge joint enterprises.*

Just outside the doors of your central office or school campus is a micro-universe enveloped by neighbors, businesses, services, organizations, and infrastructure. Local dynamics – such as politics, demographics, formal plus informal networks, and turfs or territories – spill over into the places where we lead. In this module, you will learn skills to leverage regional assets that foster collaboration and productive interactions for integrating your site with the vicinity bordering it.

Module 5: Leveraging Structures & Navigating Systems

> *Key Tenet: Leaders possess the ability to maneuver through policies, protocols, and resources to benefit their students, staff, and community and work to change systemic factors undermining the well-being and functionality of the organization.*

We didn't create the systems in which we lead, but we do have the ability to transform them to meet the needs of today's young people. Systems are composed of rules, ideologies, customs, and codes – and are unlikely to change unless the leaders therein expect and demand them to. Think of structures as a Jenga-like tower of building blocks requiring interdependent reliance to keep the institutional walls upright. Structures may be physical, such as buildings, offices, or classrooms; or they may be operational, as in how each part of the organization is interdependently interwoven. This module takes leaders through a process to break down architectural components (such as bell schedules, student placements, or teacher assignments) and systemically reconstruct how school looks and feels in the spirit of continuous improvement.

Conclusion: Strategies for Sustenance

The concluding chapter is a mini-module, in and of itself, on sustainable leadership mindsets and practices. It offers words to the wise and tips for keeping yourself centered in the midst of the chaos that only those out there in the TK-12 field can remotely imagine. If you're thinking, "I've seen it all," don't be so sure. The education game would not be complete without bugs, hackers, bots, guilds, glitches, and patches. But, as I like to say, "we *get* to do this work", as in it's an honor, a privilege, and a joy. So let's not forget to play and have some fun along the way.

▶ ENGAGEMENT MINDSETS

Whether you are interfacing with the modules in a shared, team, or large-group format, I've developed some touchstones to promote certain mindsets and attitudes that will benefit your personal and collective learning:

1. We share a "none of us is as good as all of us" mentality.
2. We shift roles between learner and expert at any given moment.
3. We prioritize active involvement because others are relying on our voices, participation, and perspectives.
4. We vulnerably share our experiences and challenges without fear of judgment or comparison.
5. We keep our own egos, biases, and assumptions in check.
6. We follow the guiding activities but also freely modify them to fit our needs.
7. We are committed to bettering our systems from the inside out.
8. We take an asset-based approach to discussing students, families, staff, and our communities.
9. We practice compassion and kindness with one another (and ourselves).
10. Nevertheless, we persist.

Game on!

References

Antonacopoulou, E. & Bento, R. (2011). Learning leadership in practice. In *Leadership in Organizations: Current Issues and Key Trends. J. Storey*. London: Routledge.

Day, D., & Thornton, A. (2018). Leadership development: the nature of leadership development. In J. Antonakis, D. Day (Eds.) *Leadership Development: The Nature of Leadership Development* (3rd ed., pp. 354–380). New York City, NY: SAGE Publications, Inc. https://doi.org/10.4135/9781506395029.n14

Game–changer. (n.d.). Definitions accessed from Collins online dictionary; Merriam-Webster online dictionary; & Urban Dictionary on July 17, 2024.

Guthrie, K.L. & Jenkins, D.M. (2018). *The role of leadership educators: Transforming learning*. Charlotte, NC: Information Age Publishing.

Ibarra, H. (2015). *Act Like a Leader, Think Like a Leader*. Cambridge, MA: Harvard Business Review Press.

Liu, Z., Venkatesh, S., Murphy, S. E. & Riggio, R. E. (2021). Leader development across the lifespan: A dynamic experiences-grounded approach. *The Leadership Quarterly*, 32(5), 101382.

Rebora, A. (March 2023). Richard Culatta on the 'transitional moment' in education. *Educational Leadership Magazine*, 80(6). ACSD.

Storey, J., Hartley, J., Denis, J.L. & Ulrich, D. eds. (2017). *The Routledge companion to leadership*. New York: Routledge.

Exploration of Self

▶ INTRODUCTION

> *Key Tenet: Leaders are keenly aware of how their personal beliefs, biases, and dispositions influence their behaviors, interactions, and execution of their professional duties and roles.*

I come from a family of educators. My parents, sister, and a couple of nieces are all lifelong teachers. I taught for a little more than a decade before going into site and district administration for another dozen-plus years. And now I'm working in higher education leadership. I know I'm in good company with many of you who also come from generations of dyed-in-the-wool career educators. History and English were my primary content areas; 11th grade my favorite group of students; alternative education settings my sweet spot; coaching and mentorship my knack; and systems change my eternal quest. Though I'd originally planned to be a high school teacher for the long run like my folks, the tap-tap-tap of leadership eventually came calling. True to my Capricornian nature, I ascended the ranks from instructional coach to vice principal to principal to district-level director to assistant superintendent to superintendent to university administrator. That's me in a nutshell for now. It's time to find out more about you.

But before we dig into your business, the reason we're starting with the Self is simple. Though we suit up in business attire and present ourselves in ways that indicate for others to "follow the leader," we're also human beings with past and present experiences that have shaped and formed our personalities, pathways, and perspectives on life. We've each had internal and external forces at play that aligned at some point to position us as school or central office leaders. Something deep within spurred you up the echelon, and someone or something outside of you confirmed that calling by recommending, mentoring, or hiring you. You may have readily embraced it or finally accepted your fate after a bit of initial kicking and screaming. Either way, kudos on grabbing for the proverbial carousel's brass ring. But to be clear: Life is not linear and not every leadership role will be a fit, so if you don't find it right away, keep searching.

Making the jump into formal leadership can feel daunting. It doesn't help that we've been conditioned within our profession to perceive the transition from teacher to administrator as *going to the dark side*. It's an almost guaranteed "joke" that your peers will make in their congratulations to you on your first assistant principalship or another entry-level leadership job. Though stated in jest and meant to be lighthearted, your first leadership challenge awaits – and gets at the crux of why transitioning into higher levels of leadership can be tricky. You are still you, but others now see you differently. That paired with your own self-doubt can be doubly challenging. You've likely heard the term imposter syndrome, those voices in our heads telling us that we're not worthy, ill equipped, or punching above one's weight. Those intrusive thoughts are just that: uninvited guests. Dismiss them now.

Instead, might you say, "Why not me?" and "If not me, then who?" and then get to work. While confidence is important, humility is equally so. Because you do have a lot to learn. A ton. But isn't that why most of us school devotees went into the field of education in the first place? Remember, you were and still are a student, a determined teacher, and now get the honor of adding being a leader to your repertoire. Exciting stuff indeed!

▶ FOUNDATIONS

The activities in this first module include several topics related to cultivating your authentic leadership self. To center our actions in theory, we will explore foundational materials, including research studies, lived and vicarious experiences, and contemporary discourse on the following themes:

- Developing professional self-efficacy in each new role you aspire for or ascend to
- Exploring psychological conditions and leadership mindsets to maximize impact
- Acquiring strategies for professional branding and preparing for promotion
- Identifying personal motivators and activators

Since there are volumes of books, articles, and videos on each of these subjects alone, what follows is meant to serve as a high-level framing that sets up the context for the exercises at the end of the module. It will not be an exhaustive literature review or formal evaluation of each field of study. However, you are encouraged to do your own deeper dive by seeking out additional materials that pique your curiosity along the way.

Professional Self-Efficacy

Reflective leaders authentically reassess their efficaciousness in relation to what their position, job, or role calls for as they climb up each rung on the ladder. How you perceive your ability to overcome challenges and activate your talents in novel situations is a combination of mindsets, experience, feelings, and observations. Albert Bandura (1997), Stanford University professor of social science in psychology and generator of the earliest research on self-efficacy in the workplace, posited that

> People's beliefs in their efficacy have diverse effects. Such beliefs influence the course of action people choose to pursue, how much effort they put forth in given endeavors, how

long they will persevere in the face of obstacles and failures, their resilience to adversity, whether their thought patterns are self-hindering or self-aiding, how much stress or depression they experience in coping with taxing environmental demands, and the level of accomplishments they realize. (p. 3)

Efficacy, primarily, is both a mental and experiential self-development process. Some of it relies on attaining knowledge or skills that you don't already possess, and some of it depends more on "will": Do you have the intrinsic motivation to stretch yourself in uncomfortable ways to expand your capacity? As such, Bandura (1997) identified four psychological conditions that shape one's self-efficacy:

1. experiencing mastery in previous realms;
2. having vicarious experiences by observing others;
3. hearing messages of confidence or encouraging words from peers or advisors; or
4. emotionally feeling ready (or realizing that you're not) that the time is ripe for a new experience.

In short, after you've done something once, you know it can be done again in the future. Likewise, if you see someone similar to yourself accomplishing a goal you also desire to accomplish, you'll internalize the idea that it's also within your reach. It can be as small as running a great staff meeting to having your dissertation approved. And each successful event compounds in interest for a cumulative sense of self-efficacy.

This is how each of the four domains may sound in your head:

- Mastery experiences: I've been really successful as an assistant principal and think I'm ready to run my own school now.
- Vicarious experiences: I've been watching how my supervisor handles the challenges in our department, and I believe I have the right skills to take over when she retires next year.

- Social persuasion: My mentor has been prompting me to apply for open positions since I've grown so much in my current role as a teacher on special assignment.
- Emotional states: Now that my kids are older, it feels like a good time in my life to take my next career step.

Of course, we don't always know what we're getting into, even when vetted through the four domains. Most people who go into site leadership come from teaching, counseling, or coaching backgrounds, which require wildly different skill sets and capacities from a management position. Just because you are an excellent classroom instructor or content area expert does not mean that you'll be a natural as a school administrator. It's even more nuanced than that at the district, county, or state agency level, which are even further removed from the students we educate.

Leader efficacy is a burgeoning field of research, but it's really just a fancy way of saying one's ability to perform a task or accomplish expected outcomes to a desired degree. Now, that said, there is a certain *je ne sais quoi* to determine whether someone is efficacious, because many traits are in the eye of the beholder. A principal, for example, may be a smash hit with the parent community but perpetually cause problems for district leadership by not following established protocols. Or a director could be excellent at meeting deadlines and submitting compliance reports while lacking compassion or kindness toward their staff. One also could be highly effective as an instructional coach, yet the crossover to a vice principalship ends up being too much of a stretch when they find out they're issuing disciplinary consequences all the livelong day. But the point is, we are not all good at the same things and that's okay.

This is more about gaining experiences that, if approached with a growth mindset, build skills that help you adapt to new situations and functions. In one smallish (8,000 students) district, I served simultaneously as the principal over two alternative education schools and as the coordinator of student expulsions... which soon turned into my next double shift as director of instructional technology and the district's strategic plan coordinator a few years later. While such leadership experience-building opportunities felt disjointed at times, those seemingly odd bedfellows were actually preparing me for an assistant superintendency in which I oversaw a likewise diverse set of seven unique instructional services departments with a relative sense of familiarity.

Practical Application

Since a sense of personal confidence is a necessary condition to gain success in your leadership role, taking an honest inventory of your baseline aptitudes is a good start. The first of its kind 30 years ago, the General Self-Efficacy Scale (GSE) developed by Ralf Schwarzer and Matthias Jerusalem (1995) is a simple 10-item rating scale that helps people determine personal levels of efficacy. There is scarcer research to be found specifically on school leaders' self-efficacy, but a more recent study conducted in Norway by Cecilie Skaalvik (2020) explored the connections between principals' feelings of efficacy related to instructional leadership using the prompts related to developing goals, motivating and guiding teachers, creating a positive and safe learning environment, and developing a collective culture. (pp. 494–95)

In Exercise 1.1, in the reproducible activities section at the end of this chapter, I have blended elements of the two scales as well as the other theoretical underpinnings mentioned in this section into a self-assessment tool for you to examine your own levels of efficacy at this point of your leadership journey. Box 1.1 is a preview of the items you will be asked to consider using a self-rating scale.

BOX 1.1 SELF-EFFICACY ASSESSMENT

Skills, Dispositions, and Aptitudes

- ❏ I know which of my talents and skills can benefit our larger organization.
- ❏ I possess and contribute essential knowledge and information that helps the school or district's leadership team make informed decisions.
- ❏ I bring unique and valuable experiences, expertise, and perspectives to the table.
- ❏ I actively engage in meetings and learning activities and apply what I learn to my day-to-day practice.
- ❏ I maintain a professional demeanor most of the time.

Interpersonal Dynamics

- ❏ I am good at building trusting relationships while maintaining healthy boundaries.
- ❏ I am politically and socially aware of group power dynamics.
- ❏ I have no problem apologizing when I get something wrong.
- ❏ I praise and recognize people publicly and coach, check in, or correct them privately.
- ❏ I care deeply about others' well-being, and it shows through my actions (in addition to my words).

Problem-Solving

- ❏ I can envision several potential remedies to contextual problems of practice, no matter how insurmountable they may seem.
- ❏ When facing opposition, I jump right in to help the team overcome the challenges we face.
- ❏ I respond quickly and appropriately when others express concerns.
- ❏ I authentically involve students, families, staff, and teachers in finding solutions to issues that arise.
- ❏ I see and frame problems as opportunities for continuous improvement.

Strategic Prioritization

- ❏ I know how to prioritize what matters, and I don't get easily distracted from that purpose.
- ❏ I am able to develop, guide, and execute a strategic plan for improved outcomes.
- ❏ I spend most of my time on high-leverage impactful leadership actions.
- ❏ I seek out and implement tools and resources that will help me organize my tasks, duties, and workflow.
- ❏ I endeavor to remove unnecessary barriers and burdens for myself and my staff so we can focus on the real work of teaching and learning.

Motivation & Morale

- ❏ I maintain a strong sense of why I want to lead, even during the hardest times.
- ❏ I am able to motivate and elicit high performance outcomes from staff in all roles.
- ❏ I listen carefully to what is being said (as well as the subtext) to better understand what an individual is experiencing and what might uplift them.
- ❏ I continually try out diverse approaches to bolster morale and encourage persistence.
- ❏ I lead through example by keeping my own motivation up.

Examination of Psychological Conditions and Mindsets

It's wholly natural to view life through your own autobiographical lens. Prismatic snapshots contribute to who you are as an individual: your upbringing, genetic make-up, physical body, race/ethnicity, personal choices, innate traits, geographic location, gender/sexuality, belief systems, family composition, and myriad other identities. While we share many of the same ingredients by simply being human, the ways we experience and express ourselves is refracted through countless filters that influence how we respond to workplace circumstances exclusively to us. In other words, each of us is walking around in our own little world interacting with every other person who is in theirs. When you think about that, it's almost miraculous that we see eye to eye on anything!

In my previous book, *Leading Through an Equity Lens* (2023), I wrote about this perceptual self-in-environment phenomenon described as "umwelt":

> To loosely borrow the term from biosemiotics philosopher Jacob von Uexküll (1864–1944), *umwelt* refers to the theory that organisms that share the same environment possess wildly different world views and perspectives based on their sensory perceptions. "Every subject spins out, like the spider's threads, its relations to certain qualities of things and weaves them into a solid web, which carries its existence" (2010, p. 53). Another way of saying this is illustrated in the aphorism that *fish can't see the water they are swimming in* or *if you want to know what water is, don't ask a fish*. Tim Elmo Feiten, 2022 posits, "The concept of *Umwelt* thus performs a double duty…on the one hand the strictly empirical study of animal behaviour and physiology, on the other hand a speculative and creative way of envisioning worlds radically different from ours."
>
> (p. 2)

This self-centeredness is normal and our default state of existence. It takes intention and attention to look into the mirror and see who's looking back at us. You may discover some unflattering truths, but uncovering them will strengthen your leadership stance. Once you give light to your shadow self, it can be tamed. To explicate it further, executive leadership coach Lolly Daskal observes in her 2017 book *The Leadership Gap: What Gets Between You and Your Greatness*: "The problem is one day, that suddenly, what once worked to propel [a high performing leaders] rise stops working. The very same traits that once worked *for* them start to work *against* them" (p. 3).

For example, look at the hypothetical leader described in Table 1.1. The left column lists their leadership dispositions and capacities. These are attributes that parallel a certain leadership archetype that tends to find success in the education field. However, when taken to an extreme, under stress, or left unchecked, those positive attributes can swing into the dark side, as illustrated in the middle column. The right-hand column contains

Table 1.1 Leadership shadow sides

Leadership trait	Shadow side	Impact on others
Precise	Critical	Fear of scrutiny or judgment; increased performance anxiety; procrastination/task avoidance
Intelligence	Know-it-all	Condescension resulting in feelings of inadequacy/unworthiness: *You must think I'm dumb.*
Decisive	Steamroller	Lack of acknowledgment for others' contributions; alternative voices/input isn't being heard; *it's my way or the highway*
Action-oriented	Impatient	Rushed or hurried; little consideration for others' readiness for implementation
Rational	Cold	Logic is valued over emotions; discounting others' feelings; dismissive of concerns
Strategic	Manipulative	Suspicions of a secret agenda; outcomes are already predetermined; false/fake attempts to get input

the potential impacts of shadowy behaviors on others in their sphere of influence.

This is your Type A, want-to-get-things-done-now, logically minded leader who comes across as very confident and persuasive. Most of the time, it works for them and the people they lead. However, but on occasion, they may appear autocratic, unfeeling, and blunt. All of us want to leave people and places better than we found them, so it's imperative to take an honest look at how your leadership temperaments can go awry.

Practical Application

Later on, in Exercise 1.2, you will take a look behind the curtain of your own shadow side by writing down traits that have both positive and negative flipsides plus the impacts on those in your care. Then you will be asked to devise concrete triggers to remind you of when your leadership attributes are trending toward liability under certain circumstances.

▶ BRANDING, PLANNING & PREPARING FOR PROMOTION

There are various twists upon the old adage that success is 10% inspiration (or genius) and 90% preparation (or perspiration). Whatever the combination, the point is that you can't expect to take your leadership to the next level unless you take personal initiative and strategic action prior to the main event. So, let's talk about how to get yourself ready for the various occasions you'll be presented with to exhibit your leadership prowess.

Branding

This section will be purposely brief simply because the idea of personal branding risks coming across as a clichéd trend in this reality show era of self-promotion. If the term is off-putting, think of this segment as conducting your own 360-degree review: a form of performance evaluation that involves gathering feedback from your co-workers, direct reports, and others you interact with. If you are afraid to find out how others experience your leadership, that could be your first clue as to how they might feel. Embracing reflective and vulnerable management practices models the spirit of continuous improvement that we hope others around us will also adopt. I'm not going to pretend it's easy to hear about your flaws, and it is all too easy to get defensive at the feedback. So, skip this one if you don't truly want to know. They don't call it growing pains for nothing.

It should go without saying, but I'll say it anyway – branding is not making up a new persona or engaging in professional cosplay. People can sniff out when you're not being authentic, so stay true to your own personality. It would be disingenuous to borrow someone else's leadership style that you admire but isn't natural to you. Instead, you must capitalize on strengths you already possess that you believe will positively impact others. An article called "Creating a Purpose-Driven Brand", posted on the University of California Berkeley's ExecEd website (n.d.), sums this up best:

> A purpose-driven personal brand is not just a showcase of skills and accomplishments, but also a reflection of one's deeper motivations and values. This kind of branding goes beyond conventional professional positioning; it connects with others on a more profound, human level, fostering trust and engagement. In a landscape where authenticity is increasingly valued, a purpose-driven personal brand can be a differentiator, leading not only to career opportunities but also to greater fulfillment and alignment in one's professional journey.

This is an aspirational view of branding that stems from your core reasons for wanting to lead in this dynamic world of educational administration. It's your moral code. Your mission. Your call. It's what you hope others will see that distinguishes you when walking into the room.

On a baser level, however, there is an aphorism that "if you're not controlling your brand, your brand is controlling you." As such, people in your sphere of influence are continually formulating their own assessments of your intentions, your values, and your worth. I'll tell you right now, you do have something to prove because administrators are frankly not the most beloved folks on the educational spectrum, especially those at the district, county office, or university level. We're perceived as "not being in the trenches" of a school site.

But whatever realm you reside in, taking care of your reputation is essential, as it will both precede and follow you along your career pathway. In the arrogance of youth, I once openly challenged our English department chair during a meeting for advocating (what I felt was) an obsolete way to teach grammar and vocabulary. I did not disagree with her very gracefully. I left that department not long after and found myself working with her in not one, not two, but three other capacities in different districts over the years. Karma will get ya.

Embodying and exemplifying a consistent brand engender trust, in that your words match your actions. Table 1.2 demonstrates how you can test the effects of your brand by documenting the qualities you think you're representing with solid proof to support your claims. If you can't think of ample evidence, you may have a branding mismatch. You can't just *tell* people what

Table 1.2 Evidence of brand consistency

Brand qualities	*Evidence*
Equity champion	I introduced the concept of an equity audit to other school principals, and some asked me to help them facilitate a data walk on their campus.
Innovator	Others inside or outside of my department adopted a technique or process I personally developed.
Organizer	The schedule I constructed streamlined our work and saved us significant time.
Trusted resource	I created a slide deck that others are now using as a template for future presentations.
Key contributor	The grant I oversee was renewed for a second term because the outcomes accomplished during the first cohort instilled confidence in our execution.
Responsible/ Reliable	I successfully met or exceeded all deadlines during our department's biggest crunch time.
Encourager	I received thank you cards from all of my mentees at the end of the year saying how much my kindness and support mattered to them.

you consider your brand; you have to live it, and have others verify it as well in order to truly count.

A Brand in Jeopardy

Having been in leadership roles for over 20 years, I'm sure I've had a lot of unflattering nicknames that I never got wind of, but there's one that stuck with me. When I was assistant superintendent of instruction, I required all of my directors to share their presentations with me prior to submitting them through the board agenda process. I'm a former English teacher, a minimalist, and a bottom-line get-to-the-point sort of person, so you might imagine how I reacted to slide decks that were anything but visually tidy, succinct, error-free, and precise. I wielded my Pilot G2 pen heavily on those PowerPoints and agenda item write-ups; one of my signature techniques was to cross out an entire slide page with a bold black vertical line.

And behold, *The Slasher* was born. At first, I thought it was kind of funny. I certainly couldn't disagree that it was true. But as I thought more about it, I realized that practice was demeaning and demoralizing to my staff and could have been handled in a much gentler way. I apologized for my approach and decided to create a self-review checklist with clear expectations for look, content, style, and so on that would set them up for success before anything hit my desk. But that nickname stuck. I am and will forever be The Slasher to some. And it's a tendency I still need to resist every day. Alas, perception is reality.

So, gear up and find out who's looking back at you in the mirror. The first part of each statement that follows is a hypothetical example of a person's aspirational brand; the second part of the statement is how they might show up when triggered or stressed, compromising their desired reputation. In other words, you want to be considered an asset, but your behavior can be a liability.

- You want to be seen as competent and capable, but you compromise that image by complaining about having too much on your plate.
- You want others to value how experienced you are, but you can act like a blowhard during staff meetings.

- You want to be known as someone with integrity and high principles, but no one ever seems to meet your standards. Thus they deem it impossible.
- You want to elicit feelings of ease and comfort in your presence, but you can be perceived as a wishy-washy people-pleaser.
- You want to appear poised and polished, but you come across as unapproachable or unavailable.
- You want to be seen as passionate and driven for a cause, but you may come off as preachy, self-important, or superior.
- Your careful, methodical, thoughtful approach to your work can seem overly cautious, slow, and uncertain among your colleagues.

Practical Application

In Exercise 1.3, you will be prompted to identify aspects of your brand that you want to highlight that make you unique, while examining how your brand can be compromised when your actions or emotional triggers send contradictory messages. Balancing your brand with staying authentic is key for consistency.

▶ ROLE TRANSITIONS

Other duties as assigned: that infamous last bullet point on every leadership-level job description. One pitfall of advancement up the management ladder is forgetting to let go of your previous role while piling on new expectations. This especially happens during internal promotions in the same school or central office department. But it can also happen within us as the lure to remain comfortable and competent by doing what you have already mastered is a compelling one. In a study on comfort zone orientation, Duke University researchers Nona C. Kiknadze and Mark R. Leary (2021) observed that

> People seem to distinguish most clearly between "low-risk" activities that clearly lie inside their comfort zone and "high risk" activities that lie so far outside their comfort zone that they regard the behaviors as impossible. Yet, this binary distinction ignores a "discomfort zone" between these

> extremes. Whereas the comfort zone involves behaviors people can perform with little or no anxiety or avoidance, the discomfort zone consists of desired behaviors that require tenacity and conscious effort to override avoidance motivation. In the discomfort zone, people must decide whether behaving in a manner that creates anxiety is worth the potential benefits.
>
> (p. 2)

Discomfort never killed anyone (as far as I know), so let's get reacquainted with Lev Vygotsky's Zone of Proximal Development, which you likely learned about way back in your teaching certification program. It includes the willingness of a learner to stretch, embrace unease, and sit with ambiguity; identifying someone with the knowledge and skills to guide you; acquiring supportive resources that advance your learning; and engaging in social interactions that allow you to work on your skills and abilities in the context of your job (Saul McLeod, 2024).

Some people stay at one site or in one position for decades, but that is becoming less common at the close of the first quarter of the 21st century. All you have to do is look at your school or district's organizational chart and see how many new leaders came onto the scene in the past few years and what the organization looked like five to ten years prior. Stephanie Levin and Kathryn Bradley, authors of a Learning Policy Institute (LPI) and National Association of Secondary School Principals (NASSP) report titled "Understanding and Addressing Principal Turnover" (2019), remark:

> Turnover is a serious issue across the country. The national average tenure of principals in their schools was four years as of 2016–17. This number masks considerable variation, with 35 percent of principals being at their school for less than two years, and only 11 percent of principals being at their school for 10 years or more. The most recent national study of public school principals found that, overall, approximately 18 percent of principals were no longer in the same position one year later. In high-poverty schools, the turnover rate was 21 percent.
>
> (p. 3)

It is somewhat surprising, given the pressures that the Covid-19 pandemic placed on school leaders, but these statistics still comport with a 2023 article by Evie Blad in EdWeek, "What New Data Show about Principal Turnover." Blad writes that, in a 2020–21 survey issued by the National Center for Education Statistics,

> 11.2 percent of public school principals left the role altogether. That's an uptick over the 9.8 percent deemed 'leavers' in the 2016–17 school year, but it's in line with trends dating back to 2008–09, when 11.9 percent of principals left the field – not coincidentally at the height of the Great Recession when state, federal, and local budgets shrunk as did K-12 administrative ranks.

However, another study, conducted by the Rand Corporation in 2023, found a

> nationally representative sample of district leaders estimated that 16 percent of their principals retired or resigned in 2021–2022, which is more than double the rate from 2020–2021. A 16 percent turnover rate translates into roughly 19,000 more school leaders leaving their position relative to the previous school year.
> (Diliberti & Schwartz, 2023, p. 2)

Whatever the number may actually be, the truth is that leader attrition is a fact of life in many institutions across the United States. In the savviest of districts, the human resources department is already one step ahead of such transitions by creating employment pipelines in both the classified and certificated management ranks.

In TK-12 education specifically, a typical advancement trajectory for an instructional leader may look like that in Figure 1.1. While those are some traditional vertical pathways, it's okay to meander, go off course, or buck convention – it's your life! But fair warning, what makes you successful in one role does not automatically or naturally transfer to the next

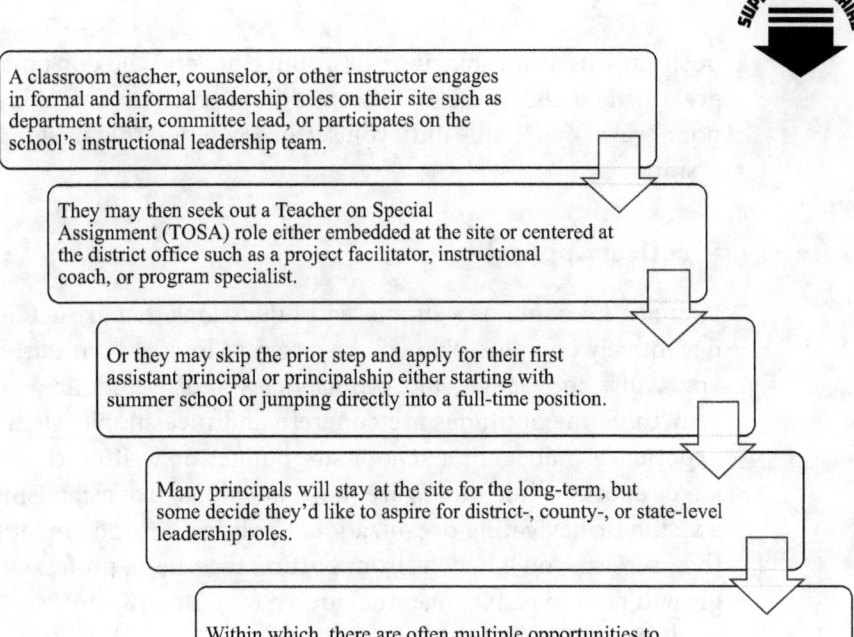

Figure 1.1 Advancement pathways

position. There are amazing classroom teachers who don't make great principals. There are also middling teachers who do. It's not always predictable until you settle down into that next leadership seat.

Practical Application

Exercise 1.4 contains a simple set of questions that are actually deceptively complex. You will be asked to look at your current key skills, knowledge, and proficiencies and predict areas for growth. Some aptitudes are concrete and measurable, such as experience managing a school site budget or writing compliance reports, while others are more nebulous, like establishing a vision or navigating organizational politics. After completing the exercise, you'll benefit from putting together a professional growth plan to gain conceptual understanding prior to real-life application in your next role.

▶ THE SIX PS OF PROMOTION

Similarly to how I wish I'd been exposed to consumer economics and personal finance back in high school, it bears going over the bottom lines for actually landing your first or promotional leadership role. That is, what should be common knowledge is preferably taught outright. This is dodgy territory because screening tools, hiring panels, and formal approval processes create a gauntlet to run that can't always be predicted. However, there are some go-to focus areas that you'll need to attend to in your preparation for the promotion process, regardless of the permutations.

You will likely need to

1. *polish* up your application materials;
2. *practice* for your interview;
3. take inventory of your online and in-person *presence*;
4. prepare to *perform* a task for the screening panel;
5. *provide* professional references or recommendations; and
6. *pursue* potential positions

P #1: Polish

Your first impression is the only impression that matters, because if your paperwork is sloppy, you won't even get past the initial screening. Triple-check spelling, grammar, correct use of vocabulary/terminology, and formatting in your cover letter, résumé, and email correspondence between you and your potential employer. Research what today's standards are for assembling your written materials so that you don't date yourself or stand out for all the wrong reasons. Materials that are clean, neat, succinct, and organized are key.

In today's market, bots and humans alike will be reviewing your application materials, so you must appeal to both. Luckily, there are some tips and tricks that should cover your main bets:

- Read the job description carefully and borrow specific words and phrases that show up as essential qualities and qualifications and sprinkle them throughout your résumé and intro letter. Be careful not to sound like a bot yourself, though; blend the terms in naturally.
- Striking the right tone is important. Project confidence not arrogance. Be friendly but not effusive. Professional yet personal. If you have a life situation that explains an anomaly in your résumé (like an employment gap) or provides a reason behind why you are seeking a new job, that may be stated but not overemphasized. This is not the place to say you had a mental breakdown, got fired, or hated your last boss, though. Sounds obvious? Unfortunately, not.
- Your résumé and cover letter should complement, not repeat, each other. The letter should explicate or highlight the successes in your work history but should also share why you are seeking a new position and *this one* in particular. Though it can be cumbersome to customize every single introduction letter to the exact title and name of the organization you are submitting it to, be assured it makes a difference. Nobody is immediately won over by a "to whom it may concern" intro for a nondescript "leadership" position (or even worse, the wrong position).

P #2: Practice

We all have different styles of practicing for an interview. Some like to write bullet notes, others longer narrative responses, and some orally in front of a mirror or with a friend. The point is we all need some practice. In the land of Google, you can prepare yourself silly by querying typical interview questions. And in the land of AI, you can even find computer-generated or crowd-sourced answers to potential questions. I've interviewed others and have been interviewed myself probably a hundred times over my career, and there are some very predictable patterns in the educational realm. I can almost guarantee what the first and last questions will be and can predict the primary themes in the middle.

If you want to spare yourself hours of research and spend your time crafting your own answers, here you go:

Question 1: *Tell us about your professional and educational experiences that have prepared you for this position in our organization.* Essentially, what they want to know is: Why this, why here, why now? Share upfront why you applied and want to work in the organization and how you've gotten ready to execute the role.

Questions 2–5:

- a) You will almost always get a question regarding a time you struggled, a conflict you had to resolve, or a problem you faced in a work situation. Be ready to present something authentic, recent, and transferable to the role you are seeking. They want to get a picture of how you deal with stress and approach solutions, and they also want to detect indicators of your leadership style (do you seem avoidant, confrontational, direct, empathetic, reflective?). Just don't pretend you've never struggled; whenever someone can't think of an answer to this question, it triggers a red flag!
- b) A specific job description-related question or two will probably show up at some point, so it's important to read the info you are provided carefully, both the "required"

and "desired" technical, managerial, and leadership skills. If possible, tuck a few key phrases from their materials into your notes or memory so you can pull them out when appropriate, for a few bonus points.
c) Organizations want to know what you know about them. Did you do your homework on the school or district? Do you know their data and stats? Do you know their challenges? Do you know their adopted curriculum or key initiatives? A website deep dive is a good way to get your intel, followed by some informational interviews if you can secure any.
d) A project-related question: Tell us about a time that you were tasked with leading a project from start to completion that you're proud of – or some variation on the theme. The panel is interested in your thought processes and organizational style. Have a ready example of something you spearheaded, not something you just participated in; it's a common mistake that leaves the panel under the impression that you haven't led anything significant yet.
e) Most of the time, you'll get a scenario, case study, or hypothetical. The situation will likely be something you'll encounter in the position. Listen carefully, ask clarifying questions if you have them, and put yourself into the shoes of a leader in those circumstances. You'll have to think on your feet as any number of issues may be presented to you.

Question 6: *Is there anything else you want to share with us that you haven't covered already, or do you have any questions for us?* Sounds easy, right? Actually, this is the toughest question to hit the right notes on. If you feel like you could expand more on one of the answers you provided earlier or forgot to say something essential, this is the perfect time to cover your tracks. It will show you are attentive to detail and reflective. It's customary these days for an applicant to bring in a list of questions they have for the panel. And, sadly, an otherwise solid interview can go south very quickly. I've seen people bring in a list of questions longer than the panel had for them. Yes, you are "interviewing" them too but keep it to fewer than three questions. I'll be frank here. Do not

- Ask a question you can Google the answer to or find on their website.
- Ask questions that feel templated and canned à la "Where do you see the organization going in the next 3–5 years?" or "What does success look like in the first 90 days?"
- Ask anything about salary, vacation, health care, and so on. Save that for the job-offer conversation when and if it comes.

Here's what you should do to make a great lasting impression: Listen to the types of questions you were asked earlier and ask them as follow-ups. "Based on question 3, it sounds like the organization is facing xx challenges, I'm wondering if you can tell me more about your needs and how the person in this role can help." Or "I'm the type of leader who enjoys community building. What kinds of things have been done in this arena so far so I can get a sense of how I might expand on your successes?" This approach has won me (and many other panels) over more than once and sealed the deal of making the candidate an offer.

P #3: Presence

You'd think by now this P would be obvious, but there are still folks out there applying for jobs who haven't cleaned up their online act. In fact, just recently, I declined to interview someone who'd shared their LinkedIn handle on their résumé. When I clicked on their profile, I found a posting frenzy of all of the rejection letters they'd received during their almost full year of seeking employment, plus a link to an article they'd written that was quite the rant about all the ways they'd been wronged by a certain higher educational institution – which just happened to be the very organization to which they were applying. My reaction: *Thank you, next.*

Now I'm not telling you to not be yourself, but if you have social media profiles that are open to the public, you need to assume that recruiters may see photos of you that are "not safe for work" (NSFW) or read threads of you venting, proselytizing, or pontificating on any manner of topic. Even sites you think are locked down can be screen-shotted, modified, or publicized. Don't fall into the trap of thinking anything online is private.

The truth of the matter is that being in a leadership position means you need to be beyond reproach, whether you like it or not. Just search the internet for ample proof.

Offline, you need to be aware as well. Curiosity is natural. Parents will look in your cart at the neighborhood grocery, and students will try to find out where you live and who you hang out with. Your own reputation is not the only thing at stake, so is your organization's image. I really don't want to hire someone who is going to get my district in the limelight for all the wrong reasons.

On the positive side, you can make your socials work for you. A LinkedIn page is pretty much expected and essential in your job hunt. It's basically a form of an online résumé but with some extras that can give a little more flavor to your personality via your posts, comments, and connections. Familiarity can also be a great asset. Human beings have what is called an affinity bias, meaning we gravitate toward those with which we feel we have something in common or shared values. *Oh, you have a BA in U.S. History, too! Cool, you also follow Simon Sinek. Hey, we both have rescue terrier mixes. I already like you.* You get the picture.

Your real-life connections also matter. You may have heard the maxim that "You are the company you keep"; in other words, those you socialize with and how people perceive them can also affect how others think about you. Especially when applying internally in your organization, if you're hanging out with a known complainer, rabble rouser, or someone who has a reputation that negatively precedes them, you may be painted with the same brush. While in the application process, you might want to distance yourself from folks with suspect profiles you aren't that close to anyway.

P #4: Perform

Not all positions will include performance tasks or presentations, but they are becoming more frequent. If the application process includes a demonstration or exhibition of your portfolio or facilitation skills, you'll need to practice and prepare. Expect it to be a little awkward. Often you're pretending to lead a staff meeting, conduct a training, or coach a colleague. Some people are very comfortable with role-playing and can jump right now; others of us aren't as natural in this mode. Fortunately, tasks are often delivered to you ahead of time so you can plan out your demo and rehearse your key points for as long as you need to get familiar with the elements involved.

Other kinds of tasks I've seen are designed to assess your written communication, organizational approaches, or basic skills. You may be assigned to write a welcome email to a parent group, interpret and explain a data-filled spreadsheet, or reconcile a challenging meeting schedule. Sometimes you have a limited amount of time to produce the submission so the interviewers can see both how you operate under pressure and how strong your skills are in that arena. It may bring back bad memories of timed multiplication table drills from fifth grade, but don't panic. Just anticipate and do your best.

P #5: Provide

I hope I'm not the only one whom this P fills with a bit of dread. Asking former and (even worse) current supervisors for letters of recommendation or to be listed as a reference feels kind of icky. But it's a necessary part of the process and doesn't seem to be going away anytime soon. I'm sure you know the drill. Choose people who have a neutral, unknown, or positive reputation in the field. Including a high-profile individual such as a superintendent can work for or against you depending on how people feel about them. The thing about letters is, we know you asked only those people who will write nice things, so they really don't add up to much in the hiring equation. Smart interviewers also call your references, listed or not; contacting former and current supervisors and weighing their input can be very influential to whether you get moved on to the final stages or not.

P #6: Pursue

Rarely does the perfect job just fall into your lap. More often, you're frequenting job websites like Edjoin or LinkedIn or executive recruitment search firms for openings. You may have to interview dozens of times before landing a position, so keep an open mind as you explore. While you're digitally searching,

Table 1.3 Professional growth arenas

Tactical skills:	Knowledge base:
• time management • prioritization • public speaking/presenting • meeting facilitation • project management • problem-solving • productivity/organization • managerial/supervisory approaches	• equity-centered practices • educational leadership principles • TK-12 state & federal policy • DEI (Diversity, Equity, Inclusion) • improvement science • college & career readiness • AI/digitally mediated learning • Instructional design
Technical skills:	**Interpersonal skills:**
• technology tools & platforms • graphic design • written communications/storytelling • data analysis/visualization • research/evaluation • grant writing • clerical/administrative	• collaboration • stress management • conflict resolution • active listening/body language • mentoring/coaching • giving/receiving feedback • self-awareness/branding • networking

think about some other unconventional ways to gain needed experiences to add to your toolkit. Ask for internal opportunities in areas you'd like to advance, such as job shadowing or subbing for another leader when they are offsite or formally asking for coaching or mentoring from those you admire. Finally, take a look at Table 1.3: professional growth arenas and think about which types of learning are most applicable to your personal leadership development plan and then draft answers to the corresponding prompts.

The 5 Ws (+an H) of Your Professional Growth Plan Prompts

1. What do you want to learn this year? What do you need to learn? Where do the two interests overlap?
2. Where might you access the material/content/coursework/training that fits your learning goals?
3. When and how frequently do you want to spend your time learning (time of day, time of year)?

4. Who will help you develop your learning plan, access resources, and monitor your progress?
5. Why did you choose the topic you chose, and how is it directly relevant to your job description or work duties?

Practical Application

Exercise 1.5 contains a series of six activities that mirror the Ps described in this section. Some of them are quick reviews of your application materials to make sure they are as spotless as can be, while others require research, reflection, and rehearsal. The good news is that once you've done the work, you can replicate or mildly adjust your materials for a number of different job openings. It's all well worth your time, I promise.

▶ MOTIVATORS AND ACTIVATORS

If you're in it for the long haul, figuring out what motivates and sustains you as a leader is essential. This is hard work. Even on a good day. Keeping your spirits up and head clear will help you contextualize what you're experiencing as you grow into your role. As educators, we know all about intrinsic and extrinsic motivation when it comes to our students. We try to instill in them a love of learning that goes beyond grades, reasons for being cooperative that reach past rewards, or behaving in ways that don't stem from only fear of punishment. Adults are no different really.

In their 2024 book, *Motivation Myth Busters: Science-Based Strategies to Boost Motivation in Yourself and Others*, educational psychology researchers Wendy S. Grolnick, Benjamin C. Heddy, and Frank C. Worrell debunk ten myths about motivation and delve into no fewer than seven motivation theories to unpack common beliefs about motivation and what the science really says. If you're interested in this topic, I highly recommend reading the whole book; for now, this takeaway sums it up: "All people are motivated, but what they are motivated for differs, and we can do something about this by promoting and nurturing their interests" (p. 38).

Intrinsic motivation is a feeling of inspiration or extra energy to complete a task because it's personally rewarding. You're engaging in the activity because of some subconscious drive as opposed to an external demand or benefit. When intrinsically motivated, the experience itself is the ultimate reward, as suggested in the examples below:

- Cleaning your house because you like it to be tidy.
- Spending time with your family because you enjoy their company.
- Playing a game because the experience is fun.

Extrinsic motivation is when you perform a duty either to secure a return on your investment or to circumvent a potentially unpleasant result. In this case, you don't finish the task because you personally enjoy it or find it satisfying. Instead, you're completing it to avoid reproach or you're hoping to earn brownie points from others you care about, as in these examples which are corollaries to the ones mentioned earlier.

- Cleaning your house so your spouse doesn't nag you.
- Spending time with your family to avoid feeling guilty.
- Playing a game because you want to win a prize or money.

While it's easy to frame intrinsic as *good* and extrinsic as *bad*, the truth is that they aren't so easily partitioned and can suggest a false dichotomy. Thus, it's possible for a leader to do a task that they weren't initially internally motivated to take on and end up finding it personally gratifying or surprisingly interesting. Or, for example, you may be intrinsically motivated to write your dissertation, but after two years of slogging, all you want to do is ring that bell and add that Ed.D or Ph.D. to your nameplate. It's also possible to love your job and want to be compensated for it at the same time. Table 1.4 contains intrinsic and extrinsic motivators at play in work situations.

In chemistry, an activator is a substance used to induce a chemical reaction and to instigate positive regulation. The term is also referenced in instructional circles as "strategies that incorporate think time and purposeful social interaction to foster emotional, cognitive, and behavioral engagement" (p. 1), according to authors Donna Mehle and Nicole Frazier (2013) of *Activators: Classroom Strategies for Engaging Middle and High School Students*. A person can be motivated but not

Table 1.4 Intrinsic and extrinsic motivators at work

Intrinsic motivation	Extrinsic motivation
• Feeling triumphant after solving a hard problem or taking on a "stretch challenge" • Knowing that your contributions added value to a team effort • Having personal pride in how an important project or product turned out • Enjoying a new learning experience or skill building opportunity • Embracing and incorporating feedback from others to improve your future growth • Experiencing a "state of flow" when fully absorbed in a meaningful task	• Hoping to be recognized for accomplishing daily work tasks • Aiming to please your supervisor to earn praise, a raise, or another tangible reward • Keeping score on how much/little attention you get versus others • Feeling driven by fear, anxiety, or avoidance of criticism or reproach • Over-reliance on others' opinions of you in order to stay invested in the time/effort • Being overly focused on your own or others' titles, status, or positionality

activated and vice versa. For example, you might be motivated to cook a meal, but it might not happen unless you get into your car to go to the store to pick up ingredients first. Then it gets dark out and you decide to order pizza instead. Your motivation simply did not manifest into action. On the other hand, you may not be motivated to exercise, yet you put your body in motion anyway and successfully complete your workout. Consciously pairing the two takes some practice.

Practical Application

There are three main components that can spur a person on: autonomy, purpose, and mastery. Feeling like you have choice, investment, and skill in an activity makes it all the more appealing. Consider the ingredients in the mix of motivators and activators and use the sentence frames to identify environmental and personal circumstances where you felt highly interested or inspired to achieve or learn recently.

Autonomy:

- I recently felt engrossed in a state of flow when I was working on…
- This week, I learned…, which sparked my interest to find out more about…
- I had a chance to experiment with, explore, or examine a problem of practice and make a recommendation to…

Purpose:

- I felt connected to the organization's goals and purpose when I…
- I saw evidence of my work contributing to the team's project when…
- I helped a team member out by…

Mastery:

- One of the goals I achieved this week was…
- I felt professionally challenged this week by…
- I learned something important from a mistake I made this week…

▶ MODULE 1 EXERCISES

The intention of the exercises to come is to find out what makes you tick and then find your niche. Each of the below set of activities relates to the content you learned earlier in the narrative sections of the module. You may need to refer back or refresh your memory if you've saved them until the end, or you can do them as you complete each section's readings.

1.1. Assessing Your Self-Efficacy
1.2. Through the Looking Glass
1.3. Cultivating Your Brand
1.4. Transition Planning
1.5. Preparation for Promotion: Six P's

Exercise 1.1 Assessing Your Self-Efficacy

Overview: Self-efficacy can ebb and flow at divergent points in your career. You may answer the prompts below differently depending on your current status in a particular position. If you've been in a job for a while, you may feel more competent or confident than if you are in your first several months. It's important to note that qualities included below are not the only important hallmarks of being an effective leader. They are representative, rather, of the demands of school and district administrators in general, and if you have other items to add that may be more valuable to your particular role or situation, you are welcome to add your own qualifiers into the mix.

Directions: On a scale from 1 to 4, rate yourself on the following items related to your professional sense of self-efficacy as it exists today:

Self-efficacy components	1 (low) – 4 (high)
1) I know which of my talents and skills can benefit our larger organization.	1 2 3 4
2) I possess and contribute essential knowledge and information that help the school or district's leadership team make informed decisions.	1 2 3 4
3) I bring unique and valuable experiences, expertise, and perspectives to the table.	1 2 3 4
4) I actively engage in meetings and learning activities and apply what I learn to my day-to-day practice.	1 2 3 4
5) I maintain a professional demeanor most of the time.	1 2 3 4
6) I am good at building trusting relationships while holding healthy boundaries.	1 2 3 4
7) I am politically and socially aware of group power dynamics.	1 2 3 4
8) I have no problem apologizing when I get something wrong.	1 2 3 4

© Copyright material from Kim Wallace (2025), Game–Changing Leadership in Action, Routledge.

Self-efficacy components	1 (low) – 4 (high)
9) I praise and recognize people publicly and coach, check in, or correct them privately.	1 2 3 4
10) I care deeply about others' well-being, and it shows through my actions (in addition to my words).	1 2 3 4
11) I can envision several potential remedies to contextual problems of practice, no matter how insurmountable they may seem at first.	1 2 3 4
12) When facing opposition, I jump right in to help the team overcome the challenges we face.	1 2 3 4
13) I respond quickly and appropriately when others express concerns.	1 2 3 4
14) I authentically involve students, families, staff, and teachers in finding solutions to issues that arise.	1 2 3 4
15) I see and frame problems as opportunities for continuous improvement.	1 2 3 4
16) I know how to prioritize what matters, and I don't get easily distracted from that purpose.	1 2 3 4
17) I am able to develop, guide, and execute a strategic plan that results in improved outcomes.	1 2 3 4
18) I spend most of my time on high-leverage impactful leadership actions.	1 2 3 4
19) I seek out and implement tools and resources that will help me organize my tasks, duties, and workflow.	1 2 3 4
20) I endeavor to remove unnecessary barriers and burdens for myself and my staff so we can focus on the "real work" of teaching and learning.	1 2 3 4
21) I maintain a strong sense of why I want to lead, even during the hardest times.	1 2 3 4
22) I am able to motivate and elicit high performance outcomes from staff in all roles.	1 2 3 4

© Copyright material from Kim Wallace (2025), Game–Changing Leadership in Action, Routledge.

Self-efficacy components	1 (low) – 4 (high)
23) I listen carefully to what is being said (as well as the subtext) to better understand what an individual is experiencing and what might uplift them.	1 2 3 4
24) I continually try out diverse approaches to bolster morale and encourage persistence.	1 2 3 4
25) I lead through example by keeping my own motivation up.	1 2 3 4
Total Score	/100

Self-evaluation			
Area of efficacy	Areas where I excel (check all that apply)	Areas to develop (check all that apply)	Notes to Self
Skills, dispositions, and aptitudes (questions 1–5)	1 2 3 4 5	1 2 3 4 5	
Interpersonal dynamics (questions 6–10)	6 7 8 9 10	6 7 8 9 10	
Problem-solving (questions 11–15)	11 12 13 14 15	11 12 13 14 15	
Strategic prioritization (questions 16–20)	16 17 18 19 20	16 17 18 19 20	
Motivation & morale (questions 21–25)	21 22 23 24 25	21 22 23 24 25	

© Copyright material from Kim Wallace (2025), Game–Changing Leadership in Action, Routledge.

Exercise 1.2: Through the Looking Glass

Remember Lolly Daskal's cautionary tale on page 19: the gifts, talents, and distinguishing qualities that propelled you into leadership may work against you if your self-awareness is underdeveloped. First, consider your own personality traits and leadership style descriptors and list them in the table below. Are you compassionate on your best days and a pushover on your worst? Do you have a great sense of humor that can now and again dip into sarcasm or bad taste? Is group collaboration your go-to mode that sometimes results in an inability to make the ultimate decision? Be honest with yourself.

Directions:

1. First, fill out the left-hand column with various leadership traits you believe you possess and regularly exhibit that are considered strengths.
2. Then, take an honest look at your shadow side and choose adjectives that illustrate how you may show up in spaces when you feel insecure, stressed, or overwhelmed and that are the flip side of the assets you listed in the first column.
3. Next, in the right column, write down some of the ways that your lapse in moderation may impact students, staff, families, or yourself.
4. Finally, pick one or two of the traits you identified and do a deeper dive into a workplace situation where your positive intentions accidentally crossed the line to the darker side.

    a. What triggered the transgression?
    b. What did you learn from it?
    c. What might you do to keep yourself in check when you notice yourself exhibiting unproductive behaviors that don't demonstrate who you want to be as a leader?

Favorable leadership trait	Negative shadow side	Shadow side: Impact on others

© Copyright material from Kim Wallace (2025), Game–Changing Leadership in Action, Routledge.

Exercise 1.3: Cultivating Your Brand

Part I: Select a word or phrase that best reflects how others see or experience you in distinct roles, conditions, or settings:

- A lifelong friend
- A loved one (parent/partner/spouse)
- Your current co-workers/colleagues
- A critic/detractor/frenemy
- Someone you supervise/manage (or parent)
- Who you are when most comfortable/at rest
- Who you appear to be when under stress

  1. Are there some commonalities or threads that seem consistent?
  2. Are there some differences that can be explained?
  3. Are you okay with the descriptors you noted or are there some you want to change?

Part II: Evaluating your leadership brand identity. Respond to the questions below to assess whether your brand is on track or needs additional development.

- What is a brand (organization or individual) that you admire? Why?
- Describe how you see your brand today.
- How far is it from what you want it to be?
- How can you take it to the next level? (Or course-correct...)
- Does your current brand need to evolve to meet your short- and long-term goals? If so, in what ways?

Part III: Your Brand in Jeopardy

Look back at the examples that illustrate how a personal brand can go off track when a leader isn't fully conscious of their behaviors. Now consider your responses from Exercise 1.2. Write down a few of your shadow side tendencies in action and how they may negate your brand reputation.

© Copyright material from Kim Wallace (2025), Game–Changing Leadership in Action, Routledge.

I want to be seen as _____
_____; however, when I _____
_____, it weakens my brand image by
_____.

I want to be known as a leader who _____
_____, but when I _____
_____, I risk compromising those ideals.

My _____ ways can appear to others as _____, so I need to be careful that I _____ in order to preserve my intentions.

Exercise 1.4: Role Transition Planning

Write down the role you currently hold and at least three areas where you excel and then answer these questions.

- ❏ What current skills, knowledge, or capabilities may translate well into the role you think you want?
- ❏ Are you aware of what you need to learn or acquire in order to be successful?
- ❏ Do you have a realistic idea of what exactly the job entails and what elements may change key aspects of your life?
- ❏ Now fill out the blank table with potential actions you might pursue to beef up your résumé to make you stand out from the crowd.

Tactical skills:	Knowledge base:
Technical skills:	Interpersonal skills:

Exercise 1.5: Preparing for Promotion

Each of the six P's described on pages 28–35 will get you ready for prime time. Put an X in the column for each of the six components to discover areas where you'll need to spend more time getting up to speed for your next gig.

Area	Still prepping	In progress	Ready for prime time
#1 Polish			
#2 Practice			
#3 Presence			
#4 Perform			
#5 Provide			
#6 Pursue			

▶ CONCLUSION

This entry-level module packs in a lot for you to consider about yourself in relation to your work. Developing self-awareness takes time, and since we're evolving and changing throughout our lives, the growth process never truly ends. What you bring to the leadership table is unique and precious. And as I mentioned in this module, you may find yourself in positions that are not a great match and other places where you naturally thrive. Knowing thyself is essential to assess whether your discomfort stems from unfamiliarity, fear of failure, or simple nerves or if it's a warning sign that the job isn't a fit. Once you know, you know. There's no shame in moving on and finding that niche. Now that we've delved into your psyche, personality, and persona, Module 2 will expand your perspective by taking a look at how you interact with others, develop peer relationships, respond to direction, build community, and solve interpersonal dilemmas.

References

Bandura, A. (1997). *Self-efficacy: The exercise of control.* New York: W.H. Freeman and Company.

Blad, E. (July 21, 2023). What new data show about principal turnover. *EdWeek.* Accessed on July 14, 2024 from https://www.edweek.org/leadership/what-new-data-show-about-principal-turnover/2023/07

Creating a purpose-driven personal brand: A roadmap for a genuine and distinctive professional identity. (n.d.). University of California Berkeley ExecEd. Accessed on July 14, 2024 from https://executive.berkeley.edu/thought-leadership/blog/creating-purpose-driven-personal-brand

Daskal, L. (2017). *The leadership gap: What gets between you and your greatness.* Portfolio.

Diliberti, M. K. & Schwartz, H.L. (2023). Educator Turnover Has Markedly Increased, but Districts Have Taken Actions to Boost Teacher Ranks: Selected Findings from the Sixth American School District Panel Survey. Santa Monica, CA: RAND Corporation. Accessed on July 14, 2024 from https://www.rand.org/pubs/research_reports/RRA956-14.html

Feiten, T.E. (Apr. 3, 2022). Jakob von Uexküll's concept of umwelt. *The Philosopher*, 110(1) ("The New Basics: Planet"). Accessed from https://www.thephilosopher1923.org/post/jakob-von-uexkull-umwelt on December 27, 2022.

Grolnick, W. S., Heddy, B. C. & Worrell, F. C. (2024). *Motivation myth busters: Science-based strategies to boost motivation in yourself and others.* Washington, DC: American Psychological Association. Accessed on August 4, 2024 from https://books.google.com/books?id=hC8PEQAAQBAJ&lpg=PT8&ots=zIWPk5c1Yq&dq=intrinsic%20extrinsic%20motivation%20myth&lr&pg=PT46#v=onepage&q=intrinsic%20extrinsic%20motivation%20myth&f=false

Kiknadze, N.C. & Leary, M.R. (2021). Comfort zone orientation: Individual differences in the motivation to move beyond one's comfort zone. *Personality and Individual Differences*, 181, 2021, 111024, ISSN 0191-8869. Accessed on July 23, 2024 from https://doi.org/10.1016/j.paid.2021.111024

Levin, S. & Bradley, K. (Mar. 19, 2019). Understanding and Addressing Principal Turnover. Learning Policy Institute (LPI) and National Association of Secondary School Principals (NASSP). Accessed on

July 14, 2024 from https://learningpolicyinstitute.org/product/nassp-understanding-addressing-principal-turnover-review-research-report

McLeod, S. (2024). Vygotsky's Theory of Cognitive Development. Accessed on November 7, 2024 from: https://www.simplypsychology.org/vygotsky.html?ezoic_amp=1&fb_comment_id=500779888714_15217241

Mehle, D. & Frazier, N. (2013). *Activators: Classroom strategies for engaging middle and high school students.* Cambridge, MA: Educators for Social Responsibility.

Schwarzer, R. & Jerusalem, M. (1995). Generalized Self-Efficacy scale. In J. Weinman, S. Wright & M. Johnston, Measures in health psychology: A user's portfolio. Causal and control beliefs (pp. 35–37). Windsor, UK: NFER-NELSON. Accessed on 11/24/23 from https://userpage.fu-berlin.de/health/engscal.htm

Skaalvik, C. (2020). School principal self-efficacy for instructional leadership: Relations with engagement, emotional exhaustion and motivation to quit. *Soc Psychol Educ*, 23, 479–498. https://doi.org/10.1007/s11218-020-09544-4

Module 2

Mobilizing Support

▶ INTRODUCTION

Upon entering my first leadership role, I was caught off guard by the sheer volume of human resources and interpersonal relations piling up on my plate. Managing staff, working with students, engaging with caregivers, interacting with the community, reporting to supervisors, and connecting with external partners are all parts of an administrator's daily routine. For an introvert, even a sociable one like myself, I sometimes found it taxing. In the first year or two in your new position, you will be tempted and tested many times over. You'll be tempted to make your mark, introduce innovation, or implement needed initiatives sooner than later. However, in a new environment, it's absolutely instinctual for people to pose challenges for you to overcome so that they can find out who you are, what you believe, and how you lead. It's often unconscious; most people are not cooking up random issues for you to wrangle (though a few do come with hidden agendas), but they are looking at you to support them in their own jobs. And they are often eager to have you address their unmet needs.

Some things they throw at you are rooted in unresolved issues their exiting leader left behind. It's not uncommon for a pendulum swing to happen in the hiring process; if the past principal was too lax, they're looking for someone stricter and vice versa. It's an even bigger hurdle if the departing leader was beloved and they want you to be just like them. Any way you slice it, everyone involved will be simultaneously going through the transition process right along with you. Fortunately, I figured out early on that simply being with my colleagues provided a relieving balm. I relied on my fellow principals to work through dilemmas I didn't know how to handle yet, access resources, and build my leadership muscles and brain power. Ultimately, we made each other better leaders and it's a practice I've sought out in every position thereafter.

You can probably think of an immediate inner circle of mentors, supporters, colleagues, and friends who provide a regular sounding board for your professional challenges pretty easily. As a newer administrator, you will likely lean more heavily on your peers with more experience and then pay it forward to others in your wake later on. Reciprocity is essential. It's not enough to just have friends, confidantes, or acquaintances; mobilizing support goes well beyond that. There's an old saying that if you look behind yourself and no one is following, then you're not really a leader. Allies are earned not automatic. Learning how to catalyze others' peak performance to increase impact is an important and acquired skill set. We can also learn important lessons from others (even when not intentionally seeking support) if we push ourselves. Sometimes the naysayers and critics as well as people we don't personally know, such as scholars and authors we respect, can illuminate our thinking and provide alternative reasoning that broadens our perspectives.

Seeking out formal and informal relationships that support you as you're supporting your school community adds years of professional knowledge and wisdom to your arsenal. There are many types of collectives you might seek out, form, or join, such as affinity groups (e.g., racial/ethnic, linguistic, gender-specific); Communities of Practice (career-stage, role-alike, or cross-regional); Professional Learning Communities (PLCs); affiliate organizations on education-related topics (e.g., instructional strategies for English language learners or serving students with special needs); topical groups like technology users or communications strategists; or any other network or cohort of specialists honing their craft in company with one another. These spaces offer safe places to learn, share, and solve problems as well as engage in communal camaraderie. Though their goals, design, and purposes may be distinct, each, when done well, builds capacity, bolsters morale, and makes leadership less isolating.

▶ FOUNDATIONS

The exercises in this second module focus on how to devise support mechanisms and goad them into action. To provide a solid foundation for the content, we will explore these topics and more:

- Building widespread capacity in your organization by putting the theory of collective leader efficacy and social mobilization into action.
- Intentionally constructing your team composition and defining functional roles to accomplish desired outcomes.
- Raising self-consciousness about how others experience your leadership via a variety of conceptual models.
- Setting and maintaining boundaries within your leadership and management roles.

The research base is deep on much of this subject matter in the business world but is a bit scarcer when applied specifically to school and systems leaders. So, much of what follows will be a presentation of some of the high-level principles transported into the world of educational administration.

Collectivism

The basic concept behind collective efficacy centers on the premise that individuals who have a common interest form an alliance and decide to pool their diverse talents and expertise in order to increase the impact or outcome of a shared mission. To help illustrate this in action, consider these examples:

- A group of neighbors decides to come together to beautify a common area and plant a community garden near the local elementary school, utilizing their joint vegetation

knowledge, carpentry, and management skills to staff the volunteers and complete the project.
- Members of a political action group supporting a certain candidate for the local school board tap each individual's capabilities and assign appropriate roles (e.g., letter writing, phone banking, tabling, fundraising) with the intention of getting their contender elected.
- Students organize a rally to raise awareness about interrupting the school-to-prison pipeline and identify peers who can serve as social media ambassadors, keynote speakers, audio-visual technicians, and speech writers to execute their public event.

These circumstances exhibit similar key conditions: an element of choice, optional participation, knowledge of how one's own skills or talents might contribute to an effort, desire for positive change, and a clearly outlined objective.

When translated into a school setting, it might look like a team of teachers staying after school each Wednesday to collaborate on unit plans with each person offering ideas for instructional strategies, assessments, and curricular ideas with the goal of improving student learning. Or it could be a group of school psychologists who, in a training program on identification of students with special needs, study the topic together, determine a few ideas to implement, and come back together to review the results to recommend piloting a new districtwide process. A cross-collaboration team of classified staff in the main office pulls together parent volunteers to help them revise their back-to-school registration day protocols to maximize efficiency and troubleshoot the past year's enrollment issues. The iterations are endless.

The specific topic of collective teacher efficacy is borne out of how teachers feel about to what extent they contribute to student learning outcomes and is based largely on the 12-item Collective Teacher Beliefs questionnaire developed by Roger Goddard et al. (2015). As this survey is now over two decades old, and cultural responsiveness and educational equity were both fledgling fields in the early 2000s, some of the questions may not garner the same responses today. The ingredients for any collective efficacy model rely on both "will" and "skill" to actuate results: in the case of teaching, the focus should be squarely on yielding improved student learning and behavioral outcomes. And indications that this support structure is effective are promising. Over the past few decades, studies by John Hattie, legendary researcher and director of the Melbourne Educational Research Institute at the University of Melbourne, have greatly influenced our understanding of the factors that most influence student achievement. His earlier work, *Visible Learning* (2009), a nearly 400-page tome synthesizing over 800 meta-analyses relating to achievement, placed "self-reported grades" at the top of the list for maximum impact at 1.44 (noting that anything over an effect size of 0.40 is in the zone of desired effects).

Partly as a result of Rachel Eells' 2011 meta-study on Collective Teacher Efficacy (CTE), Hattie (2016) recalculated his initial ranking of 195 effects to situate CTE as the singular factor with the most dominant force in determining students' educational trajectories, and the effect size was 1.57 (Donohoo et al., 2018). Simply put, as in his earlier work, he concluded: "What teachers do matters" (2009, p. 22). And the magnitude of their doing so as a collective supersedes several external factors and uncontrollable circumstances related to students' home environments, socio-economic status, or caregiver involvement.

Eells 2011 dissertation purports that the concept of teacher efficacy centers on the belief an instructor holds about their ability to effectively help students meet learning targets. Though she doesn't express it outright, I'd add an equity stance to that assertion, which I used as the basis of my previous book, *Leading Through an Equity Lens* (Wallace, 2023). Educational equity will be realized through teacher collective efficacy when

> Dimensions of privilege and oppression (e.g. race, ethnicity, socioeconomic status, gender, sexual orientation, religion) are not predictive of or correlated with educational outcomes, broadly defined, in any significant way, and where all learners are able to participate fully in quality learning experiences.
> (Poekert et al., 2020, pp. 541–542)

What we can control outweighs what we can't, thus weakening the argument that student groups deemed "at risk", "disadvantaged", or "deficient" in various ways will never academically catch up to their peers and will stay in a perpetual state of "achievement gap."

Furthermore, Eells claims that

> When efficacy is considered at the school level, it is an organizational property reflecting beliefs about the capability of the school to achieve its goals. Since teachers interact and collaborate within schools with varying degrees of success, it is valuable to examine efficacy at both the individual and collective levels.
>
> (p. 53)

This makes for a complex situation that Eells describes as human agency operating at three separate levels:

> *Personal agency* refers to acts that a person does intentionally. People cede personal control for responsibilities to *proxy agency* when they believe that another person has better ability, or if the task at hand seems particularly difficult or onerous and they don't want the responsibility. When responsibility is shared with others, in the belief that, as a group, they can make desired progress toward a common goal, *collective agency* emerges.
>
> (Bandura, 2001) (pp. 16–17)

This trio of agencies centers on *I*, *them*, and *we*.

1. I am able do [fill in the blank] perfectly well on my own (and thus don't need or want anyone else involved).
2. I can't or don't want to do [fill in the blank], so I'll leave [that thing] up to them to figure out.
3. We have a diverse collection of abilities that will help us accomplish [fill in the blank] together.

Now each statement reflects two sides of the same coin. In the first circumstance, your actual job may be so specialized that it's appropriate to do tasks on your own. On the other hand, if you are one of many others who perform the same duties and you hold back your expertise, others are left without the benefit of shared knowledge. In the second case, you're not treading into territory you have no business being in; also, spending inordinate amounts of time learning a skill that you will use rarely is neither efficient nor wise. But that must be true; otherwise, you may be passing the buck on something well within your domain simply because you feel it's not worth your energy or is otherwise undesirable. The third situation is the Goldilocks of the model: we all do what we're good at and that contributes to the whole. Ideally, it's the right fit for everyone. The only caveat is that group work can be messy, stressful, or uncomfortable when you have to rely on people who may have different styles, approaches, and personalities when it comes to completing a task. It takes some getting used to!

Let's ground this theory in practice. A teacher operating in the realm of personal agency independently prepares lesson plans, creates instructional activities, or writes assessments for use in their own classroom with just their students. This perspective is self-centered: me, my kids, my room, my choices, my impact. The second category shows up in the exact opposite, but similarly isolated, fashion. It's their kids, their subject area, their grade level, or their classroom environment. In other words: not my business, not my problem. The third domain is where collective efficacy lives. As a grade level, subject area, school, department, or district, we decide as a group what the best approaches to teaching are, try them out with our students, review the results together, and adjust for future instruction. This is also known as the PDSA model of continual improvement. We Plan, we Do, we Study, we Act. In other words, a group of professionals takes collective responsibility for every student's success and failure, regardless of whichever place they inhabit within the ecosystem.

Collective Leader Efficacy

Now that we've laid the groundwork on personal efficacy and teacher collective efficacy, it's time to fully focus on the topic that former principal and author Peter DeWitt examines. In his first article on the subject, "Many hands make light work," DeWitt (2017), defines *collaborative leadership* as "the purposeful actions we take as leaders to enhance the instruction of teachers and build deep relationships with all stakeholders through understanding self-efficacy and building collective efficacy to deepen our learning together" (p. 30). DeWitt discusses the consequences of school leadership self-efficacy which, on the bright side, fosters job satisfaction, heightens motivation, increases confidence, boosts persistence, and creates greater collective capacity. Comparatively, when leader self-efficacy is not present in the school, administrators exhibit insecurity, reactivity, a lack of commitment, or engagement in individual pursuits or just plain gives up due to burnout. This is not to say that if you go it alone, you will fail as a leader. Rather, your impact may be limited to your own turf. When you eventually go away, so goes your legacy.

How many times have you witnessed this scenario? A site, district, or central office leader arrives on the scene with a well-intended plan of action that erases or upends the previous administrator's likewise well-intended plan of action. Shampoo, rinse, and repeat – sometimes this happens on an annual basis. This churn can be avoided if the collective culture intercedes and the incoming leader is savvy enough to take inventory before implementing new initiatives.

While a certain amount of research has been conducted on collective teacher efficacy, the concept of collective leader efficacy is still in its infancy. "Collective Teacher Efficacy and Its Enabling Conditions" (2023), a paper that Illinois educators Christine M. Anderson, Kelly H. Summers, Ryan D. Kopatich, and William B. Dwyer presented at the American Educational Research Association, broaches the subject here:

> School leadership sets the tone and narrative of the school. Implicit in the framework...is a collective teacher efficacy culture that subsists on trust and agency where all practitioners are students of their craft, and they systematically reflect on instructional practices in light of the evidence of learning. The collective efficacy narrative insists that organizational learning as well as student learning are the primary business

of the school and that all students can learn, despite the fixed challenges that may present themselves.

(p. 13)

An educational research team led by Roger Goddard et al. (2015) found that

1. School principals' instructional leadership is positively and significantly associated with teacher collaboration for instructional improvement.
2. Teacher collaboration is positively and significantly related to collective efficacy beliefs.
3. Instructional leadership is positively and significantly related to collective efficacy beliefs through its effect on teacher collaboration.
4. Collective efficacy beliefs are positively and significantly associated with differences among schools in students' fourth-grade mathematics and reading achievement.
5. Both instructional leadership and teacher collaboration are positively and significantly related to student achievement through their effects on collective efficacy beliefs.

(p. 510)

In other words, what principals do matters, too. As instructional leaders of the school, they recognize, equip, support, and encourage teachers to collaborate on their lessons, sharpen their techniques, and engage in deeper learning themselves to show up in the classroom better each day. Ideally, the site administrator protects their teachers' time and space as much as possible to create conditions that send a clear message: our core focus is on student learning.

In 2018, Hattie et al. expanded on the critical role that school leaders play in prefabricating the right atmosphere:

> School leaders must work to build a culture designed to increase collective efficacy, which will affect teachers' behavior and student beliefs. The power and promise of collective efficacy is that it can be influenced within schools, so

focusing on it as a change point is a viable path to greater student achievement, greater commitment to learning, and a more inviting place to come and learn.

(p. 44)

I'm no statistician like Hattie, but I'm quite curious about what the magnified effect size might be if we engaged in collective leader efficacy alongside teachers' collective efficacy.

It got me wondering, if a group of teachers as facilitators of learning currently make the greatest impact on student achievement, how might leaders collectively craft and sustain conditions that are *in service of* meaningful teaching and learning experiences? Breaking down the three-part phrase collective/leader/efficacy is an important part of the sensemaking process. Each word in and of itself can have multiple definitions, parts of speech, tenses, connotations, and interpretations depending on your personal schema and context. So, let's take a look at how these terms will be used to foster a common understanding as delineated in Figure 2.1. When blended together, the compound noun Collective-Leader-Efficacy means in its elemental form: *An intentional collaborative of school and district leaders committed to leveraging their combined aptitudes in order to produce the greatest degree of impact on teaching practices and student outcomes.*

Referring back to the examples posed at the beginning of this module and the features of collectivism, think about ways in which you may already be involved in continuous improvement

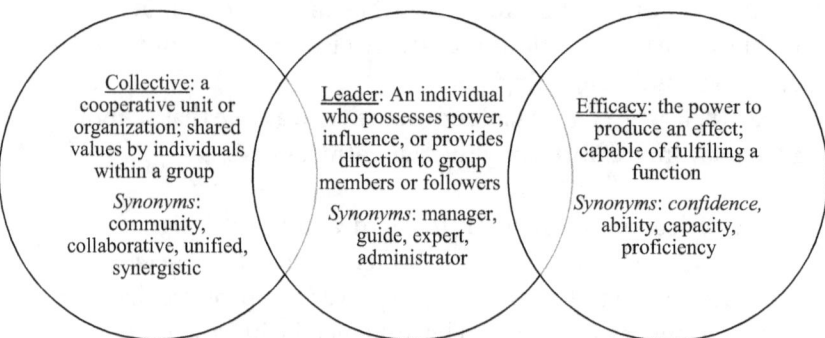

Figure 2.1 Collective leader efficacy definition of terms

efforts with your colleagues and how you might bring all of these dynamics intentionally into play:

- ❑ I am choosing to be part of this group or team on my own accord.
- ❑ I fully participate in activities because I want to learn in community.
- ❑ I bring knowledge, skills, or talents that contribute to shared efforts.
- ❑ I am motivated to make positive changes in my setting.
- ❑ I will help keep myself and others on track to meet our objectives.

Practical Application

Time to branch out from Goddard's (2002) original 12-item Collective Teacher Beliefs questionnaire. How much are leaders, as a unit, able to influence desired outcomes or institutional practices? They can explore this by rating their responses to questions posed in Exercise 2.2 related to the following:

1. Cultivating conditions that maximize student learning outcomes
2. Communicating to students that the district's adults believe in them
3. Showing cultural responsivity to student behaviors in equity-centered ways
4. Customizing central office protocols and procedures that facilitate learning
5. Promoting deep understanding and mastery of academic concepts for all students
6. Modeling ways for students to think critically
7. Introducing new programming that reflects creativity and innovation
8. Being able to make students feel safe, welcome, with a sense of belonging at school
9. Sanctioning time for role-alike staff to collaborate with and support each other
10. Agency to influence governing board decisions that affect their sites

▶ TEAM ROLES, FUNCTIONS, AND RESPONSIBILITIES

To set the stage for this next section, I will cite, for the third time in a book I've written, Mike Schmoker's (2004) powerful three-word phrase *clarity precedes competence*. Role confusion is, unfortunately, a common liability in leadership. Sometimes it's hard to know exactly what your position calls for, especially when it seemingly calls for you to be *everything, to all people, all the time*. Instead of taking it all on yourself, which is a bona fide recipe for early burnout, take some time to understand where you might expect to get support in your efforts to support others. It's about knowing one's specific job duties but also about establishing and maintaining appropriate boundaries.

The first time I was assigned my own administrative assistant, I struggled with letting go of what I'd always done for myself: calendaring meetings, taking notes, scheduling appointments, preparing documents, organizing materials, making copies, and many other clerical tasks. Part control-freak, part-novice, part-workhorse, I luckily lost a few battle royales to my graciously assertive and highly capable admins. Once I finally figured out that (a) they could do their jobs better than I could, (b) it was within their scope not mine, and (c) I needed to spend my time developing new capacities, it all came into sync. This small example illustrates that everyone has a critical part to play in the organization and discernment between responsibilities is required for proper functioning.

Going back to the premise that *leaders collectively crafting and sustaining conditions in service of supporting teacher instruction will only magnify the positive effects on student learning*, site and central office leaders may need to reorient their current understanding of what service actually means. As DeWitt says in his 2021 book *Collective Leader Efficacy*,

> Collective efficacy is about fostering leadership, independence, and interdependence among teachers, and it is also about elevating the power of the collective. School leaders need to engage in joint work with teachers and staff within

their schools that involves inquiry cycles of learning if they are to have a true impact on student learning.

(p. 4)

Note that this explanation includes the word *independence* alongside *interdependence*. This needs further explication, lest people see this as an either/or paradigm. As in, you are either a solo artist or a nameless band member. Individual talents and skills must be refined before contributing to a group. And participation on a team helps you develop independence in executing your particular area of work successfully.

The National Institute for Excellence in Teaching (2022) published a piece called "Dismantling the Culture of Nice" on how collective leader efficacy is meant to increase student achievement when those involved do it with candor and trust. They cite several reasons why systems should engage in reciprocal learning models:

- To increase the impact of the team through shared learning experiences
- To drive improvement efforts by working collectively as a high-functioning team
- To support the development of a shared leadership mindset
- To develop a culture of learning and leadership
- To identify and develop practices that support a positive impact on teaching and learning

And the ways in which such collectives can accomplish their goals:

- Setting directions
- Charting a clear course that everyone understands
- Establishing high expectations and using data to track progress and performance
- Developing people through providing teachers and others in the system with the necessary support and training to succeed

- Making the organization work, ensuring that the entire range of conditions and incentives in the school fully supports teaching and learning (p. 1)

A study commissioned by the Australian Council for Educational Research Ltd. illustrates this in practice. Researchers Kerry Elliott et. al. (2022) investigated how a group of leaders supported by a Menzies Foundation "Incubator" developed collective efficacy mindsets at the school, leader, and teacher levels. They provide us an important distinction between "[l]eader development [which] involves developing individual leaders' mindsets, behaviours, and other intrapersonal attributes [and] leadership development [which] involves developing the relationships, systems, and contexts in which individual leaders are nested" (p. 11). Furthermore, they found:

> In the context of the Incubator, it has become evident that cultivating collective efficacy involves three distinct aspects of leadership: *leadership of self, others and systems* [emphasis added]. Leadership of self involves understanding and developing individual attributes that contribute to building collective efficacy. Leadership of others involves creating the learning conditions in which others (individuals or teams) can develop the capabilities identified as relevant to cultivating collective efficacy, and also creating relationships that lead to the emergence of collective efficacy. Leadership of systems focuses on making changes to aspects of the school systems which contribute to cultivating collective efficacy. Changes to systems may include ways of working, processes and policies, governance, etc.
>
> (p. 11)

This trifecta of self-efficacy, leadership in service to others, and multilayered systems thinking is necessary to impact the greater organization. Therefore, strong collective leadership models need to attend to each to codify long-term structures and reach aspirational solutions, as will be discussed in Module 5.

Teaming Up

Have you ever been on a team where the roles were blurry, confusing, or non-existent and no one was sure what to do? Role clarity is a major element to successful teamwork. Leaders naturally want to help, engage with, and carry out a defined continuous improvement shared mission. Set them up for success by identifying who should be included in planning, execution, feedback, and support. The collaborative structures in the matrix below will help your team to clarify the boundaries between different job functions and determine what is needed from each group or individual involved. Later on, you will have an opportunity to apply the model in Table 2.1 to an upcoming initiative in your organization.

More often than not, in the educational sphere we inherit teams rather than construct them from scratch. They often pre-date and preexist our entry into the system, and we are plugged in wherever assigned. While you may not have total control over team membership, especially when it is something as fixed as a grade-level team or a curriculum council composed of elected

Table 2.1 Functional role quadrants

Leaders are the initiators and designers of an implementation plan. Their role is to • zero in on the "why" and "what" of the strategy • align staff to the goals, vision, and mission • inspire motivation and uplift morale • establish expected outcomes based on whole agency commitments • offer long-term perspectives on the work • mediate external circumstances that may hinder implementation efforts	**Implementers** are the people who carry through the plan. Their role is to • tackle the "how" of the implementation plan by breaking down goals into concrete steps • strategically organize, assign, and coordinate workflow • orchestrate short-term objectives and keep goals on track • address internal issues to enhance productivity and efficiency • ensure high-quality deliverables and outcomes

(Continued)

Table 2.1 (Continued)

Recipients are the intended audience the implementation is meant to impact. They	**Contributors** are other people involved in sustaining the plan's long-term success. Their role is to
• participate in piloting/prototypes
• provide feedback on how things are going at various intervals
• share problems or issues they're encountering or grappling with
• benefit from the plan in tangible, concrete ways
• share ideas for future iterations, adjustments, or expansions	• possess a high-level knowledge about the initiative's purpose and intentions
• connect organizational efforts they are involved in with the initiative, when appropriate
• publicly champion and elevate the initiative's accomplishments
• offer relevant resources to aid implementation efforts

department chairs, other opportunities await. Short-term committees, task forces, advisory councils, working groups, and other involvement efforts can and should be intentionally designed to include as many of the roles outlined in Figure 2.2 that apply to the team's objectives when implementing a new plan or enterprise.

Don't stop here, though. Selecting people who fit various demographics or play certain professional roles alone won't suffice in making the collaboration truly effective. You will also need to identify people from the above categories who might play a dual or triple role based on natural or learned talents or orientations illustrated in Figure 2.3. Game–Changing leadership relies on serious strategic thinking. Chess playing, even. Consider all your possible moves, then reconsider them and reconfigure your game board to predict outcomes.

Highly functioning teams must document why they exist by outlining their goals, purpose, and expected outcomes. This may take more than one meeting, so don't rush it; take time to get it right. Establish a flexible decision-making process upfront so that there are no quibbles or curve balls that skew team relationships. This is accomplished by communicating openly and frequently during and in between meetings to

Designers: blend artistic and practical design skills to conceptualize structural and visual elements

Decision-makers: those with social, political, and economic capital

Project manager: plans, organizes, oversees, and helps execute details

Resource managers: responsible for ensuring that needed resources to be successful are intact

Evaluators/monitors: assess intended versus actual impacts of the implementation on recipients

Content/Technical Experts: individual(s) with knowledge, experience, or skills related to the initiative

Negotiators: employee association designees to provide input on job expectations or other contractual conditions

Documenters: take meeting notes, send reminders, report benchmarks, milestones, goals & timelines

Troubleshooters: serve to problem-solve issues during early implementation phases

Figure 2.2 Additional functional team roles

clear up any concerns, gain clarity, and engage in sensemaking. When issues inevitably arise, handle them professionally and promptly. Festering or lingering tensions will only mount otherwise. Finally, each member must commit to doing their individual parts to support the whole team. Coming to meetings prepared is non-negotiable.

Once you're in the room together, team meetings should be a means to an end, not the main event. My (educated) guess is that you attend multiple meetings a day – some productive, some not so much. Standing meetings, in particular, can be a challenge because people feel compelled to meet, whether or not there is anything relevant to discuss. The intention here is to make every meeting meaningful through purposeful design and clear intentions. Prior to putting together an agenda, see if you can answer each of the questions posed in Figure 2.4. If you find

68 Game–Changing Leadership in Action

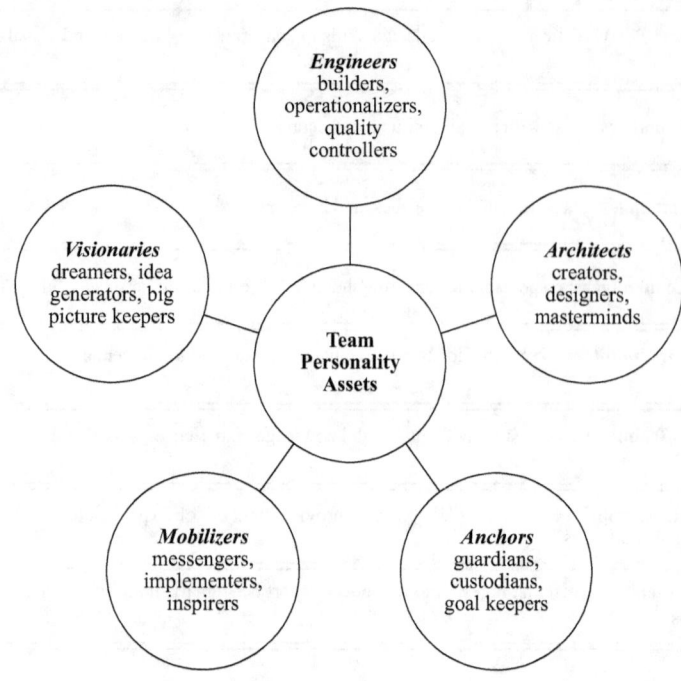

Figure 2.3 Leveraging team personality assets

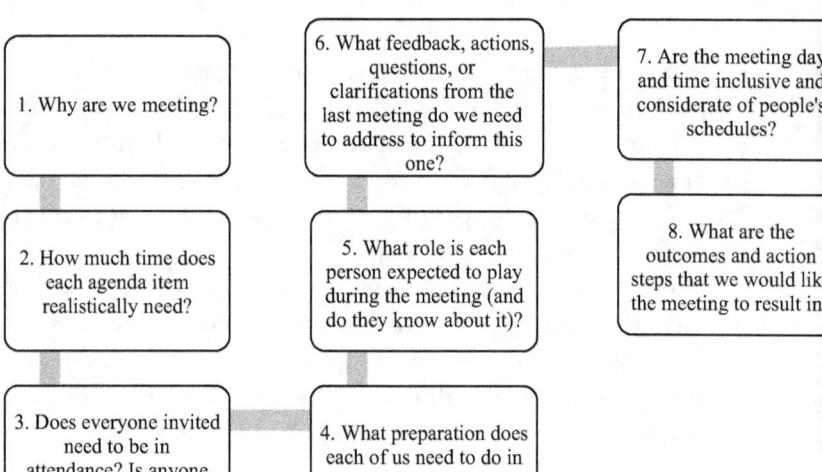

Figure 2.4 Essential questions for meeting development

yourself at a loss for any given component, think it through before calling the team together.

We're all professionals, right? Famous last words. Thinking that your team will organically figure out the right components is a common mistake. What typically happens is that a team runs afoul of one or more of these key elements and is faced with the clunky business of backtracking to set up norms, expectations, and outcomes. It's way better to get off on the right foot with established expectations. The hypothetical team described below is an example of what happens when role clarity and project management skills are lacking.

> You are a project manager at the County Office of Education and have assigned your team to develop a presentation on a new statewide policy that will affect your partner districts. Alice (the overachiever) is putting in way more effort than is needed into trivial details of the project, slowing the rest of the team down. Biv keeps attempting to insert unconnected elements that are particularly interesting to him but aren't adding value to the overarching policy components goals. Carlos is investing large amounts of time on perfecting early versions of a draft document rather than waiting to do the finishing touches after the content is developed. Debra is still rehashing past projects that have no bearing on this one and continually questioning the purpose of the assignment. Eddie just wants everyone to be happy and spends a lot of his time smoothing over or trying to fix the group's problems at the risk of non-completion on his own part.

As their manager:

1. How would you help each individual team member function more effectively?
2. What processes might you recommend that result in a high-quality final product?
3. What assets can you leverage from each team member's strengths to optimize their collective work?
4. What elements might be missing that need to be incorporated to get the team unstuck and back on the right path?

Here's an example of a team that knows its reasons for being. A fifth-grade teacher meets with his grade-level team after school to review the results of a common assessment they all conducted the previous week to gauge student growth on a set of math standards. He finds that his students did well in all areas except two and asks the other teachers whose students excelled on those items for details on how they designed their instruction. The other teachers share their different strategies while he takes notes and asks questions to understand their approaches better. He returns to his classroom a few days later and blends a combination of their methods within his unique teaching style, does a quick check for understanding, and finds that the students' grasped the concepts much better this time around. As a result, his interdependence on his colleagues enhanced his independent effectiveness with his own class.

Now, let's overlay this same scenario with a leadership lens. The school's Instructional Leadership Team (ILT) is composed of a vice principal, principal, school counselor, and grade-level leads from kindergarten through sixth grade. They meet every two weeks to develop a culture of Collective Teacher Efficacy (CTE) that mirrors their own Collective Leadership Efficacy (CLE) model at the central office. The principal and vice principal also meet with the district's ILT to learn beside their fellow site administrators and the instructional services team (teachers on special assignment [TOSAs], content area experts, and departmental administrators) in order to calibrate, consult, and coach each other on ways to implement CTE and CLE support systems at their sites.

The principals return to campus, meet with their school's ILT to share what they learned and at the same time the grade-level teacher leaders work with their colleagues to discuss problems of practices and agree on tactics they will try before coming back together to review artifacts and assessment data. Finally, and most importantly, the classroom teachers try out strategies and tools to help their students achieve instructional objectives. And then the continuous improvement cycle flows back up to the site ILT and district ILT to examine cumulative effects on student learning throughout the elementary campuses. Table 2.2 depicts the progression between the groups.

Table 2.2 Progression of systemic learning

Collaborative Structure	Collective Roles & Responsibilities
District Instructional Leadership Team (DILT): Associate Superintendent Departmental Directors Content Area Experts Instructional Coaches Principals Assistant Principals	• Governance and decision-making • Textbook/materials/technologies adoptions • Professional development, training, support • Implementation planning and execution • Responding to site needs and requests • Troubleshooting system-wide issues • Allocation of district resources to address localized problems of practice • Staffing and human resources services • Guidance on new policies and protocols • Technical expertise
Collaborative Structure	**Collective Roles & Responsibilities**
Site Instructional Leadership Team (SILT): Administrators (principal/asst. principals) Counselors Specialists Grade Level/Dept. Team leads	• Apply rationale and details from centralized direction, decisions, and directives to site • Provide site-based reinforcement of training & ongoing job-embedded professional learning activities • Communicate what's tight and loose within their campus locus of control • Come to consensus on delivery methods, timelines, and implementation of new programs, projects, policies, etc. • Create feedback mechanisms to report out issues needing resolution

(Continued)

Table 2.2 (Continued)

Collaborative Structure	Collective Roles & Responsibilities
	• Make and uphold agreements for putting policy into practice • Measure progress and report back to district ILT
Content Area/Grade Level Instructional Team (CAIT; GLIT: Content Area Teachers Grade Specific Teachers Special Educators Paraeducators Teachers on Special Assignment (coaches, specialists)	• Identify essential teaching and learning objectives • Devise differentiated instructional strategies to reach students equitably • Develop and analyze results of common assessments to evaluate student mastery of material • Customize interventions and acceleration opportunities • Engage in co-teaching, shadowing, lesson study, and/or peer observations to inform practice • Study/research a topic of shared interest • Mentor, coach, or provide moral support to one another • Conduct consultancy protocols on problems of practice • Measure progress and report back to site ILT

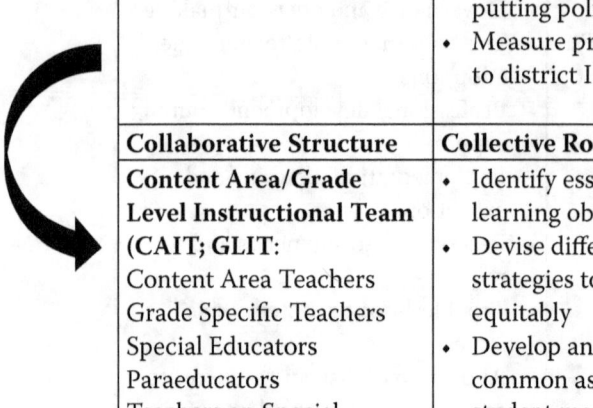

Case Study

Imagine that a site attendance team at a continuation high school has discovered that student absences are due primarily to mental and/or physical health barriers. After researching the root causes further, they decide to allocate part of a campus wing to host a wellness center that addresses student and family basic healthcare needs. The Site Instructional Leadership Team (SILT) includes the principal, assistant principal, and social worker. They convene the Content Area Instructional Team (CAIT) team, including department chairs, the school nurse, and counselor. They present a plan to the director of student services, who brings the idea to the District Instructional Leadership Team (DILT) for consideration. Once the plan is approved, the DILT works with the site to initiate the wellness center design and completion. Figure 2.5 outlines who on the team is responsible and accountable for specific tasks for implementing their plan.

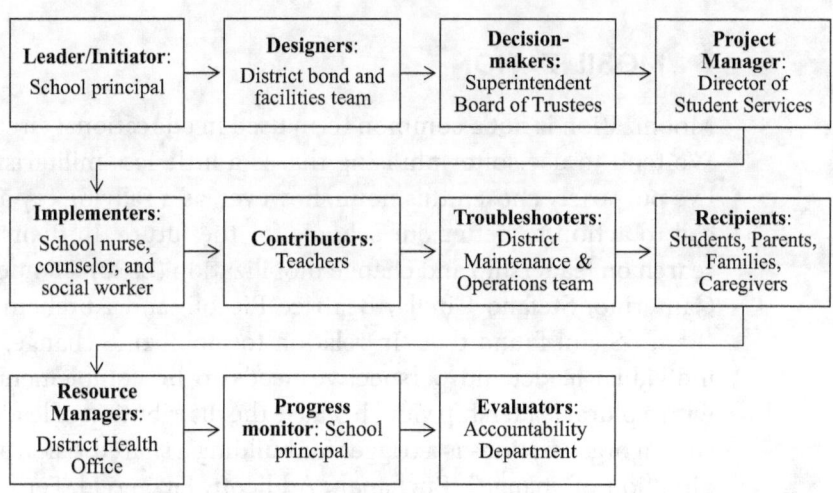

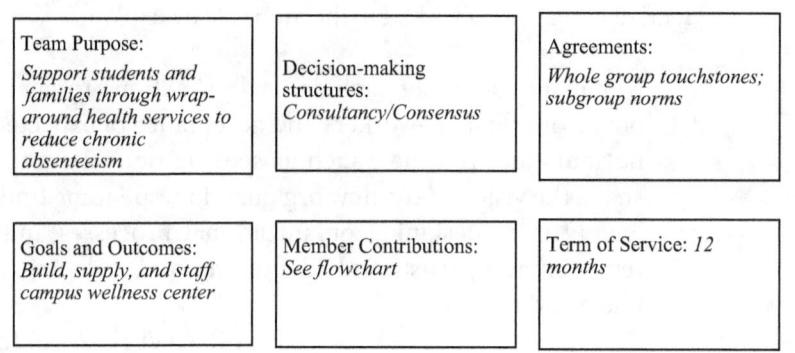

Figure 2.5 Team roles, functions, and operations

Roles: notetaker, facilitator, decision maker, contributors

Skills/Knowledge: facilities experts, health providers, consultant

Diversity of Perspectives: heterogeneous representation, equity of voice

Team Composition: Site staff (3); District leaders (3); Caregivers/Students (3)

Practical Application

Exercise 2.2 invites you to create your own model for collective continuous improvement for a team that you lead or facilitate. You may want to adopt a traditional PDSA structure or meld suggestions from this segment to develop a customized version to meet your specified purposes.

▶ MOBILIZATION

Mobilization is not a common term used in educational circles. We tend to use softer phrasing that is a little less militaristic. I've purposely chosen this noun, however, as a rallying cry and call to action to better our schools for the future. In their research on leadership and change mobilization (2020), Filomena Canterino, Stefano Cirella, Beatrice Piccoli, and Abraham B. (Rami) Shani found that "In relation to mobilizing change, an individual leadership perspective needs to be complemented with a plural leadership view, because the distribution of leadership in organizations is a trigger for building a shared vision and direction of change" (Buchanan, Addicott, Fitzgerald, Ferlie & Baeza, 2007) (p. 42), which is why the preceding section on collective efficacy is pivotal. Furthermore, they explain,

> Mobilizing activities include leaders' actions to gain support from their co-workers and acceptance of expected behaviours and routines, such as seeking out others to help shape the vision of the new organization, spending time and energy in re-designing organizational processes and systems, creating trust, and identifying and reducing resistance and inertia.
>
> (Battilana et al., 2010) (p. 43)

Reflecting on the before-times when you were not in a leadership role, recall the people who were in the front of the room and their range of effectiveness at enlisting widespread support. I'm sure you've witnessed situations where all you could hear were crickets and other times when the leader sparked enthusiasm and energy toward a cause. Note the differences between the two ends of the spectrum. What made people avoid eye contact in the first situation and jump out of their seats in the second? What were the asks involved? What were the commitments expected? How did people view or experience the leader outside of the room? What other dynamics were at play? Game–Changing leadership requires being adept at selecting the right topics and modes of implementation that will inspire others to join them.

In a small case study from England conducted in 2020, Chris Brown, Stephen MacGregor, and Jane Flood concluded:

> When it comes to distributed leadership an ability to influence is vital. This is because, even in collaborative situations, those who are more influential will ultimately steer decision making if they are: 1) accepted as leaders; and 2) if they are able to impact on a range choices and/or actions through engaging with numerous others throughout the school.
>
> (p. 9)

Simply put but not necessarily simple to execute. First, how will you know if you are 'accepted as a leader'? Second, how will you measure 'impact on a range of choices and/or actions'?

While humans are naturally wired to share a collective purpose (even if it's merely survival or subsistence), it truly depends on the leader to bring them into the fold. In an *Annual Review of Psychology* report (2018) on social mobilization, Todd Rogers, Noah J. Goldstein, and Craig R. Fox note that

> Most people have powerful psychological needs to belong, to be well regarded by others, and to see themselves as positive contributors to relevant social groups. Such needs make most people especially responsive to social mobilization interventions that are particularly personal, entail social accountability, harness positive social norms, are identity relevant, and leverage social networks.
>
> (p. 20)

This all bodes well for becoming a mobilizing leader. You have been chosen to lead, and others are poised to allow you to do so. So why do these two underlying forces not always translate to results? The criteria spelled out in the latter part of the quotations from Canterino et al. and Rogers et al. hold some keys to success. Canterino et al. include these *levers* for mobilizing support:

1. *Help shape the vision of the new organization.* Visioning processes are uplifting and imbued with optimism. Tap into the hopes and dreams of students, parents, community members, and staff by including them in establishing the foundational principles of your organization.
2. *Spend time and energy in re-designing organizational processes and systems.* Once a solid vision is in sight, strategic action must follow. Involve others in the evaluation and alignment of practices, protocols, and procedures that embody the school's goals and values.
3. *Create trust.* Communicate clearly and honestly. Be a person of your word. Apologize if you make a mistake. Follow through on your commitments. Embrace transparency. Flatten the hierarchy. If, and when, trust is broken or falters, do your best to repair harm.
4. *Identify and reduce resistance and inertia.* Resistance comes from a variety of sources and is exhibited in overt and covert ways. Stagnation is likewise an enemy of evolution. Pull out the roots rather than address the outward symptoms to sap their influence.

Rogers et al. add these *components* to the mix:

1. *Make it particularly personal.* It's natural to want to have 'skin in the game'. Rarely do people engage in activities outside of their normal scope unless they have an intimate reason to do so. Therefore, a leader must strike a chord in the group they are attempting to unite toward a movement by personalizing the issue to their own lives.
2. *Entail social accountability.* None of us wants to be the only one doing all of the work, so there must be procedures in place to ensure that contributions are balanced and, if not, readjust expectations in alignment with outcomes.
3. *Harness positive social norms.* Cooperation. Collaboration. Compromise. Charity. Connection. These are all part

of the social contract we uphold while in community. Appeal to people's collective goodwill and their behaviors will follow (alongside the accountability measures above).
4. *Identity relevancy.* Identity can be innate or acquired. Many characteristics such as race, gender, sexuality, or other naturally occurring attributes often create kinship with others of our tribe. Likewise, ethos such as belief systems, morality, and personal convictions can also be a big part of what drives us to take initiative.
5. *Leverage social networks.* The work will always be bigger than we are. After starting small with a guiding coalition of true believers, smart leaders stimulate a ripple effect by encouraging others to spread the word and galvanize additional actors to jump into the ensemble on stage.

Practical Application

These nine characteristics for mobilizing support unlock your leadership potential to share the struggles as well as the wealth in good company. Exercise 2.3 equips you for a joint prospect you'd like to spearhead in your school or system. In conjunction with the research cited, you'll need to take an honest look behind yourself to see if anyone is following.

▶ THEORETICAL PARADIGMS

Binary thinking can be a liability, but comparisons exist for good reason! In order to understand light, you must know what dark is. To truly feel joy, it's critical to have experienced sorrow. Failure and success go hand in hand as well. As such, this next section will examine three theoretical paradigms that underscore a continuum of leadership capabilities and capacities that influence relationships with supporters. The first is a concept originally introduced in Liz Wiseman's book *Multipliers* (2013) as a supervisory dynamic occurring in the corporate realm. Wiseman later teamed up with Lois N. Foster and Elise Allen (2013) to collaborate on a book called *The Multiplier Effect: Tapping the Genius Inside Our Schools*. In it, they explore the impacts of being a "multiplier" versus a "diminisher" on staff engagement and outcomes. The second construct will be related to leadership as opposed to management roles. While there is no seminal authority on the topic in the educational realm, there has been much banter about instructional leadership as the preferred operating mode to the lesser-evolved manager of things. My take: you absolutely need both. Finally, we'll touch upon the nuances between setting boundaries while remaining accessible and how to not mix up the two. Knowing what your lane is and how to stay in it is crucial for leadership longevity.

Multipliers vs. Diminishers

As examined in Module 1 in the branding section, most leaders want the people they serve to see them in a certain light. Unless we've done some of the hard work of self-evaluation, we may not know whether our natural, learned, or chosen leadership style is one that encourages others to do their own best work or actually squashes spirit, creativity, and drive. In *The Multiplier Effect*, Wiseman, Foster, and Allen (2013) assert that,

> because Multipliers are leaders who look beyond their own genius and focus on extending the genius of others, they get more from their people. Multipliers get so much brain power from their people that they essentially double the size of their staff for free [at an effect size of 2.3].
>
> (p. 4)

By contrast, Diminishers eke out only about 40% of their staff's capabilities and intelligence. While a bisected approach may not capture the complexities of leadership, Multipliers, taken as a whole, exhibit a more spacious, collaborative, and empowering stance than Diminishers, whose approaches seem bent on controlling and constraining others' efforts. Wiseman et al. categorize the two types of leaders based on five main disciplines: (1) gatekeepers vs. talent finders, (2) tyrants vs. liberators, (3) the know-it-all vs. the challenger, (4) decision makers vs. community builders, and (5) the micromanager vs. investor (p. 8).

There are, of course, leaders who straddle the two definitions depending on the circumstances. For example, I generally don't see myself as a micromanager, yet when someone is starting a job or is an employee who has not delivered on expectations in the past, I supervise them more frequently and double-check their work until they are familiar with the tasks or processes and regularly produce predictable outcomes. Likewise, if you are in a crisis situation and a decision needs to be made immediately, you may not have the luxury of time to involve many others. The point is, do you behave in diminishing ways more often than not, as a standard, rather than as an exception to the rule?

Most leaders perceive the way that they lead as effective or necessary to get the job done, and much of it is based on their personality and strong suits. But we are here to learn from the people we support. As Wiseman et al. also note,

> Uncovering and understanding the mindsets of Multipliers is the key to unlocking the Multiplier Effect. Our assumptions drive our behavior. Our behavior triggers reactions in others, causing them to either step up and operate at their best, or to retreat, giving us a fraction of their true capability.
>
> (p. 12)

I've borrowed from Wiseman et al. (2013) to explain how Multipliers and Diminishers may show up in relation to collective leader efficacy (in Table 2.3).

As mentioned earlier, depending on moment-to-moment situations, it's possible that each archetype can fluctuate between columns, especially when operating within stressful conditions. Under fire, leaders may tighten, instead of loosen, their grip in an attempt to squelch controversy or dissent. Alternatively, others may rise above their own fear of exposure fueled by imposter syndrome and rely on the brainpower and moral support of other leaders to tackle the problem at hand. There is no exact formula to performing your best, but it does begin with self-knowledge of your own tendencies and weak spots. When exposed to the light, our Jungian shadow selves' energy can be defused.

Table 2.3 Traits of multipliers and diminishers in leadership collectives

Diminishers		Multipliers	
Islanders	Operate their own school or department as if disconnected from (or exempt from) the rest of the organization	Bridge builders	See their school or department's contributions as interdependent with the success of the whole organization
Subversives	Believe that they alone know what's right; disregard the district's adopted approaches in order to do their own thing	Connectors	Influence the organization to adopt research-informed practices that benefit all involved
Monopolizers	Attempt to influence self-serving outcomes by dominating resources, space, conversations, and agendas to meet their own school or department needs	Teammates	Understand that the group is stronger when all voices are heard and considered before coming to consensus; follows through with what the whole has decided, even if it doesn't directly benefit them
Climbers	Seek power by advancing up the leadership ladder; cozies up with those at the top (superintendent or board members) to curry favor for pet projects	Scalers	Use their positional power to effect collective gains for the organization; set the stage to enable long term and sustainable growth even after they are no longer part of the organization

Wiseman et al. (2013) observe:

> Unlocking individual potential is not just a matter of personal will. And it is not just a matter of individual leaders, even if those leaders are Multipliers. It is a function of entire systems. This is why we need educational institutions that are Multiplier environments.
>
> (p. xi)

A healthy person spending time in a hospital has an increased likelihood of getting sick. Likewise, a highly functioning leader in a dysfunctional system is subject to being pulled down into the muck. The force of gravity is powerful and must be confronted to make authentic change. The remedy: Collective leadership in action.

Practical Application

So how do you know if you are a Multiplier, a Diminisher, or something in between? Exercise 2.4 offers a continuum with several examples of multiplying or diminishing behaviors that frequently occur in school and district leadership settings. Plus, you'll intentionally develop ways to nudge yourself toward the multiplier characteristics on the spectrum and set up some alerts to keep from drifting into diminisher territory.

▶ LEADERSHIP VS. MANAGEMENT

Well *versus* may be overstating it. While the terms are sometimes used interchangeably, the differences between leadership and management are distinct. Simply put, leaders zero in on the *what* and *why*, and managers focus on the *how*. This can be concretized as leadership being an executive direction role and management to operationally implement. The leader envisions and the manager executes. The leader designs organizational goals, a manager establishes benchmarks to meet them. The leader sets the conditions and managers sustain them. As a practical matter, leaders must possess diverse management competencies; likewise, managers must harness essential leadership dispositions. And our aim is to be able to shift between them fluidly and capably as called for.

Say that you are facilitating a parent meeting at Back to School Night. You start off by presenting the school's vision and the year's goals and celebrating achievements from the previous spring. Then a parent raises their hand to ask about the new dress code policy. In that moment, you swap your leadership hat for your management one and explain how the guidelines will be supervised and monitored. And so on throughout the rest of the meeting: you inspire, then explain; you motivate, then address concerns; you share long-term strategic goals, then action planning steps. You probably aren't even aware you're doing it, but well worth self-evaluating where you operate from the majority of the time – and whether the mode serves the appropriate function in the appropriate space.

Michael Connolly, Michael Fertig, and Chris James (2017) assert the difference between educational management and educational leadership and the importance of educational responsibility:

> In essence, educational management/administration entails being assigned and carrying the responsibility for the proper functioning of a system of some kind in which others participate in an educational institution. Carrying this responsibility is a state of mind not an action. Educational leadership on the other hand is the act of influencing others in educational settings to achieve goals and thus necessitates actions.
>
> (pp. 11–12)

The above delineation is corroborated by Osias Kit T. Kilag et al. (2023) in their systematic literature review on educational leadership and management:

> Educational leadership and management (ELM) is a complex and multifaceted field that has received considerable attention from researchers, policymakers, and practitioners in recent decades. The role of the educational leader has become increasingly important in shaping the direction, culture, and performance of schools and educational

institutions. Effective leadership and management can lead to improved student outcomes, teacher satisfaction, and organizational effectiveness.

(p. 264)

Becoming facile at balancing the two roles is the desired state of equilibrium in educational administration. If you are the sole person in your role at a school site or department, you will naturally need to take on both sets of attributes to get the work done. However, it becomes important to separate them when (a) there are several managerial jobs in one department or at one campus (e.g., principal primarily as leader, assistant principals as managers; or director as leader and their reporting administrators as managers) or (b) you lean too heavily into a space that's not meant for you.

For example, a superintendent should not be spending copious amounts of time on the fine details of a curricular adoption or completing compliance activities when they should be out front instilling confidence in the district's direction. Nor should a leader delegate management processes to others who aren't equipped or have the positional authority to execute a task successfully, like asking your admin assistant to write up your teacher evaluations. Now think about your current role and whether your alignment is on track or needs some synchronization.

Leadership + Management Scenarios

You may not be old enough to remember, but back in the 1970s, the *Choose Your Own Adventure* book series was all the rage. In this rudimentary RPG (role-playing game), you took on the protagonist's identity and were presented decision-making junctures with a few options to choose from which propelled you to chapters with different endings. As a throwback to that era, I will present three case study scenarios with administrators at different levels navigating the nuances between leadership and management situations. There is no one correct answer to the direction each fictional leader might go, but there will be different outcomes or consequences as a result of their decisions.

The three case studies present you with opportunities for determining how different leadership or management moves might actualize one's sought-after outcomes. After reading each vignette, consider the root issues at the center of the dilemma and develop leadership and management maneuvers that help resolve the concerns presented.

- ❑ List a few of the management issues you identified in each case study.
- ❑ What managerial moves could be utilized to address the dilemma?
- ❑ List a few leadership issues you identified in each case study.
- ❑ What leadership moves might be employed to respond to the situation?
- ❑ What are the pros and cons of each move?

CASE STUDY 1: MIDDLE SCHOOL PRINCIPAL

Keisha has just been named the principal of Roundtree Middle School where she was previously a 6–8 grade arts electives teacher. During her first meeting with the site's content area department chairs, she delivers information about two new district initiatives that are expected to be implemented that fall. Immediately, people raise concerns about the timelines, preparation needed, lack of resources, scheduling impacts, and other problems they see with the plan. While she understands – and even agrees with many of their objections – she also knows that in her new role she has to support the policies and dictates from the central office. The English and math department chairs, who hold the most sway in the room, openly challenge Keisha to "stand up against" and "protect us from" the district. Now she needs to respond.

CASE STUDY 2: HIGH SCHOOL TEACHER-LEADER

Roberto chairs the science department at a large suburban high school. There are 14 teachers in the department spanning four grade levels (9–12) and covering several scientific domains: earth/physical science, biology, environmental science, chemistry, and physics. Recently, their state's universities changed the science graduation requirements for students to meet minimum enrollment eligibility, which will also inadvertently impact the site's current staffing configuration. Traditionally, the most senior teachers have been allowed to petition for whichever classes they want to teach most, leaving the newest teachers whatever courses remain unclaimed. However, human resources has reported that the most recently credentialed teachers have the right authorizations to teach in the new integrated science pathways approved by the universities, while some of the veterans do not. This creates tension and conflict amongst the team during department meetings as they are drafting schedules for the upcoming school term. Roberto needs to devise a process to both meet the bureaucratic regulations and keep department morale intact.

CASE STUDY 3: CENTRAL OFFICE ADMINISTRATOR

Timar is the director of instructional technology at an urban school district. She successfully led the district through serious challenges that remote learning posed during the pandemic by introducing several digitally mediated tools to better support student and teacher learning environments. Now that students are back on campus in person and several of the site technology licenses that were purchased at a steep discount during Covid-19 are up for full-price renewal, she is recommending discontinuing four learning platforms that data analytics show are not proving a good return on academic investment in regard to student growth and frequency of instructor usage. Yet there are some schools that are superusers and log onto the programs daily as part of their lesson design. There are also parents associated with all 37 sites who spend time with their children in the portals after school hours to stay up to date on their learning progress. While these benefits are real, the district needs to use its resources wisely and appropriately. Timar and her team need to figure out how to scale down these adopted tools in ways that don't disrupt instructional needs of teachers and learning supports for students.

Each of these case studies illustrates on-the-job problems of practice that present learning opportunities and strategy development. There are no shortcuts or magic potions, however, so also be prepared to clearly explain your thinking, what elements you weighed for decision-making, and how this is the best choice considering the circumstances. Let go of the illusion that you can please everyone – a necessity for long-term sustainability as covered in the final section of module 2.

Boundaries vs. Accessibility

Fact: It feels great to be needed. To be the person who can make things better. The one whom others turn to for answers. But it can also be addictive. Maybe not clinically so, though perhaps bordering on Pavlovian. Ring that renowned bell and certain types come running, tails wagging, mouths salivating. We leaders get a serious buzz off of finding solutions, bringing order to chaos, and tackling problems large or small. Oxytocin. Cortisol. Adrenaline. Most of us get a kick chasing that natural high – and that's good because leadership is not for the faint of heart. People like us, and other first responders, actually run *toward* danger, and it's okay to a degree. But not at the risk of losing yourself in the process of supporting others. Martyrdom: not recommended and to be avoided at all costs.

Fact: There is only one of you. And you simply cannot be all things to all people. It's exceedingly easy to get lost in the shuffle of what is required of us versus how others expect us to meet their own needs. That's where boundaries come in. Boundaries often include intangible mental, physical, and emotional perimeters people set up to guard or preserve their own wellness. Lack of development or awareness of your personal thresholds for things like socializing, service, networking, or other outward facing activities can lead to inundation, burnout, or overcommitment. Sometimes you have to draw the line, set limits, say no, take a break, delegate, or let go. In truth, you are not only doing this for yourself but also modeling for those who are watching.

Leadership in the age of cell phone technology has transformed our ways of working, living, and being. Whatever your role – caregiver, partner, friend, or professional – there is a certain expectation to be reachable, available, and responsive at a rate unprecedented in human history. Case in point: I once had a supervisor who held our weekly executive team meetings on Fridays at 5 pm. If that's not clear value statement, I don't know what is. Kathrin Reinke and Gisela I. Gerlach, in their (2022) study on bi-directional boundaries between the home and workplace, affirm the idea that

> Employees may discern supervisor availability expectations either from supervisors' explicit statements or by observing the supervisors' own work-nonwork availability, interpreting that as representations of what supervisors expect from others (Fishbein and Ajzen 2010). To show aspirations for performing effectively, employees feel pressure to fulfill their supervisors' expectations.
> (p. 699)

With my own staff, I tried breaking the mold of constant connectivity by requesting that all directors, managers, and principals refrain from emailing or tagging people on shared documents over the weekend or on holidays. They could work if they wanted or felt they needed to, but they weren't allowed to impose that on anyone else. As Reinke and Gerlach (2022) conclude:

> Organizations should create working conditions that allow employees to segment work from nonwork domains to the extent of their preferences, while allowing for integration of nonwork matters into work. Facilitating these boundary management behaviors contributes to employees' well-being, which in turn is linked to job-related outcomes such as performance and turnover intention. (Wright & Huang, 2012)
> (pp. 711–12)

Unplugging can be restorative and re-energizing when Monday morning inevitably arrives.

People exist on a spectrum of thresholds for the amount of proximity they can tolerate in both work and personal relationships. And we all have cultural, familial, and experiential constructs about what constitutes healthy, normal, or comfortable. At work, boundary crossing may occur when others seem to want or need excessive amounts of your attention or time or you feel you must attend every single school event without fail. Or answering their messages within minutes of seeing it, à la "Did you see my email/text/instant message/comment/tag?" Or it might tread into personal territory when someone relies on you as their private therapist, financial advisor, or confidante. Once you've set that standard, scaling it back is exceedingly difficult.

The best advice I can give is to do what feels right on your own terms. I've been in situations where others felt disappointed or rejected when I set boundaries for myself by not being accessible to talk at a late hour or rescue them from a quandary. I'm going to tell you straight up: some will never be happy. I found that out as a superintendent many times over. In reality, the more I tried to stretch beyond my boundaries, the worse it got. Attending to 43 schools, plus five board members, and my executive cabinet was a tall order. There were ample opportunities for people to feel they were being slighted or overlooked. This is why I left this hardest interpersonal leadership challenge for the end of Module 2. It's easy to run afoul even with the best of intentions.

Accessibility is associated with exuding approachability, whereas availability is linked more to time and vicinity. Leaders display accessibility when they act in accordance with Maximizer characteristics such as friendliness, humor, and putting people at ease. Availability, on the other hand, prioritizes carving out time for relationships, making it clear how you can be reached, and demonstrating visibility in spaces where it matters most. Paired, the two are powerful strategies that you can carry out on your own terms. In the article "Inclusive Leadership in Thought and Action," Quinetta Roberson and Jamie L. Perry (2022) suggest that

> a leader's discernable presence and readiness for consultation on any issues helps to communicate norms of availability and accessibility ...[and] that a leader's attentiveness to, and encouragement of, opportunities to improve work processes and achieve group goals convey norms of openness that embolden employees to take risks.
>
> (p. 761)

A hallmark of accessibility is humble leadership. These folks openly share about making mistakes and the lessons gained from them. They show their own humanness, flaws and all. They apologize when wrong. Reveal strength through vulnerability. Think about celebrities like Taylor Swift, Dolly Parton, or Oprah Winfrey – each of whom is known for exposing their heartbreak and struggles on very public stages. And they are loved all the more for it. Being accessible doesn't mean compromising your personal safety or boundaries, though. And it also doesn't mean that you bare it all in every situation or put yourself at serious risk of exposure. Take it from someone who regrettably has.

In an attempt to make myself relatable in one of my senior leadership roles, I came up with an idea to make a "Top ten things you don't know about Kim Wallace" list and share it with the organization as part of my introduction to the district. In it, I shared some personal details that I felt were benign, a little bit funny, and somewhat self-effacing to show that I was a real person behind the title. Without going into the sordid details, let's just say that a couple of the items became regular fodder for the teachers' association Facebook page during a time of tumultuous salary negotiations. And if you've never had a malicious meme made of yourself, then you haven't truly experienced the pitfalls of being a public figure. I put myself out there and I took it in the teeth.

Having an open-door policy can also easily be twisted into something else the moment you need to close that door to mentally regroup, eat a snack, or take a breather. Therefore, availability should also be meted out and meticulously managed. It might be as formal as establishing office hours or a known time when you are free for unplanned office drop-ins. Or it could be a regular part of your schedule, such as doing double duty as recess monitor while conferencing with staff out on the playground. Visibility is a key component of availability. In a study on principals' practices that influence teacher turnover in urban schools, Amy Millet Scallon, Travis Bristol, and Joy Esboldt (2023) found:

> Teachers saw leaders engaged in public actions that demonstrated student support and expressed appreciation that their principal's value of centering students was not limited to "behind closed doors." Several teachers talked about the different locations throughout the school in which they had grown accustomed to seeing their principal throughout the day. From walking the hallways to dropping in on classrooms, teachers spoke positively about being able to see their principal participating in meaningful action…Teachers also talked positively about the variety of tasks in which their principals participated. While teachers mentioned responsibilities and

work such as leading staff meetings and administration, most positive comments centered on teachers' perceptions of principals being visible as they did little things.

(p. 94)

There is a time and place for the myriad leadership responsibilities and duties throughout the day. Organizing your time to maximize your impact includes showing up and being present when you're engaged in the interpersonal parts of the job and returning to your desk to tend to the non-public duties when the hustle and bustle of the school day is at a low(er) simmer.

Practical Application

How do you discern the what, when, where, why, and how of boundary setting and keeping? Table 2.4 offers some areas for consideration. You may nod along as you read the left side of

Table 2.4 Brokering boundaries

Leadership duties. You are responsible for	Boundary breakers. You are not responsible for
• Organizing and coordinating the work • Communicating mission, goals, and vision • Connecting to community/context • Making assignments and delegating tasks • Allocating and managing resources • Problem-solving and responding to needs • Managing and reporting progress • Motivating staff to accomplish objectives • Nurturing strengths and identifying improvements • Representing and advocating needs	• Having every answer/solution • Putting everyone else first • Knowing how to do everyone's job • Always being on stage or up front • Making everyone happy • Sacrificing your own health and well-being • Addressing factors/conditions out of your control • Solving everyone else's problems • Controlling other adults' behavior • Being superhuman • Tackling every single wrong in the system

the table. All's well. Then the right side elevates your heart rate. Easier said than done. In Exercise 2.6, you will develop a plan around a few of the items that you struggle with most. This will set you up for positive and healthy interpersonal relationships with your staff, supporters, students, and supervisors and earn the social capital needed for long-lasting leadership.

▶ MODULE 2 EXERCISES

Practice makes progress. Your performance outcomes are contingent on how well the traits and behaviors described in this module are developed within the domain of interpersonal connections. When novices try out different approaches and strategies, learn lessons, and begin to see patterns of how the game is played, they eventually become skilled performers. The mental muscles built during the growth process will eventually become automated as an individual levels up into new efficacies as a game-changing leader. The exercises contained in Module 2 connect to the content you learned earlier through the foundational material, including evaluating beliefs about your own agency and consciously constructing a fully functioning team. We'll delve further into the mirror images of multipliers vs. diminishers and leaders vs. managers before supporting your boundary-setting goals throughout these activities:

2.1. Leader Belief Questionnaire
2.2. Teaming Up
2.3. Mobilizing Support
2.4. Multiplier Effects
2.5. Leadership + Management

Exercise 2.1 Leader Belief Questionnaire

In Module 1 exercise 1.1, you answered prompts related to your own self-efficacy, whereas Exercise 2.2 intends for you to gauge how much the leaders in your organization are able to collectively influence desired outcomes or institutional practices that affect your schools. You'll probably have to estimate or make educated guesses on some and use them as a good opportunity to probe into the topic as you learn more about your ecosystem.

Criteria	Scale 1–5 (*minimally to significantly*)
1. To what extent are site administrators in your district able to cultivate conditions that maximize student learning outcomes?	1 2 3 4 5
2. To what extent does your organization directly or indirectly communicate to students that the district's adults believe in them?	1 2 3 4 5
3. To what extent are leaders prepared to respond to student behaviors in equity-centered ways?	1 2 3 4 5
4. To what extent can your school staff customize central office protocols and procedures that facilitate learning?	1 2 3 4 5
5. To what extent are leaders successful in promoting deep understanding and mastery of academic concepts?	1 2 3 4 5
6. To what extent do leaders model ways for students to think critically?	1 2 3 4 5
7. To what extent does your school's programming reflect creativity and innovation?	1 2 3 4 5
8. To what extent are leaders able to help students feel safe and welcomed and have a sense of belonging at school?	1 2 3 4 5
9. To what extent are leaders encouraged to collaborate with and support each other?	1 2 3 4 5

Criteria	Scale 1–5 *(minimally to significantly)*
10. To what extent are leaders able to influence governing board decisions that affect their sites?	1 2 3 4 5
Scoring 40–50: High collective efficacy 29–39: Medium collective efficacy 28 or under: Low collective efficacy	_____/ 50

Exercise 2.2 Teaming Up

The first part of this exercise is best applied contextually. When you have the opportunity to build a new team, convene a task force, or reconfigure an existing group structure or purpose, you'll be well served by approaching the task theoretically before selecting the individuals to participate. Fill out the framework below to establish a clear rationale for the team's existence. In the boxes, you'll begin to identify people who may fit into the ensemble in order to execute a shared purpose.

Using the model in Figure 2.3, create your own flowchart with the people involved in an existing initiative or campaign you have under way. If there isn't anyone assigned to a certain section, think about who can fill that gap to keep your implementation moving forward.

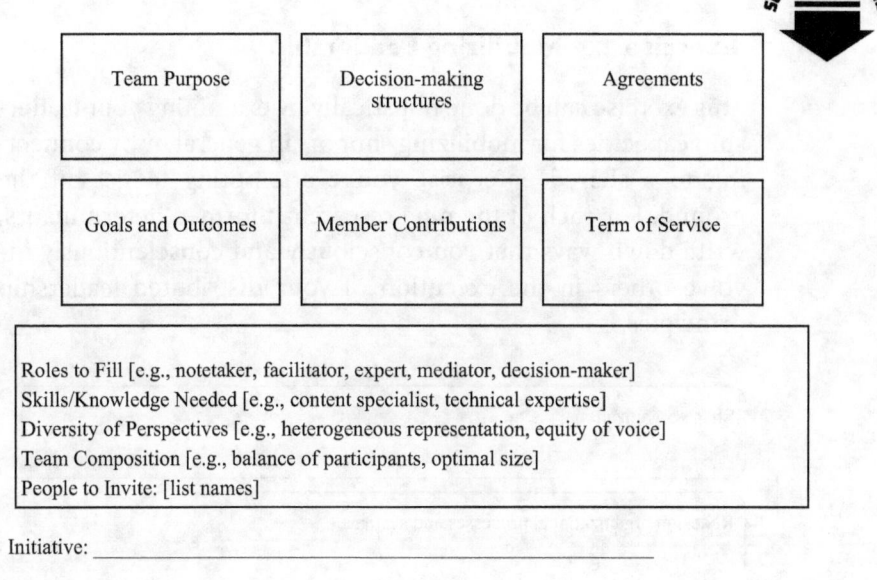

| Team Purpose | Decision-making structures | Agreements |
| Goals and Outcomes | Member Contributions | Term of Service |

Roles to Fill [e.g., notetaker, facilitator, expert, mediator, decision-maker]
Skills/Knowledge Needed [e.g., content specialist, technical expertise]
Diversity of Perspectives [e.g., heterogeneous representation, equity of voice]
Team Composition [e.g., balance of participants, optimal size]
People to Invite: [list names]

Initiative: _____

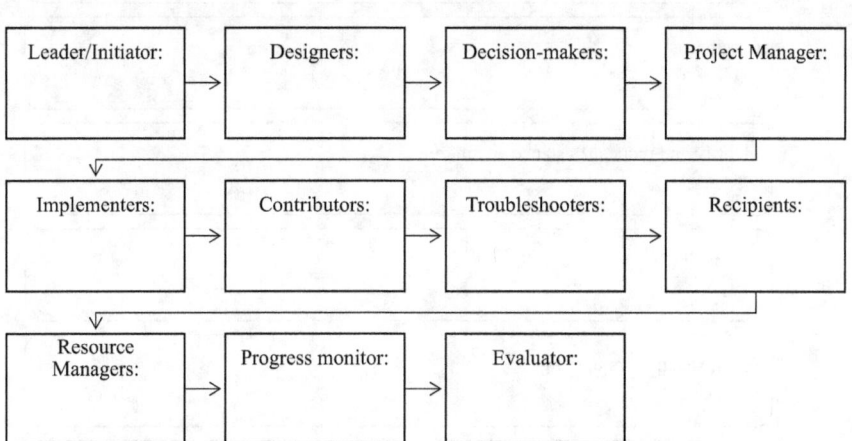

© Copyright material from Kim Wallace (2025), Game–Changing Leadership in Action, Routledge.

Exercise 2.3 Mobilizing Leadership

This exercise can be done holistically by examining your leadership capacities for mobilizing support in general or by connecting to a shared enterprise you're attempting to get off the ground. For each of the nine research-informed determinants, write down ways that you consciously and conscientiously involve others in the execution of your distributed leadership principles.

Shape organizational vision

Redesign organizational processes and systems

Create trust

Identify and reduce resistance and inertia

Personalize

Entail social accountability

Harness positive social norms

Identity relevance

Leverage social networks

© Copyright material from Kim Wallace (2025), Game–Changing Leadership in Action, Routledge.

Exercise 2.4 Multiplier Effects

Reflecting on your overall leadership style, identify where you usually fall on the continuum below in relation to each of the contexts based on the frameworks described in Table 2.2. Then jot down some notes next to each scenario with some concrete strategies you might employ to keep yourself right of center as much as possible and appropriate to the conditions or circumstances in which you find yourself. The righthand box on the continuum indicates Multiplier behaviors, the left box represents Diminisher actions, and the middle box is somewhere in between.

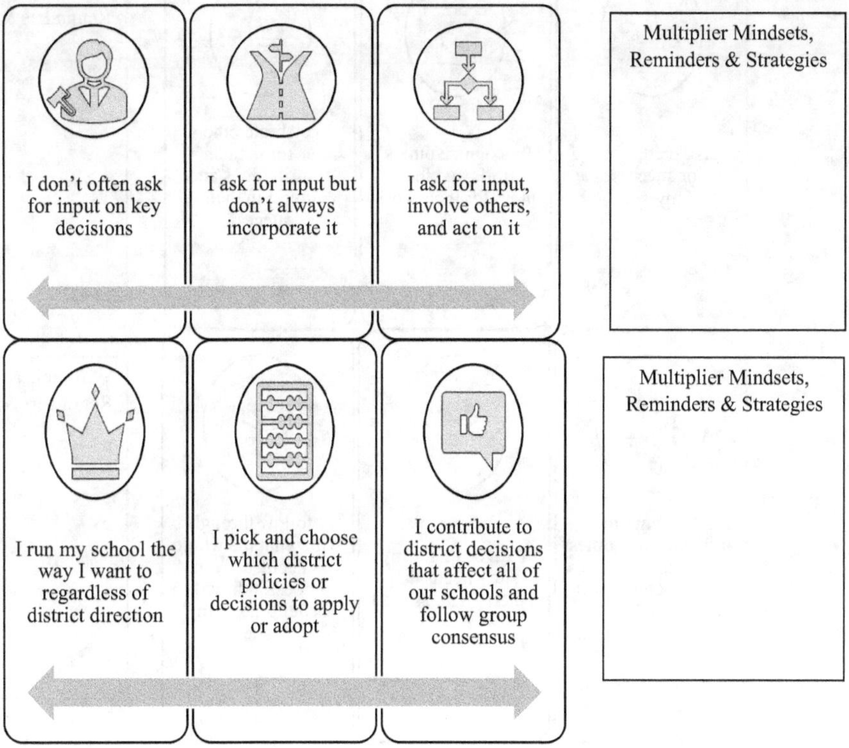

I don't often ask for input on key decisions	I ask for input but don't always incorporate it	I ask for input, involve others, and act on it	Multiplier Mindsets, Reminders & Strategies
I run my school the way I want to regardless of district direction	I pick and choose which district policies or decisions to apply or adopt	I contribute to district decisions that affect all of our schools and follow group consensus	Multiplier Mindsets, Reminders & Strategies

© Copyright material from Kim Wallace (2025), Game–Changing Leadership in Action, Routledge.

			Multiplier Mindsets, Reminders & Strategies
I compete with colleagues to secure the best hires for my site	I collaborate with my peers to determine which candidates fit which sites best	I actively seek attracting the highest-quality employees for our district overall	
I take credit for the major successes at my site	I recognize others' efforts and thank them for their work	I celebrate others for their contributions and invest in their success	Multiplier Mindsets, Reminders & Strategies
I attempt to influence outcomes and attain resources that meet my own school or department needs	I advocate for my site's needs that others share as well	I follow through with what the whole has decided, even if it doesn't directly benefit me or my site	Multiplier Mindsets, Reminders & Strategies

© Copyright material from Kim Wallace (2025), Game–Changing Leadership in Action, Routledge.

I try to associate with higher-ups to advance my own power and influence

To gain resources for site projects, I lean into relationships that will benefit the cause

I use positional power to effect collective gains for the organization

Multiplier Mindsets, Reminders & Strategies

© Copyright material from Kim Wallace (2025), Game–Changing Leadership in Action, Routledge.

Exercise 2.5 Leadership + Management

In the table below, write down some skills and practices you want to learn and incorporate into your game–changing leadership repertoire based on the three categories listed on the left side.

My leadership responsibilities	
My management responsibilities	
My boundary breakers	

▶ CONCLUSION

So much of educational leadership revolves around people. Though this module mostly focuses on the adults in the system, it does so for the benefit of students. Everything you do from your leadership seat should stem from that purpose. I think you may know what I mean when I say the kids are the easy part. Yes, there are some challenging adolescent behaviors and attitudes that push our buttons, but even the toughest cases pale in comparison to some of the adult interactions we encounter. By helping the individuals closest to the children manage their own emotions, set healthy boundaries, and resolve conflicts, we are clearing the path forward for a productive learning environment for all.

This concludes the first domain of the Game–changers framework. In the next two modules, we'll move into the second domain of environmental conditions. In Module 3, analysis of setting, you will explore your locale, noting the ways in which people interact within the backdrop of your school or worksite. Module 4 follows focusing building awareness of the surroundings, such as the landscape, infrastructure, and physical conditions bordering your buildings. These often less explored ecosystems in the study of administrative leadership are meant to open all five senses to possibilities and potential for school improvement efforts.

References

Anderson, C. M., Summers, K. H., Kopatich, R. D. & Dwyer, W. B. (2023). Collective teacher efficacy and its enabling conditions: A proposed framework for influencing collective efficacy in schools. *AERA Open*, 9. Accessed on July 25, 2024 from https://doi.org/10.1177/23328584231175060

Bandura, A. (2001). Social cognitive theory: An agentic perspective. *Annual Review of Psychology*, 52, 1–26.

Battilana, J., Gilmartin, M., Sengul, M., Pache, A. & Alexander, J. A. (2010). Leadership competencies for planned organizational change. *Leadership Quarterly*, 21(3), 422–438.

Brown, C., MacGregor, S. & Flood, J. (2020). Can models of distributed leadership be used to mobilise networked generated innovation in schools? A case study from England. *Teaching and Teacher Education*, 94, 103101. https://doi.org/10.1016/j.tate.2020.103101

Buchanan, D.A., Addicott, R., Fitzgerald, L., Ferlie, E. & Baeza, J. (2007). Nobody in charge: Distributed change agency in healthcare. *Human Relations - HUM RELAT*, 60. 1065–1090. https://doi.org/10.1177/0018726707081158

Canterino, F., Cirella, S., Piccoli, B. & Shani, A. B. R. (2020). Leadership and change mobilization: The mediating role of distributed leadership. *Journal of Business Research*, 108, 42–51. https://doi.org/10.1016/j.jbusres.2019.09.052

Connolly, M., James, C. & Fertig, M. (2017). The difference between educational management and educational leadership and the importance of educational responsibility. *Educational Management Administration & Leadership*, 47. Accessed on August 15, 2024 from 174114321774588. https://doi.org/10.1177/1741143217745880

DeWitt, P.M. (Sept/Oct. 2017). Many hands make light work. *Principal*. NAESP.

DeWitt, P.M. (2021). *Collective leader efficacy: Strengthening instructional leadership teams*. Thousand Oaks, CA: Corwin.

Dismantling the culture of nice to build collective leader efficacy (2022). National Institute for Excellence in Teaching (NIET) Accessed on November 19, 2023 from https://www.niet.org/assets/Resources/Learning-Acceleration-Resource-Building-Collective-Efficacy.pdf

Donohoo, J., Hattie, J. & Eells, R. (2018). The power of collective efficacy. *Educational Leadership*, 75(6), 40–44. https://www.ascd.org/el/articles/the-power-ofcollective-efficacy

Eells, R. (2011). *Meta-analysis of the relationship between collective efficacy and student achievement.* Unpublished doctoral dissertation. Loyola University of Chicago. Accessed on November 20, 2023 from https://ecommons.luc.edu/cgi/viewcontent.cgi?article=1132&context=luc_diss

Elliott, K., Hollingsworth, H., Thornton, A., Gillies, L., Henderson, K. (2022). School leadership that cultivates collective efficacy: Emerging insights 2022. Australian Council for Educational Research. Accessed on November 19, 2023 from https://doi.org/10.37517/978-1-74286-694-9

Fishbein, M. & Ajzen, I. (2010). *Predicting and changing behavior: The reasoned action approach.* New York: Psychology Press.

Goddard, R. (2002). A Theoretical and Empirical Analysis of the Measurement of Collective Efficacy: The Development of a Short Form. *Educational and Psychological Measurement*, 62(1), 97–110. https://doi.org/10.1177/0013164402062001007 (Original work published 2002)

Goddard, R., Goddard, Y., Kim, E. S. & Miller, R. (2015). A theoretical and empirical analysis of the roles of instructional leadership, teacher collaboration, and collective efficacy beliefs in support of student learning. *American Journal of Education*, 121(4), 501–530. https://doi.org/10.1086/681925

Hattie, J. (2009). *Visible learning: A synthesis of over 800 meta-analyses relating to achievement.* Abingdon, UK: Routledge. Accessed on November 12, 2023 from https://apprendre.auf.org/wp-content/opera/13-BF-References-et-biblio-RPT-2014/Visible%20Learning_A%20synthesis%20or%20over%20800%20Meta-analyses%20Relating%20to%20Achievement_Hattie%20J%202009%20...pdf

Kilag, O.K.T., Manguilimotan, A.M., Maraño, J.C., Jordan, R.P., Columna, P.A. & Camaso, M.F.A. (2023). A conceptual framework: A systematic literature review on educational leadership and management. *Science and Education*, 4(9), 262–273.

Poekert, P. E., Swaffield, S., Demir, E. K. & Wright, S. A. (2020). Leadership for professional learning towards educational equity: A systematic literature review. *Professional Development in Education*, 46(4), 541–562. https://doi.org/10.1080/19415257.2020.1787209

Reinke, K., Gerlach, G.I. (2022). Linking availability expectations, bidirectional boundary management behavior and preferences, and employee well-being: An integrative study approach. *J Bus Psychol*, 37, 695–715. Accessed on August 17, 2024 from https://doi.org/10.1007/s10869-021-09768-x

Roberson, Q. & Perry, J. L. (2022). Inclusive leadership in thought and action: A thematic analysis. *Group & Organization Management*, 47(4), 755–778. Accessed on August 17, 2024 from https://doi.org/10.1177/10596011211013161

Rogers, T, Goldstein, NJ, Fox, CR. (2018). Social mobilization. *Annu Rev Psychol*, 69(1), 357–381. https://doi.org/10.1146/annurev-psych-122414-033718. Epub 2017 Sep 25. PMID: 28945979.

Scallon, A. M., Bristol, T. J. & Esboldt, J. (2023). Teachers' perceptions of principal leadership practices that influence teacher turnover. *Journal of Research on Leadership Education*, 18(1), 80–102. https://doi.org/10.1177/19427751211034214

Schmoker, M. (2004). Learning communities at the crossroads: A response to Joyce and Cook. *Phi Delta Kappan*, 86(1), 84–89. Accessed on August 14, 2024 from https://doi.org/10.1177/003172170408600114?journalCode=pdka

Visible Learning. (2016). Hattie Ranking: Backup of 195 effects related to student achievement. Accessed on November 12, 2023 from https://visible-learning.org/hattie-ranking-backup-195-effects/

Wallace, K. (2023). *Leading through an equity lens*. Bloomington, IN: Solution Tree Press.

Wiseman, L., Foster, E., & Allen, L.N. (2013). *The multiplier effect: Tapping the genius inside our schools*. Thousand Oaks, CA: Corwin.

Wright, T. A. & Huang, C.-C. (2012). The many benefits of employee well-being in organizational research. *Journal of Organizational Behavior*, 33(8), 1188–1192.

Module 3

Analysis of Setting

▶ **INTRODUCTION**

Picture all of the schools you've attended and worked at throughout your life. In total, I've matriculated through one preschool, two elementaries, one middle school, one high school, and four colleges. I've taught in nine secondary classroom spaces, coached across five schools, and worked at three central offices, inclusive of four California school districts plus one university. In sum, that's almost 50 years (and counting) of time spent on school premises. Though I'm not a trained interior designer or master architect, I certainly have logged well over Malcolm Gladwell's supposed 10,000 hours of what it takes to master a concept – in this case, school ecosystems – a premise made popular in his 2008 book *Outliers*. Truthfully, I didn't think much about the buildings or passageways while I was inhabiting them as a student or teacher. As a kid, I just showed up and readily accepted in whatever room I would spend the year. As a high school teacher, I was similarly assigned a classroom (sometimes shared with another teacher) that I did my best to make inviting, warm, and safe.

Only when I became a leader did I begin to see the wider school environment as a complete habitat that existed outside my own door. My scope expanded overnight to include every corner of campus from managing multistory buildings and monitoring open spaces and common facilities to the minutiae of patching fences, filling gopher holes, and expunging graffiti from bathroom walls. All schools don't look alike but many have similar features: a parking lot or traffic roundabout out front, an administration building, multiple classrooms, a cafeteria/gym, a library media center, bathrooms/locker rooms, and outdoor physical education or play facilities. School infrastructure and exterior structures are often funded by publicly voted state and local bonds that pass every blue moon to modernize existing property or build new construction. Consequently, across the U.S., children and grown-ups spend time in schools that may be over 100 years old or barely one.

The socio-politics of school funding, however, is not the primary concern of this module. I mention it only to suggest that a multipurpose room (MPR) does not possess the same quality, look, and feel of every MPR universally. Yours may be a gorgeous specimen with state-of-the-art design, yet mine might be of a 1960s vintage that looks and feels every single one of its dogged years of service. While we may not have much control over every aspect of the locations where we land, we do have a responsibility to create optimal learning environments for our students and teachers. And environmental conditions, one of the lowest rungs on Maslow's hierarchy of human needs, are the bottom-line basics warranting our attention throughout Module 3. As such, this chapter will cover

- Schools as ecosystems, broken down into geographic locale, physical location, physical environment, and sociocultural environment;
- Uncovering the game–changing potential for leading and learning in digitally mediated and virtual spaces;
- An eight-stage data-informed protocol for walking your equity talk
- Universal design principles as the root of Universal Design for Learning (UDL) practices on campus

▶ FOUNDATIONS

Schools as Ecosystems

School campuses, along with central and county offices and institutions of higher education, can be construed as educational ecosystems. The National Research Council of the National Academies (2015) depicts learning ecosystems as "the dynamic interaction among individual learners, diverse settings where learning occurs, and the community and culture in which they are embedded" (p. 5). Marijke Hecht and Kevin Crowley's (2019) article, which unpacks the learning ecosystems framework, acknowledges several reasons why we cannot simply create replicable approaches to such ever-evolving environments:

> Challenges persist because learning ecosystems are complex – by which we mean they are dynamic, non-linear, and unpredictable (Yoon, 2011); they are continually undergoing changes that amount to more than the sum of their parts (Johnson, 2008). Therefore, we cannot expect, as we might with a complicated problem, to come up with a set of instructions to solve educational problems and expect them to remain solved, nor can we easily replicate these efforts across space and time effectively.
> (Snyder, 2013) (pp. 267–68)

Emphasis on the part that says *expect them to remain solved*. School settings as ecosystems are living, breathing organisms that are on the receiving end of human interactions. They age, break down, get fixed up, add extensions, and absorb the loving blows of learning as it happens in real time and space. Consequently, there is no single playbook to follow but rather an impetus to "read" your setting on a continual basis to exercise leadership opportunities in this domain.

To distinguish Module 3 from Module 4, which pertains explicitly to the external surrounding community, the ecosystem metaphor described here will be contained to the actual physical and virtual locations where instruction, play, activities, events, and other formal and informal learning activities take place. From the parking lot to the playing fields (and everything in between), educational ecosystems include people, spaces, resources, and services. Social strata, customs, politics, hierarchies, and other intangible or underlying forces also take up residence here.

Owing to the very real phenomenon of teaching and learning settings expressing their own personality, the activities in this module require customization on your part. A director of an early learning center leads within an entirely different atmosphere than a principal at a juvenile justice institution, for instance. Likewise, leaders across the globe operate within their own unique settings. All these dynamics and more will be addressed in this section with a concentration on four elements borrowed from the literary definition related to storytelling settings that follow:

1. Geographic locale relates to macrocosmic locations like regions, counties, towns, or provinces as well as smaller-grain sizes such as a city block, apartment building, or park. The locale is where your campus is centered within a nested circle of Saturn-like rings comprising the neighborhood, district, county, and state emanating outwards. (The outer realm features will be examined in greater depth in Module 4.)
2. Physical location consists of the "things" and "objects" on site. Your school or workplace is an aggregate of classrooms, offices, cafeteria, library, locker rooms, and lab buildings as well as playgrounds, common areas, landscaping, infrastructure, passageways, and outdoor spaces. It also contains materials and resources, such as emergency preparedness supplies, safety mechanisms, technology infrastructure, electrical wiring, ventilation, and plumbing systems.
3. Physical environment is a combination of the aforementioned things and objects plus how humans interact with them. How a site is laid out, flows, and functions affects how people navigate and experience their learning or working spaces. The campus's birthdate, levels of maintenance and repair, degree of sanitary conditions, and range of appealing sensory factors such as green spaces, clean air, natural lighting, and other tangible, observable features all impact the ways we feel while in the milieu.

4. The social and cultural environment is the mood and atmosphere infusing the site. People and events are influenced by climate, topography, habitat, and the other elements described above which, in turn, mold the tenor, vibe, and ambiance within a space. This environmental feature is the most abstract and most difficult to measure because much of it is invisible to the naked eye. It requires using all five senses plus your sixth sense of instinct and intuition to really see what's going on.

Now we'll apply these descriptors to a fictitious school to illustrate how environment and experience are intertwined.

Case Study

In the world of fiction, all good stories being by painting the scene. After which, the reader or listener is oriented to the plot, characters, themes, conflicts, and varying points of view. As you read the vignette of Fox Hedge School, note the multiple clues about how the setting attributes inform your initial understanding of their educational environment.

> Fox Hedge is a pre-K-8 Alternative Education Center that offers a personalized hybrid model of instruction. Students meet one on one with their assigned grade-level teacher, who designs appropriate learning goals and monitors and assesses academic progress. They also attend small group classes twice a week for lab science, arts, and mathematics. Parents seeking out this small school in rural western Wisconsin vary in political or ideological stance and range from liberals to libertarians and those who possess religious beliefs on a wide spectrum as well. There are also medically fragile children, students with special needs, and those who have farming or family business duties and other unique circumstances that make Fox Hedge an appealing option.
>
> However, it is not without its challenges, including parental resistance to standardization or conformity, and some students experience levels of isolation and feelings of exclusion emanating from enrolling in an atypical learning environment compared with their peers. The staff strives to support very diverse needs built on belonging and inclusion related to environmental factors, including its remote location, distance from state-of-the-art resources, and philosophical differences about the purpose and goals of public education.

Analysis of Setting 109

Geographic Locale
Rural unincorporated town
Main industries: forestry, logging, farming
Large Midwestern state, USA

Physical Location
K-8 Alternative Education School
Two main buildings with cubicle spaces for teacher/student weekly sessions, library/computer lab, three small group classrooms and a communal garden plot

Physical Environment
Built in the 1970s, no recent building upgrades
Few extra-curricular spaces due to instructional model requiring minimal time on site

Social & Cultural Environment
Tight-knit community of families that have chosen to homeschool, ranging from politically and socially conservative to liberal
General feelings of mistrust or suspicion toward traditional public schooling

Figure 3.1 Four elements of setting scenario

Figure 3.1 contains the basic ingredients of this school's story by applying the four elements of locale, location, physical, and socio-cultural environments into an illustrative model.

Imagine that the new head administrator at Fox Hedge wants to become more aware of how the four elements interface. As in every environment, there are assets to leverage and gaps to fill. Using a SWOT analysis tool, leaders can begin to pull the environmental threads apart that make up the composite fabric of the campus. Using the boxes labeled Strengths, Weaknesses, Opportunities, and Threats, the school director and teacher-leader team document the forces in action as demonstrated in Table 3.1.

After the in-depth analysis of their setting, the leadership team decides to prioritize reorganizing the site with the resources they already have to open up more gathering spaces for students and families to build connectedness. At the same time, they will pursue the longer-term approach to secure

Table 3.1 SWOT analysis of Shady Hedge School

Current strengths	**Current weaknesses**
– Centralized location near a bus route makes for easy access – Separate K-3 building and 4-8 building allows for appropriate grade span segmentation – Library/media center offers resources not found in every home – Community garden has become an integral part of the K-8 curriculum – School climate surveys show students and families feel physically and emotionally safe while on campus	– Limited classroom space = fewer group classes than we'd like to offer – Insufficient bathroom facilities for K-1 students and those who are medically fragile – During extreme weather conditions, the internet and electricity go out for days – Lack of play, lunch, and social spaces impacts student and family bonding – Itinerant educational model can make the school feel transactional rather than a true community
Future opportunities	**Pending threats**
– Consolidate vacant 1:1 instructional cubicles to maximize and open up additional space – Raise funds for picnic tables and benches for the garden to create a gathering area – Secure high-capacity generator for electrical backup during inclement weather – Seek permission to expand site's footprint from district officials – Apply for bonds or grants to modernize the physical plant with renewable energy and sustainable resources	– Little anticipated funding to take care of deferred building maintenance – Unpredictable grade-level enrollment from year to year makes it hard to plan for facility needs – Climate change is weathering buildings at a faster rate than the district's maintenance crew (of one) can keep up with – Parent volunteerism for campus projects has dwindled

funding for higher-cost resources like upgrading the HVAC (heating, ventilation, and air conditioning) unit and a more robust internet infrastructure.

Practical Application

In Exercise 3.1, you'll get a chance to conduct a similar thought experiment for your own site within the framing of a SWOT analysis. Just remember to keep it focused on the physical and virtual spaces' impacts on your school community before interpreting what the human interactions mean.

▶ GEOGRAPHICAL LOCALE

It's unwise, if not impossible, to discuss setting in a vacuum from what surrounds it, so though geographic locale will be more of a focal area in Module 4, it bears cursory attention here as well. Where people live, work, and learn happens in context. How schools are built is often in direct alignment with their geographic location. An expanded view of geography, including climate, seasons, landscape, natural features (e.g., rivers, mountains, cliffs), flora and fauna, human-made elements (e.g., dams, properties, highways), and many other topographical conditions, all affect how schools are constructed to weather and operate in the elements. From sprawling suburban campuses to remote one-room schoolhouses, our regional locations impact what we learn, how we learn, and even why we learn.

Walking into a native or tribal school in the Yukon is going to look and feel very different from a D.C. public school building. The former needs to be equipped for heavy snow, extended sub-zero winters, and account for significant commutes or access challenges, while the latter, set in a densely populated southern U.S. location, may be antiquated and overcrowded. From an enrichment perspective, the Yukon offers endless outdoor learning adventures and lessons, and D.C.'s museums, monuments, and multiculturalism are unparalleled. Every locale possesses both assets and obstacles no matter where you are on the

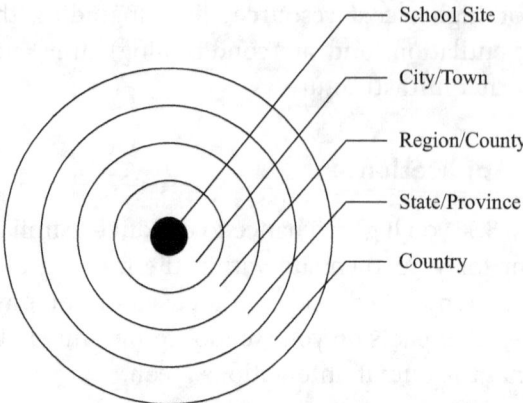

Figure 3.2 Nested layers of environmental settings

planet. There is no perfect place where the grass is greener, and that's why context matters so much. The goal is to leverage your environmental assets and resources and minimize your constraints and hurdles. Imagine a bull's-eye, as illustrated in Figure 3.2, with your site tucked into the center and enveloped by increasingly expanded entities.

Physical Location and Environment

After we establish the backdrop against which our schools are oriented, it's time to zoom in on the campus itself. Aashna Khurana's (2022) article on converting physical spaces into learning spaces notes:

> Not many people have focused on the pertinence of utilizing the physical space as a learning resource in improving teaching-learning experiences. Despite school buildings being the most expensive asset of a school, this resource has received scant attention. A handful of architects, who have explored the school's entire physical environment as a learning resource focused on the structured spaces (interior and exterior of school infrastructure) and loose spaces (open spaces like playgrounds, and courts). The spaces offer myriad opportunities that complement instructional

delivery and aid the information given in the textbooks. The three-dimensional space, if utilized well, can offer a multi-sensory experience and distinct space for a child to experience learning and supplement the unidimensional learning material and blackboard teaching.

(p. 2)

As indicated in the book's introduction, we must blend our leader, teacher, and student selves on a daily basis. However, owing to familiarity, it's easy to become attuned or even immune to our physical environment. The first time you are in a place, you notice many novel sensory features that eventually fade into the background once you know the place better. For game-changing leaders, this means identifying and re-envisioning your campus learning spaces to bring a live heartbeat to your architecture. If the ideal is for students to receive active and engaging instructional methodology, we should also translate that into adult experiences.

School Climate

While there is a dearth of formal educational leadership research related to physical environment alone, much has been written on the topic of the effects of school climate on student achievement and attendance, especially related to mental health, bullying, discipline, and safety and security. It's widely understood that conditions of psychological and physiological welfare are interdependent with one's situational reality. Based on data collected from U.S. Department of Education School Climate Surveys, the National Center on Safe Supportive Learning Environments (2022) reports four circumstantial findings that directly impact human wellness:

- Physical environment can be related to both student achievement and student behavior.
- Physical environment is related to teachers' levels of absenteeism, effort, effectiveness in the classroom, morale, and job satisfaction.

- Decent, safe, and secure facilities are essential to successful educational programs.
- Physical environment of schools is affected by school funding and the local policy in the surrounding neighborhoods in which the schools are located.

(no p. #)

In short, spaces and places hold a certain caliber. Maybe nobody warned you that you would become a plant manager as well as a leader, but it comes with the territory. People of all ages need a sense of belonging and inclusion that can be accomplished through adaptively arranging your physical setting. The challenge in front of you is to figure out how to shape those components on the ground. I must confess: Easier said than done.

Even though there are a few actions you can tackle at a grassroots level like special event setup and breakdown or rudimentary décor and beautification, much of our environment is controlled and managed centrally related to maintenance, repairs, and safety. Not only is the central office responsible for adhering to laws, policies and procedures regulating school design, construction, and upkeep, there are commonly union contracts in places that restrict this work to bargaining unit employees. And if you, like me, have ever found yourself on the wrong side of the local fire marshal for excessive student artwork and fabric window coverings in an attempt to make your classroom feel homier, I offer my condolences.

So, it's important to manage expectations here. You may not be able to allow students to paint a colorful mural on the blacktop or parents to fill potholes in the parking lot, but you can determine what's in your locus of control and maximize efforts in those directions. The first step is to find out (a) what you can do without seeking permission, (b) what you can do if requested through a specific organizational protocol, and (c) what is totally off-limits. Then proceed accordingly. I don't encourage vigilantism, but you may need to push at some boundaries to get past what often seems to be a default "no" to outside-of-the-box facilities requests.

Practical Application

Exercise 3.2 presents you with an open-ended environmental needs assessment tool to use internally at your site on a topic of your choice. You may want to audit your school's emergency preparedness plans and supplies in the case of environmental liabilities in your area, such as earthquakes, tornadoes, hurricanes, extreme drought, wildfires, and excessive winds. Or you might decide to evaluate the site for nuanced patterns like wayfinding, sensemaking, and flow. It could be simply that you've had several complaints about a certain facility that needs rehabilitation and it's time for action. The purpose of this activity is to select an area of interest and involve your school community by first assessing the environmental situation and then generating ideas to rectify or alter the spaces in question.

Socio-cultural Environment

Why does any of this matter anyway? Because when young people and grown-ups alike feel ownership, pride, and connection to school, everyone benefits. The systematic review and meta-analysis that Ming-Te Wang et al. (2020) conducted on the effects of classroom climate on children's well-being

> poses positive classroom climate as one effective method for promoting youth's academic achievement, socioemotional development, and mental health, especially during adolescence. While it is no small feat putting research into practice, the evidence suggests that when classrooms are high in quality, children are more likely to strive for and achieve success.
> (p. 17)

In their ASCD online column, "Tending to Learning Environments," Douglas Fisher and Nancy Frey (2022) concur:

> The people who use a space can form attachments to it because of the relationships contained within. They see themselves and their identities represented in it and find

> the space to be useful and positive. The way we create a learning environment with ourselves and our students in mind can transform it from a space to a place, one that is meaningful to students personally and emotionally. Students deserve to step into places that value them and amplify their voices. Educators deserve to work in places that bring out the best in them.
>
> (no p. #)

Stay here for a moment to let the space-to-place concept sink in. Think about your own experiences as a student, teacher, and administrator in spaces that felt like places where you belonged and times that they did not. What made the difference between the two? Climate, to be sure, is far from static. It can and does change regularly and thus must be cultivated and cared for. Taking frequent vital signs of your site can help leaders develop insights into the spaces where kids and adults feel safe, happy, and at ease as opposed to places where danger or fear lurks.

There are dozens of school climate measurement tools in the field that can be employed to calibrate perceptions of school connectedness. However, there are limitations to surveys related to typically low response rates, accuracy of self-reporting, and difficulty interpreting valid patterns from the data. Plus, they are often issued only at specific grade levels or once a year, which offers us just a snapshot of what was going on exactly at that moment but is not necessarily an overall portrait of institutional health.

Instead, just like taking your temperature, gauging barometric pressure, or checking the day's air quality index, you can paint a more comprehensive picture of ecosystemic trends as they fluctuate over time. Table 3.2 illustrates how a site administrator might quickly check on ten preselected environmental attributes that contribute to the functioning of the school at the beginning of each week.

Practical Application

Borrowing from the ideas listed in Table 3.2, Exercise 3.3 prompts you to craft your own temperature and pressure gauges

Table 3.2 Weekly environmental conditions checklist

Physical/Tangible components	Atmospheric/Climate components
☐ Measure Air Quality Index (AQI) in open spaces, playground, classrooms, labs, etc.; check for predictions of wildfires or pollution events that could trigger health concerns	☐ Check on and report progress to staff who've requested repairs or maintenance via work orders and follow up with custodial or operations for completion
☐ Watch temperature/weather/natural disaster forecasts and make alternative plans for inclement or extreme weather conditions	☐ Check anonymous online portal for student or staff submissions regarding areas to watch out for on campus that feel unsafe or need supervision
☐ Check for Wi-Fi, cable, or electrical outages; ensure platforms are up and running; report any connectivity issues to the central office	☐ During breaks/lunch, walk campus perimeter and take note of any "hot spots" of activity that could signal impending conflicts or escalation
☐ Remove or request disposal of any unusable or broken furnishings or equipment that pose safety threats	☐ Observe body language, facial expressions, and language that reflects a group's mood or collective vibe
☐ Document needed repairs, damage, graffiti, or vandalism and report to authorities asap	☐ When encountering staff and students, ask how they feel and if there is anything you need to be aware of

to predict shifts in the physical environment or school climate that might need attention. You will scan your setting for a handful of potential issues that may interrupt or interfere with working and learning conditions and head them off at the pass to maintain homeostasis.

Leading and Learning in Digitally Mediated Spaces

One's physical location isn't the only space that game–changing leaders need to tend and nurture. The technological environment also plays a big role in teaching and learning. There are myriad terms that capture learning that takes place using technology off-campus: virtual, remote, online, distance learning, blended, hybrid, cyber-schooling, e-learning, and so on. In a systematic literature review, researchers Vandana Singh and Alexander Thurman (2019) collected 46 definitions from 37 resources on the topic of online learning and settled on this overarching depiction:

> Education being delivered in an online environment through the use of the internet for teaching and learning. This includes online learning on the part of the students that is not dependent on their physical or virtual co-location. The teaching content is delivered online and the instructors develop teaching modules that enhance learning and interactivity in the synchronous or asynchronous environment.
>
> (p. 302)

I don't fancy myself as an early adopter of technology or even in the early majority. As a fence-sitting later end user, I tend to not even pay attention to new technologies until they are societally widespread. Once everyone around me has already tested the waters, I'm finally ready to jump in. However, I've always been interested in educational progress, and I wrote my 2012 dissertation on teachers and technology barriers to ascertain whether generational differences had a discernible impact on the instructional uses of digital tools in the classroom. (It did.) However, that didn't automatically translate into widespread implementation until the pandemic intervened.

No matter where you are in the world, I will surmise that few, if any, educators were spared the effects of the Covid-19 pandemic on their organizational settings and operations during the spring of 2020 and beyond. Some of those impacts had a lasting legacy as students and adults alike were catapulted into innovative instructional environments as a matter of fact, not by choice. According to Josh Howarth's blog post[1] on Exploding Topics, the statistics between 2020 and January 2024 are no less than astounding: the EdTech market is now worth $340 billion and its usage in K-12 schools increased 99% since 2020.

Andrew A. Tawfik, Craig E. Shepherd, Jessica Gatewood, and Jaclyn J. Gish-Lieberman (2021) probed into first- and second-barrier orders to teaching in K-12 online learning in an urban school setting during the 2019–20 school year. First-order or "extrinsic barriers, are obstacles to technology integration that are external to a teacher's control" (p. 926), while second-order barriers "stem from personal beliefs, values, and dispositions regarding the role of technology in education settings" (p. 927). For more information on Peggy Ertmer's (1999) original development of this theory, I have written extensively in my first two books by Solution Tree on the topic as well as added a third-level barrier regarding institutional obstacles that pose unique challenges to working and learning environments. In this case study, Tawik et al. noted that

> In terms of first-order barriers, the study highlights the importance of (a) time needed to design and adapt instructional materials, (b) accountability within an online format, and (c) administrator support in the communication process. For second-order barriers, teachers commented on how they perceived online learning to impact important teaching activities (e.g., accountability, timeliness of feedback) and the teacher student dynamic. Finally, they commented on the challenge to support the socio-emotional component of students and parents in online learning, which is important for school culture and community.
> (p. 925)

While the support of administrators was not the focus of this study, it does bear mentioning that first-order barriers were mitigated by leadership helping to communicate the what, why, and how of the shifts to virtual instruction and, "despite several challenges (e.g., accountability, access, and accommodation), many teachers, students, and families navigated this transition" (Tawfik et al., 2021, p. 925).

It wasn't easy. And definitely not without costs. While some young people thrived in these new spaces, others felt detached, disengaged, and unable to connect – literally and figuratively. Equity gaps between students living in economically diverse circumstances had differing access to high-quality instruction. Schools scrambled to purchase as many Chromebooks, laptops, and tablets as they could get their hands on, not fully anticipating the lack of internet infrastructure in outlying communities and other under-resourced locales. Other basic needs such as school breakfast and lunch programs, counseling services, special education support, and general safety and stability that students relied on were suddenly cut off or minimized to degrees of ineffectualness. This lack of structure and supervision also allowed unfettered access or limitless time spent on entertainment, gaming, and social media. Physical classrooms are far from distraction-free, but behind the boxes on Zoom, students could be (and often were) playing video games, watching YouTube, or surfing all kinds of websites that the teacher in their own Zoom box simply couldn't visually observe like they could in brick-and-mortar classrooms.

Whole societies became untethered to the usual physical activities that tend to ground us in our relationships with each other in our shared material and natural world. In terms of this particular environmental state of affairs, Mira Yemini, Laura Engel, and Adi Ben Simon (2023) likewise claim,

> Such a profound and widespread experiment with distance learning and new technologies has not previously occurred in human history. As physical mobility was halted worldwide by the pandemic, daily life became more locally and community-bound. For much of the world, the disappearance of normal physical commutes between home-work-school and the elimination of the traditional physical buildings where work and school occur reoriented notions not only of where teaching and learning should take place, but also placed new recognition on the importance of environmental connections and "being in nature." At the same time, while life during the pandemic emphasised local connectivity, there was simultaneously an explosion of emphasis on connection via technologies, including WhatsApp, FaceTime, social media, Zoom, etc. These dynamics – given life by the global pandemic – have widened awareness, recognition and discussion of the role of the physical school in community spaces, and shown how different modes of teaching and learning are possible.
>
> (pp. 4–5)

It is likely that contemporary scholars and researchers will endlessly debate the impacts of (over)abundant technology use on our brains and bodies, especially related to children's growth and development. As much as we know to be concerned, time will only tell how these changes will manifest as potentially permanent evolutionary adaptations. The fact is, we have entered a historical epoch where technology is part of our make-up and so integrated that we don't even think about its presence most of the time.

Though many kids, parents, and classroom teachers were relieved to revert to more traditional means of instruction post-pandemic, the infrastructure of virtual environments is here to stay. Instead of closing down schools entirely in the event of snow or other inclement weather, they simply shift to online instruction for the days affected. When families need (or choose) to travel, kids may still be able to access materials and lessons in digitally mediated formats. Students who are hospitalized, injured, or chronically ill can now find fully remote learning opportunities that just didn't exist in widespread ways in the pre-2020s. The pandemic opened our eyes and widened our minds to envision schools in ways that better reflect the needs as well as the realities of our greater society. We've already been online shopping, conducting market research, creating and consuming original content, debating current events in the news, engaging socially with media, banking, and Googling for decades now. Education was the final frontier to break down the walls between real life and, well, real life online. In preparation for the next two sections of this module, you may want to consider how digital environments also pose leadership challenges that warrant creative solutions in addition to more tangible terrestrial features.

Walking the Equity Talk

Commonly referred to as equity audits, data walks, or asset mapping, all are variations on similar themes. The general idea is to explore a setting-specific problem of practice (PoP) posing obstacles within the teaching and learning environment. The word "walk" is not to be taken literally, though there may be aspects of the event you design that include walking through classrooms or other parts of campus. Think rather of walking the equity talk as a mental exercise or occasion to push pause on the inner workings of your site to witness ways in which people are acting in congruence with the environment or not. *The Principal as Leader of the Equitable School*, published by the Ontario Principals' Council (2012), explains the rationale behind conducting such inquiry-based data-focused activities:

> School teams rely heavily on data collection in developing evidence-based school improvement plans. Data are used to identify and remove barriers to student achievement, to raise awareness about discriminatory practices, and to encourage conversations and collaborative actions about equity issues. Disaggregation of the data allows teams to do a gap analysis and to target specific areas that require improvements. In this way, staff can intentionally effect change for students who are underserved and foster their success. Walkthroughs allow principals and teachers to engage in dialogue and reflection about critical aspects of school improvement – students, curriculum, and achievement. The school improvement planning process is the vehicle for translating collected achievement data into constructive change in the classroom and the school.
> (p. 120)

If we really want to get at the root of certain types of issues that persist for certain populations on your campus, you may consider doing an action-research event at your school. An equity data walk can unearth core issues that may be obstructing access and opportunity for your most marginalized students or families. In the next eight subsections, I will pair each item's general description with a fictional case study to ground the content in practice. While you will work through each stage in sequence, per Figure 3.3, this set of pre-planning questions encapsulates the main components you'll eventually need to account for:

☐ **Why** are you focusing on this specific PoP? (Establish and explain a clear rationale for focusing on the equity concern.)

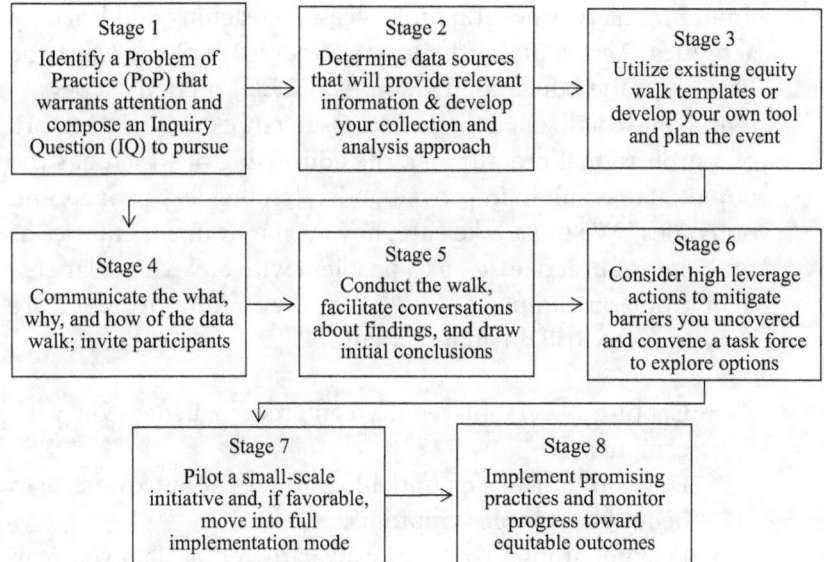

Figure 3.3 Equity data walk protocol stages

- ☐ **Who** will participate in the equity walk? (Instructional Leadership Team, site administrators, teachers, counselors, support staff, parents, community members, district office leaders, students, etc.)
- ☐ **What** will they be looking for and at? (e.g., examining data sets, listening to a focus group, reading qualitative testimonials, interpreting survey results, reviewing student study team notes)
- ☐ **When** will it happen? (time frame: before, during, after school, evening, on a weekend; month or season)
- ☐ **Where** will it take place? (specific location on or off campus: classroom, lab, library media center, gym, fields, etc.)
- ☐ **How** will you conduct the walk? (logistics, participant roles, agenda, tools and materials, contingency plans)

Stage 1: Identifying the Problem of Practice

The first stage is for your leadership team to isolate an equity-centered problem of practice (PoP) evident in your setting. This identifies hurdles or barriers that are intentionally or unintentionally preventing full access to teaching and learning activities. According to the framework (2016) of the Carnegie Project on the Education Doctorate (CPED), a PoP is "a persistent, contextualized, and specific issue embedded in the work of a professional practitioner, the addressing of which has the potential to result in improved understanding, experience, and outcomes." We must take care, however, to frame inequities as problems of practice, *not* as a problem with any particular student group on campus or families in the community. Here are some ways to drill down into a PoP:

- Capture observable equity-centered challenges on your campus.
- Develop hunches or initial hypotheses about root causes behind the visible symptoms.
- Document intel you've already gathered or data you plan to collect before settling on your exact PoP.
- Anticipate responses from your school community and how you might frame your walk to get buy-in.

Problem of Practice Exemplar:

> Our leadership team is concerned that the placement of our special education classrooms poses a significant equity concern. Based on the data we've collected, including mapping the distance to accessible restrooms, proximity to handicapped parking spots, and lack of exposure to and interaction with general education students, our physical environment may be limiting students with moderate to severe disabilities to engage in the least restrictive educational setting. Staff and parents have also been asking us to address this apparent exclusion from the main parts of campus and non-compliance with Individual Education Plans (IEPs). Therefore, we're proposing an investigation into the matter.

After you've composed a PoP statement, turn it into an inquiry question that will be the focal point of your walk. When crafting your question, start with an interrogative like *how*, *to what extent*, *why*, or *what if*. Also, be specific about the equity-related

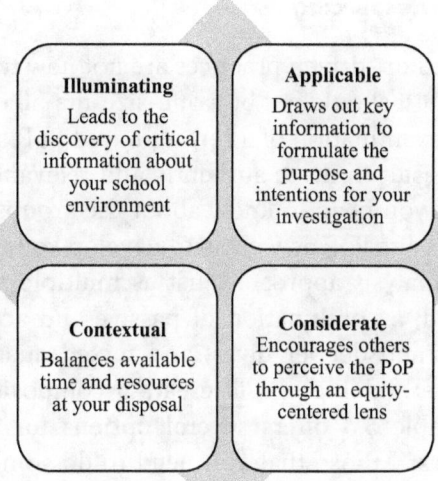

Figure 3.4 Inquiry question criteria

issue, the student group(s) you are attempting to support, and the adults involved. Finally, make sure it's open-ended, leaving room for possibilities and avoiding foregone conclusions. Effective inquiry questions should also consider the four criteria contained in Figure 3.4.

For the PoP outlined in the earlier example, the leadership team in the exemplar composes a couple of inquiry questions to potentially pursue:

- In what ways might we re-envision our campus layout to be more inclusive and accessible and to foster a greater sense of belonging for our students with special needs in advance of the new school year?
- How might we conduct a comprehensive site audit to identify buildings, resources, and structures that would benefit our students with special needs in the short and long term?
- To what extent does our current campus footprint facilitate or hinder integration of students with special needs and general education students, and where are the areas we should focus on first?

Stage 2: Data Resourcing

Data-informed or -driven practices are not new to educational leadership, but it should not be a one-size-fits-all endeavor. For each unique examination of a setting-based PoP, starting from scratch will result in more authentic and relevant approaches to learn what you need to know about the groups or topics at the center of your PoP as well as to develop your discrete collection and analysis approach. Just as multiple measures are recommended, a combination of passive and active sources, quick checks and deeper dives, and mixed quantitative and qualitative methodologies will create a composite picture of the scene. Table 3.3 offers several options for deliberation. Active sources – those that you need to do some legwork to accomplish – are indicated with an (a) next to the item, and passive sources – information you can tap that is already in existence – are indicated with a (p).

Continuing the thread of the data walk exemplar, the figurative site leadership team settles on four approaches to probe into their inquiry question, including the tools and resources outlined below:

Table 3.3 Multiple measures for data collection

Quick checks	Deeper dives
o Surveys/exit polls (a)	o Community mapping exercises (a)
o Participation/attendance rates (a)	o Qualitative feedback (a)
o Website click-throughs (p)	o Listening tours (a)
o Time logged onto a platform (p)	o Demonstrations/hypotheticals (a)
o Standardized assessment scores (p)	o Ethnographic studies (a)
o Master schedule/course enrollment (p)	o Focus groups (a)
o Demographic/census data (p)	o Interviews (a)
o Dashboard information (p)	o Observations (a)
o Resource purchases/cost summary (p)	o Reflection sessions (a)
o Graduate/dropout/completion/attrition rates (p)	o Longitudinal trends analysis (p)
	o Transcript reviews (p)

1) Site maps, including classrooms, common spaces, offices, bathroom facilities, entrances, exits, parking lots, play areas, and hallways:
   a. Clean version with current campus layout
   b. Marked-up version with areas for investigation
   c. Blank version for ideation
2) Student Information System spreadsheet containing a list of students with IEP designations, disaggregated by race, gender, and grade level
3) Caregiver Focus Group Questions:
   - Based on your experiences, share some supportive features we have on campus?
   - Based on your experiences, share some features that present obstacles to your child and/or family?
   - What suggestions do you have for improvements?
   - If you had to choose one location or specific area for us to focus on, what would it be and why?
4) Look-For, Listen-For Observational Tool to be used for a week to inventory daily interactions and notice trends around selected campus locations as described in Box 3.1.

BOX 3.1 LOOK-FOR, LISTEN-FOR OBSERVATIONAL TOOL

Overview: A "look for, listen for" observation event means actively paying attention to visual and auditory cues in a given situation, deliberately searching for particular sights and sounds to gather information. Essentially, it's a focused observation method that utilizes both sight and hearing to gather details on process and content in a specific setting.

Key Tenets
1. Be specific about what you see and hear.
2. The tool is not meant to be evaluative. Don't interpret or judge; just describe.
3. Observe patterns and avoid overgeneralizing from a single comment or incident.
4. Note strengths as well as areas for growth.

Prompts: As you observe, use any of the following questions to help you document your observations through different lenses:

- At different points in the day, what is the mood, vibe, or energy of the space you have been assigned?
- To what extent do students with special needs interact with their general education peers in the space? When do they cross paths the most? The least?
- What physical barriers did you notice getting in the way of productive interactions or engagements?
- Did you observe active indicators of inclusion or involvement of students with special needs in the space by their general education peers or adults?

Part I: Observation *Name:* _____
Location: _____ *Time:* _____
Date: _____

Look Fors "I Saw"	*Listen Fors "I Heard"*
☐ Interactions between staff and students ☐ Peer interactions ☐ Access to facilities and wayfinding ☐ Socio-emotional visual cues (facial expressions/body language) ☐ Ability to navigate spaces ☐ Content of signage, artwork, décor ☐ Other visible observations	☐ Use of asset-based and deficit-based language ☐ Verbal instructions/directions/prompts ☐ Tone(s) of voice(s) ☐ Vocal expressions (shouts, laughter) ☐ Invitations to engage ☐ Inclusion in activities ☐ Other auditory observations

I noticed:

I wonder:

Part II: Group Summary Form: *After discussing each observer's individual notes from the week, the team will complete one summary chart interpreting the data they collected.*		
Campus location(s):	*Observation data (examples, direct quotes, or summary)*	*Themes or initial conclusions about what the data indicates*
Environmental elements that foster inclusion and belonging		
Infrastructure or physical features presenting barriers		
Interpersonal interactions observed in the space		
Visual and auditory indicators of integration and involvement		
Other observations of note		

Part III: Idea Generation

1) As a group, brainstorm some approaches, strategies, or additional activities that may shed more light on addressing the problem of practice.

2) Which, if any, of these ideas might we pursue as next steps?

3) What, when, and how will we communicate our findings and recommendations to the extended the school community?

Stage 3: Equity Walk Design

There is no right or wrong way to do your walk. Think creatively, personalize the experience, and be inventive. That said, many organizations already supply free access to digital or reproducible templates, toolkits, and guidance documents on the topic of data walks to advance equity. Wherever you can find pre-existing resources like the ones listed below, pick and choose certain elements that fit your needs.

Resources:

- ✓ Education Trust-West Data Equity Walk Toolkit (https://west.edtrust.org/data-equity-walk-toolkit/)
- ✓ University of Wisconsin Madison Tools for Practicing Data Equity (https://researchdata.wisc.edu/uncategorized/tools-for-data-equity-part-2/)
- ✓ U-Penn Centering Racial Equity Through Data Integration https://aisp.upenn.edu/aisp-toolkit_5-27-20/)
- ✓ Digital Promise Data Ready Playbook (https://digitalpromise.org/inclusive-innovation/data-ready-playbook/)

The design that the case study team decides to embark upon contains four main components that will be executed over the course of a week:

1) Site staff, including the principal, counselor, IEP case workers, teachers, and campus supervisors, will fill out observation templates of "look fors" and "listen fors" during passing periods, breaks, and before- and after-school activities to document levels of inclusion of students with moderate to severe special needs in various settings Monday through Thursday of the chosen week.
2) The site team will meet to discuss the passive data sources they gathered prior to the walk (campus map analysis and demographic reports on students with IEPs) in relation to the active data compiled from the observation forms to draw initial conclusions.
3) To test out their inferences, on Friday the team will host a caregiver focus group with parents and guardians to confirm or re-evaluate their findings.

4) Finally, the principal will hold a community engagement event to share the equity walk results and involve stakeholders in strategizing ways to reconfigure the physical campus to enhance inclusivity and belonging.

Backward-Mapping the Event

In preparation for your event, Figure 3.5 backward-maps the planning process and suggests time frames to get your team ready. Developing pre-walk checklists can also ensure that you've crossed your t's and dotted your i's before the walk occurs.

<u>Resource Checklist</u>: List all the tools and materials needed and prepare the location for the visit:

- ☐ Technology devices, pens, notepads
- ☐ Data presentation materials: forms, charts, displays, other tools
- ☐ Snacks, water, other comforts
- ☐ Space organized for optimal participation
- ☐ Back-up plans

<u>Inclusive Engagement</u>: Have you…

- ☐ Consciously partnered with staff, students, and families in the equity walk design?
- ☐ Taken special needs into consideration when choosing a location?
- ☐ Invited an equitable representation of the community impacted by the issue?

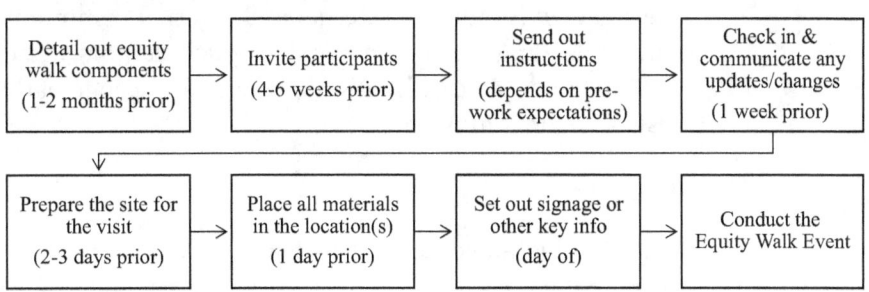

Figure 3.5 Backward-mapping the walk

- ☐ Planned how to monitor voices in the space to elicit balanced participation?
- ☐ Provided for accommodations that respect diversity (translators, accessibility, neutral settings)?
- ☐ Communicated in jargon-free, understandable language?
- ☐ Decided how to involve participants in developing post-walk recommendations?
- ☐ Determined ways to show authentic appreciation for participation?
- ☐ Pre-scheduled follow-ups with the results, actions, or next steps?

Stage 4: Communicate Intentions and Rationale

Communicate what factors have inspired your team to launch the data equity walk you plan to carry out with your school community. Depending on the audience, you'll want to customize your messaging to the level of involvement different people may have. Outline your internal and external communications plan elements based on the categories that follow:

For those external to the event:

- Explain the PoP and inquiry question in simple language to orient people to the site-specific situation you are attempting to research.
- Send out previews prior to the interactive event via newsletters, video messages, website, and social media posts to share why your school is doing the walk and what you hope comes out of it.
- If the walk is complex, controversial, or high-stakes, set the stage with multiple internal and external communications leading up to the event to quell rumors or to acclimate people to why it's happening and gauge early resistance or confusion.

Content Checklist:

- ☐ Provide a high-level summary regarding why your school is doing the walk.
- ☐ Present the PoP in easy-to-understand terms.

- ☐ Share what you hope comes out of it.
- ☐ Ask for moral support.

Strategy Options:

- ☐ Newsletter item/memo
- ☐ Video message
- ☐ FAQs page on website
- ☐ Board presentation

For those participating in the event:

- Invitations to join must clearly explain what the event is about and what participants will be expected to do, along with the purpose, goals, and intentions.
- Prepare participants with talking points to explain what's going on to those who aren't involved but may be aware of or see the walk in action.
- Send reminders, touch base, answer questions, and provide detailed logistical information to support full participation prior to the event.

Content Checklist:

- ☐ Provide background information on the PoP and why it was selected.
- ☐ Establish purpose, goals, and intentions of the walk.
- ☐ Outline specific reasons why they are being invited.
- ☐ Give detailed explanation on what participants will be expected to do.

Strategy Options:

- ☐ Craft invitations with info on the who, what, where, why, when, and how of the event.
- ☐ Offer talking points on basic elements of the walk.
- ☐ Send frequent reminders, including requests for any pre-work required.
- ☐ Provide logistical information to support full participation prior to the event.

Box 3.2 is a sample principal memo and draft agenda for participants based on the running case study.

> ## BOX 3.2   PRINCIPAL COMMUNICATION
>
> *From: Principal Curry*
> *Re: Data Equity Walk Memo*
> *Dear Campus Climate Committee:*
>
> *I am inviting you to participate in a special event at Howard Middle School on Friday, September 26, 2025. We will be embarking on our school's first data equity walk to help us better understand how to create a more inclusive campus climate for our 6th- to 8th-grade students. Since the concept of a "data equity walk" may be new to you, in essence it's a process of examining data to pinpoint areas where certain student populations may be underserved and require different approaches to be more successful – in this case, fostering stronger connections between our students with special needs and their peers.*
>
> *Specifically, the placement of our special education classrooms poses a significant equity concern on campus. Based on data we've collected already, our leadership team recognizes that our physical environment may be limiting students with moderate to severe disabilities to engage in the least restrictive educational environment. Staff and parents have also been asking us to address this apparent exclusion from the main parts of campus and compliance with Individual Education Plans (IEPs). Therefore, we're proposing an investigation into potential ways to reconfigure or reallocate classroom assignments and/or other facilities to develop remedies or interventions to rectify the problem by next fall. The inquiry question guiding our observation is: In what ways might we re-envision our campus layout to be more inclusive and accessible and to foster a greater sense of belonging for our students with special needs in advance of the new school year?*
>
> *After collecting sufficient data on our school setting using a "Look for, Listen for" observational tool between September 22 and 25, we will host a parent focus group panel on September 26 to learn more about their experiences on our campus – a detailed agenda is included on p. 2 of this memo. In order to prepare for the event, we'd like each participant to review the following data resources attached in advance:*
>
> 1) *Number of students on IEPs as reported in the Student Information System (SIS), disaggregated by race, gender, grade level, and special education designation*
> 2) *Site map with entry points, classroom assignments, facilities access, and wayfinding*

3) Compilation of the week's observation notes on the inclusion of special education students in general education activities such as recess, lunch, sports, and clubs

I appreciate your willingness to participate in Howard's inaugural data equity walk and share your perspectives, expertise, and ideas for improvement. Please find attached some key documents to help orient you to the process, and please feel free to reach out with any questions you may have prior to the event.

Data Walk Agenda Howard Middle School		
Location: Counseling Office Conference Room Resources: Notetaking device; data sources		
Agenda Item	Process	Time
Orientation and Expectations	Introductions Set norms and group agreements Frame goals and intentions	9:00–9:30 am
Grounding Activities	Review and discuss pre-walk data Calibrate notetaking expectations	9:30–10:45 am
Equity Walk Event	Conduct focus group panel with parents of students with special needs	11:00–12:30 pm
Lunch	Host lunch for observation team and guest panel members	12:30–1:15 pm
Closing	Debrief panel discussion Develop next steps	1:20–2:15 pm

To orient you to the purpose and parameters of our walk, the FAQs that follow should help:

Q: What is a Data Equity Walk?
A: A "data equity walk" is an interactive activity where a group of people, like educators, community members, or students, analyze educational data to identify and discuss disparities in student outcomes across different demographic groups. The goals are to understand and address equity issues within the data by collectively

> identifying solutions to close achievement gaps. Essentially, it's a process of examining data to pinpoint areas where certain student populations might be underserved and require targeted interventions.
>
> Q: How do we frame a problem of practice (PoP)?
> A: A problem of practice is a persistent, contextualized, and specific issue embedded in the work of a practitioner, which has the potential to negatively impact understanding, experience, and outcomes. Inequities must be framed as problems of practice, not as a problem with any particular student group related to racial, ethnic, or linguistic background, familial composition, or exhibited behaviors. The true causes of a problem may not yet be fully understood and, if we aren't careful, can lead to exacerbation of the problem or misguided attempts to confront an incorrectly defined issue.
>
> Q: What will we be doing during the observation?
> The leadership team will invite a group of caregivers representing diverse student needs (including disabilities related to physical, cognitive, learning, autism spectrum, and social-emotional mental health) to share their perspectives and experiences regarding the pros and cons of the physical layout at the middle school. They will be asked four open-ended questions:
>
> - Based on your experiences, what are some supportive features we have on campus?
> - Based on your experiences, what are some features that present obstacles to your child and/or family?
> - What suggestions do you have for improvements?
> - If you had to choose one location or specific area for us to focus on, what would it be and why?
>
> You will be provided a notetaking tool to capture key themes during the caregiver focus group panel discussion and will learn more about how to use it during the pre-walk prep time outlined on the agenda.

Stage 5: Conduct the Event

Since you've already done so much to prepare during stages 1–4, you're more than ready to conduct the event itself. Equip participants with the resources you've selected, engage in agendized activities, and facilitate group conversations about your collective findings. Remind everyone of the ground rules and functional roles of team members by providing support materials like these:

A) Communicate Participant Expectations:
   ✓ Complete all pre-walk activities provided prior to the event.
   ✓ Arrive on time, ready to learn.
   ✓ Stay in the role you've agreed to play (or were assigned).
   ✓ Maintain an inquisitive mindset throughout the walk.
   ✓ Commit to staying for the duration of the event.

B) Establish Common Agreements:
   1. All participants stand on equal ground.
   2. We use asset-based language and maintain positive attitudes toward students, families, teachers, and support staff.
   3. We shift roles between learner and expert at any given moment.
   4. We use a variety of data sources to inform our direction.
   5. We refrain from jumping too fast to conclusions, and we remain open to discovering novel solutions.
   6. We ask questions when we don't understand or when we need more clarity.
   7. We monitor our emotions and support others with theirs if difficult feelings come up.
   8. What is said in the room stays in the room.

Stage 6: Propose High-Leverage Actions

While you may have had some anticipated outcomes from the walk in mind prior to the event, you now have a much fuller picture of the scope of your PoP and very likely already began discussing ideas with the team to pursue. Before you conclude the day's activities, build in time to brainstorm potential actions that address the PoP moving forward. Use the pre-work information, what you uncovered during the event, and the dialog that took place immediately afterward in the debrief. Write down any and all ideas without discarding any at this time. Later on, the site leadership team will review the suggestions and formulate a plot to propose.

Table 3.4 Obstacles and opportunities

Obstacles	Opportunities
Grounds/surface maintenance in disrepair (uneven pavement, cracked blacktop, pitted fields, etc.) preclude inclusion for students with disabilities in games and group activities	Submit facilities repair requests to address the identified surfaces in order of priority to maximize inclusion and access for all students
Crowded hallways and loud acoustics during passing period contribute to or exacerbate anxiety and discomfort for students with special needs	Redesign passageways with clear signage, painted directions, and student volunteers manage traffic flow (like a street intersection) to ensure safety and security
Classrooms designated for students with moderate/severe IEPs are located in the portables on the perimeter of campus and the percentage of time they have to interact with general education peers is less than 15%.	Commission a site redesign contest partnering student leadership team representatives and students with special needs to improve inclusion opportunities by 35%.

For instance, the team in our fictional scenario may have learned, through the weeklong site observations and the parent focus group session, that there are three main obstacles and opportunities they might consider taking action toward (Table 3.4).

Stage 7: Pilot a Solution-Seeking Initiative

The brainstorming session is the launching point for testing out one of your highest-leverage actions on a trial basis. Fair warning: you may/will not get it exactly right. No solution ever works perfectly out of the gate. That's why a small-scale endeavor is recommended. During this period, your hypotheses will be verified or denied or something in between. A pilot evaluates the new initiative on a limited scale to identify its strengths, weaknesses, gaps, and opportunities. Embracing a continuous improvement mindset and being open to what the pilot is telling allow you to make the necessary pivots as information emerges.

As the closing example from the case study team, they decide to work through the second proposal, embedding some aspects of the third proposal from Table 3.4. As such, the principal issues this challenge to the student body:

> Form a team of up to six students (equally balanced between students with special needs and general education peers) to propose a hallway traffic flow implementation model for the three main hallways on campus. In one month's time, we will host an evening to display everyone's prototype. The top three contenders will then be selected to pitch their plan in front of a 'shark tank' panel for consideration. The team whose model is selected will be involved in the execution of their plan.

Stage 8: Implement

If you decide to move past the pilot stage into full implementation, Table 3.5 outlines suggested next steps of the process alongside the example from the case study.

Table 3.5 Implementation stages adapted from Leading the Launch (Wallace, 2021)

Steps	Case study scenario
Involve collaborators	Hold a community forum to gather input and ideas on potential campus layout options to advance inclusivity and access.
Gather and analyze inputs	Review feedback and consult with facilities department to determine feasibility of proposed options.
Make a decision	Commit to a direction on which option provides the most benefits compared to the costs involved.
Plan and deliver professional learning	Dedicate time on each monthly staff meeting to develop approaches to meet the goal of a 35% increase in positive interactions, problem-solve issues and adjust as needed.
Implement the initiative	Officially implement the initiative school-wide prior to the fall semester.
Provide ongoing support	Measure impacts and orient new staff and families to the philosophy, space use, and mindsets needed for the implementation to remain successful.

Practical Application

Walking the equity talk is a dynamic (and possibly quite addictive) process. As in any continuous improvement model, once you have a developed one solution to a PoP, it will spawn many more inquiries. We shouldn't be satisfied with moving the needle for one group of students, as there are many, many more also waiting for change. But once you've introduced and embedded the equity walk mindsets and processes into your practice, it will become your way of being, your way of leading. Go forth and interrogate, iterate, instigate, and innovate using Exercise 3.4 as a guidepost. If you're not quite ready to execute the whole process, you will find an abbreviated cross-observation version in Exercise 3.5. Or you can use elements from both!

▶ UNIVERSAL DESIGN FOR LEARNING (UDL) SPACES

You've likely heard of the pedagogical approach called Universal Design for Learning (UDL), popularized in 2008 when CAST (Center for Applied Special Technology) published their UDL Guidelines 1.0. UDL has become a widespread movement in Pre-K-12 educational circles. The theory is predicated on three main principles that make education more accessible to all learners: multiple means of (1) engagement (the "why" of learning), (2) representation (the "what" of learning), and (3) action and expression (the "how" of learning). UDL invites educators to deliberately tailor instructional experiences that anticipate and attend to learners' multifaceted needs. The goal is to mitigate manufactured environmental impediments that may get in the way of a student's natural ability to access information, find personal meaning, and apply prior knowledge to novel situations (Stapleton-Corcoran, 2022; Burgstahler, 2021).

What you might not know is that UDL germinated from a seed planted by architects, product designers, engineers, and environmental design researchers at the Center for Universal Design (CUD) at North Carolina State University in 1997. They established seven principles for the universal design of products or operations as a means to create inclusive and functional environments for all individuals who come into contact with public spaces. The descriptors in Box 3.3 are directly from the CUD website, and I've provided examples in italics of how their applications might show up in our school environments.

> **BOX 3.3 UNIVERSAL DESIGN PRINCIPLES IN EDUCATIONAL SETTINGS**
>
> Principle 1: Equitable use. The design is useful and marketable to people with diverse abilities.
>
> *Example: A library-media center possesses technology, equipment, and furniture that students can access regardless of their differences in abilities, such as wide doorways, low shelving, voice to speech software, audiobooks, large print, digital aids, braille, and leveled readers intentionally placed right alongside conventional print materials.*
>
> Principle 2: Flexibility in use. The design accommodates a wide range of individual preferences and abilities.
>
> *Example: A counseling office or wellness center that offers quiet decompression spaces with low lighting and beanbags, an art therapy station, a circle of chairs for small-group discussion, and closed-door offices for private sessions.*
>
> Principle 3: Simple and intuitive use. Use of the design is easy to understand regardless of the user's experience, knowledge, language skills, or current concentration level.
>
> *Example: A district displays the lunch menu on their website and in each school's cafeteria with photographs of food items for sale with easy-to-understand pricing and payment information that can be translated into languages other than English with the click of a button.*
>
> Principle 4: Perceptible information. The design communicates necessary information effectively to the user regardless of ambient conditions or the user's sensory abilities.
>
> *Example: Each main hallway has an interactive map kiosk presenting essential information about campus locations, navigation, and safety routes people can interact with via pictorial, verbal, and tactile modes.*
>
> Principle 5: Tolerance for error. The design minimizes hazards and the adverse consequences of accidental or unintended actions.
>
> *Example: The front office and locker rooms contain failsafe equipment such as an automatic defibrillator device that uses step-by-step voice*

> instructions, pulses, and beeps to help people at any age or cognitive ability administer life-saving CPR in the event of a medical emergency.
>
> Principle 6: Low physical effort. The design can be used efficiently and comfortably and with a minimum of fatigue.
>
> Example: Automatic doors, touch screens, escalators/elevators, curb cuts and ramps, automatic sinks and soap dispensers, lighting sensors, levered handles, and voice-controlled technologies.
>
> Principle 7: Size and space for approach and use. Appropriate size and space are provided for approach, reach, manipulation, and use regardless of the user's body size, posture, or mobility.
>
> Example: Every classroom is equipped with adjustable tables, counters, and work surfaces that can accommodate a variety of seating options that welcome wheelchairs or other mobility devices and students of all stature (in lieu of one-size-fits-all individual student desks).

UDL is often employed as a precursor to referring students to more specialized educational interventions and services by ensuring that the general education environment is already accessible, comfortable, and equitable; presuming that making the regular classroom setting inclusive of students' unique and differentiated learning needs, the number of misplacements in more restrictive special education assignments will be significantly reduced as a result. Special educator Aashna Khurana (2022) confirms that

> Often, the first step to inclusion is the physical access and reduction of physical barriers that can affect the participation of the learners in a school. Therefore, school spaces need to be intentionally designed or adapted to be accessible and flexible. This requires the schools to identify spaces that would need restructuring to reduce existing infrastructural barriers or proactive planning of new indoor, outdoor and digital spaces incorporating UDL guidelines and checkpoints.
>
> (p. 5)

In alignment with UDL guidelines, Khurana suggests several no- to low-cost ideas for integrating UDL into the physical setting:

- Creating spaces that use locally abundant resources to build school infrastructure and support skills of locals
- Transforming school spaces like classrooms, playgrounds, courts, and washrooms into learning spaces
- Encouraging teaching-learning in natural settings amidst nature whenever possible
- Leaving some spaces as "mystery spaces" to allow creative use, "get away spaces" for students to disconnect and reconnect with peers, and "collaborative spaces" to support work in small groups
- Creating welcoming classrooms that offer varying levels of tasks, sensory experiences, scaffolds, and set individualized expectations from each learner
- Allowing effective and efficient use and management of classroom resources (including technological aids), such as ensuring accessibility for all learners, keeping them in spaces accessible to all learners, and having a variety of learning aids to support spiral learning
- Varying the level of sensory stimulation, demands, and requirements for tasks
- Creating spaces that are learner-friendly, minimizing distractions for sound- and light-sensitive learners, and allowing access to the buildings
- Creating/improving accessibility and user-friendliness, such as having wide doors and hallways and automated doors.

(pp. 3–5)

When a district I served in passed a several hundred-million-dollar bond, I routinely asked students as young as kindergarten what they would like to see in the modernization of their own campuses. Aside from the refreshingly frequent requests to build a roller coaster or install a waterslide on their playground, kids often had ingenious as well as practical plans for the usage of their spaces. High on the list: cleaner/better bathrooms; cafeteria set-ups that were more functional; improved fields and play equipment; and more student lounges or hangouts. Imagine if you similarly issued a design challenge to your students to create a school of their dreams. What might they say? What are the possibilities?

In a paper on innovative learning spaces, Irit Sasson, Itamar Yehuda, and Shirley Miedijensky (2022) discuss:

> Because classroom climate is derived from an ecological paradigm, aspects of the physical environment highly relevant to innovative learning spaces are part of the concept, such as classroom appearance, furnishings, size, physical resources, and even heating and ventilation (Evans, Harvey, Buckley & Yan, 2009). Franklin and Harrington (2019) developed a new rubric for evaluating teacher and student roles and responsibilities, also relevant to this study, which delineates four domains of successful classroom practice: classroom teaching and learning; classroom behavior management; classroom environment –social aspects; classroom environment–physical space.
>
> (p. 726)

Of the four domains outlined by Franklin and Harrington (2019), three are setting-dependent: behavior management, social interactions, and substantial attributes of the classroom environment. Behavior management is a real and ongoing process and can be exhausting to maintain. Modeling, correcting, and teaching about what constitutes appropriate peer cooperation occur on a near minute-to-minute basis in many classrooms. Respecting our shared spaces and materials provides ample opportunities for continued growth as well.

If teachers are expected to facilitate learning in accordance with UDL principles, they will need support and training in these arenas in addition to the curriculum and instruction zone. As Erin Stapleton-Corcoran, instructional designer at the University of Chicago, reminds us on the Center for the Advancement of Teaching Excellence website (2022): "Keep in mind that UDL is a process and can be implemented incrementally and in a series of iterations. You can start with small changes that align with UDL principles, and revise over time" (no p. #). By asking the following, administrators can play a key role in mentoring teachers to envision and plan for instructional adaptations that otherwise could breed chaos if not carefully constructed:

1. What might it look like to elevate the spheres of positive behavior management and productive peer interactions?
2. What needs to be physically in place in your classroom for your lesson plan to roll out successfully from start to finish?
3. What adjustments or interventions might be viable when and if things go off script?
4. How will you prepare your students in advance for these kinds of instructional shifts and establish their expected participation and responsibilities?
5. How might we involve parents and caregivers so they understand primary aspects and goals of your upcoming lessons and can do some frontloading at home?

Practical Application

Exercise 3.5 combines the various UDL strategies mentioned in this section and prepares leaders to lay the foundations of universal design in their workplace locations. You will identify one learning space on to apply the seven principles and determine what supports might be proactively developed to activate UD in advance of incorporating the L piece of the puzzle.

▶ MODULE 3 EXERCISES

Throughout module 3, you were encouraged to ponder your geographical locale, physical setting, socio-cultural environment, school climate, universal design principles, and virtual learning spaces in unconventional ways. To cement your understanding about the spaces and places we inhabit, this set of exercises is intended to bring the perceptible and discernable characteristics of your campus to the forefront rather than the background of teaching and learning experiences.

3.1. Setting SWOT analysis
3.2. Environmental needs assessment tool
3.3. Climate checklist
3.4. Data equity
3.5. Cross-observational exchange
3.6. Universal design principles practical application

Exercise 3.1 Setting SWOT Analysis

You've read the case study on Fox Hedge Alternative School. Now it's your turn to inspect the environmental elements of your own site. Independently or with a team, write down the benefits your physical spaces afford students and staff as well as the barriers or challenges they pose. Then select one or two ideas from the future opportunities quadrant and draft a proposal for consideration.

Current strengths	Current weaknesses
Future opportunities	Pending threats

Course of Action:

1) Immediate:

2) Short-term:

3) Long-term:

Exercise 3.2 Environmental Needs Assessment Tool

This exercise gives you a chance to test out the feasibility of different ideas for enhancing your physical environment and spearheading change efforts at the site. By first conducting a needs assessment with input from families, students, and staff, then prioritizing with your leadership team, and finally running the ideas up the chain for approval, you can take greater charge of your physical environment. Since there are many directions you can go with this exercise, the prompts below are broadly phrased to leave open-ended responses that invite possibility. Just pick a place and get going.

1. Area(s) for investigation:
2. Reasons/rationale for choosing this location/topic:
3. Current status of environmental situation:
4. What's working well in the space(s):
5. Constraints of the space(s):
6. Is the area (select as many that apply):
   ☐ Dangerous/condemned
   ☐ Unsightly/unkempt
   ☐ Insufficient/inadequate
   ☐ Inequitable for students or staff
   ☐ Unusable/non-functioning/damaged
   ☐ Vacant/underutilized
   ☐ Other: _____
7. Potential approaches/renovations:
   ☐ General clean-up
   ☐ Decluttering/reorganization
   ☐ Disposal/removal
   ☐ Maintenance work order
   ☐ Facilities request
   ☐ Community project
   ☐ Other: _____
8. Initial steps: _____
   _____

Exercise 3.3 Climate Checklist

In Table 3.2, you were provided with a sample environmental climate checklist that a site administrator might use to predict, plan for, and respond to both physical and atmospheric conditions on their campus. You may want to keep or replicate some of the ideas from the example or customize the ten items to match your own purposes. In each of the boxes, write down some procedures that can be quickly implemented on a regular basis (daily, weekly, or biweekly) to keep a finger on the pulse of your site.

Physical/Tangible components	*Atmospheric/Climate components*
☐ Note Air Quality Index (AQI) concerns.	☐ Check maintenance work order requests and follow up.
☐ Look for temperature/weather/natural disaster forecasts.	☐ Observe areas on campus for additional supervision needs.
☐ Test electrical, plumbing, Wi-Fi, etc. for performance issues.	☐ Note "hot spots" of activity that could signal conflicts.
☐ Remove or request disposal of any unusable furnishings or equipment.	☐ Assess the vibe or undercurrents in different spaces.
☐ Document needed repairs, upgrades, or damage and report to authorities.	☐ Ask students and staff how they feel about specific issues on site.

© Copyright material from Kim Wallace (2025), Game–Changing Leadership in Action, Routledge.

Exercise 3.4 Data Equity Walk

The eight stages presented in this chapter on how to conduct an equity walk plus the case study detailed throughout pages 121–140 will help you create your own event using the templates and models provided for each step in the process. Answer the following questions to the best of your ability. You will go back to them for refinement as you work your way through the protocol.

Why are you focusing on this specific POP? (Establish and explain clear rationale for focusing on the equity concern.)	**Who** might participate in the equity walk? (Instructional Leadership Team, site administrators, teachers, counselors, support staff, parents, community members, district office leaders, students, etc.)
What might they be looking for and at? (e.g., examining data sets, listening to a focus group, reading qualitative testimonials, interpreting survey results, and reviewing student study team notes)	**When** might it happen? (time frame: before, during, after school, evening, on a weekend)
Where might it take place? (specific location on or off campus: classroom, lab, library media center, neighborhood gathering spot)	**How** might you conduct the walk? (logistics, participant roles, agenda, tools and materials, contingency plans)

Data Equity Walk Checklist

<u>Stage 1: Equity-Centered Investigation</u>

- ❏ Identify a school-based equity concern you'd like to understand better.
- ❏ Write a problem of practice (PoP) statement on your area of focus.
- ❏ Develop an inquiry question (IQ) to guide the design of your walk.

© Copyright material from Kim Wallace (2025), Game–Changing Leadership in Action, Routledge.

Stage 2: Identification of Data Sources

- ❏ Select one or more potential passive/active data resources for examination that inform your POP and IQ.
- ❏ Prepare data collection, analysis, and interpretation tools for participants.

Stage 3: Event Design and Preparation

- ❏ Backward-map specific benchmarks to hit prior to the event.
- ❏ Develop an agenda and schedule.
- ❏ Book locations/rooms for each phase of the event.
- ❏ Document all tools, technologies and materials needed and prepare the location for the visit.
- ❏ Detail logistical information (e.g., parking, directions, meals, expectations).

Stage 4: Communications (ongoing)

- ❏ Draft and send invitations to participants including any pre-work or foundational materials along with the event agenda.
- ❏ Schedule follow-up messaging, calendar reminders, updates, and so on.
- ❏ Compose general messaging to school community about the purpose of the walk.

Stage 5: Conduct the Walk

- ❏ Prepare wayfinding signage.
- ❏ Make introductions.
- ❏ Create/adopt norms/agreements.
- ❏ Establish goals and roles.
- ❏ Hold the event activities.
- ❏ Facilitate debrief and solution generating prompts and activities.
- ❏ Organize closing appreciations.
- ❏ Share next steps.

© Copyright material from Kim Wallace (2025), Game–Changing Leadership in Action, Routledge.

Stages 6–8: Initiative Implementation

- ❏ Select one promising idea to pursue.
- ❏ Plan and pilot the selected initiative on a small scale for a limited time period.
- ❏ Review feedback, data collected, and determine whether to abandon the endeavor, expand the pilot, or implement it widespread.
- ❏ If moving forward, identify professional learning needs, communications, and other preparatory activities to set everyone up for success.
- ❏ Implement the initiative and monitor progress frequently to ensure its effectiveness and expected impacts.

Exercise 3.5 Cross-Observational Exchange

For Exercise 3.5, you are invited to find a partner school to visit and host a visitor on your own site to broaden your respective perspectives. Think of this as your own mini "foreign exchange" experience, in which you will go out in to the field and come back with fresh eyes on your school grounds. If your district is large enough and you have enough geographical diversity among your schools, seek out a partner who is willing to engage in a cross-observation with you in exchange for the same. If you need to reach out to someone in a nearby district instead, that's perfectly fine, too. The goals of this cross-observation are two-fold: (1) You each get to witness elements you might want to incorporate or leverage at your own site, and (2) you'll mutually benefit from seeing your own locale through new lenses. The template below is meant to be modified to fit your needs, but here are some general areas to spark ideas.

Elements	Site 1	Site 2
Campus layout features		
Use of natural environment		
Utilization of learning spaces		
School resource management		
Condition of facilities		
Architecture and design		
Americans with Disabilities Act (ADA) accessibility		
Equity and inclusion of students with special needs		
Safety and security features		

(Continued)

Elements	Site 1	Site 2
Wayfinding and signage		
Traffic flow (parking, drop off/pick-up, throughways)		
Common areas and large group spaces (library, gym, courtyard, fields)		
Locations of support services, administration, counseling, health/wellness center		
Geographical limitations impacting physical or functional operations		

Reflections:

1) Perspectives gained about my own site that were enlightening to me:

2) Observations from peer's site that might be adapted or incorporated in my setting:

3) Immediate, mid-term, and long-term actions to pitch to staff, families, and students for potential campus improvements:

Exercise 3.6 Universal Design Principles Application

Select a learning context that you'd like to investigate for potential transformation related to the seven principles of Universal Design (1997). Write down the type of space it is (e.g., classroom, theater, campus commons, career-technical education (CTE) facility, gymnasium) and identify what currently exists and what gaps need to be filled before implementing UDL as an instructional method.

1) Area under consideration: _____

2) Instructional goals/outcomes: _____
_____

Principle 1: Equitable use. The design is useful and marketable to people with diverse abilities.
Current status:
Potential improvements:

Principle 2: Flexibility in use. The design accommodates a wide range of individual preferences and abilities.
Current status:
Potential improvements:

Principle 3: Simple and intuitive use. Use of the design is easy to understand regardless of the user's experience, knowledge, language skills, or current concentration level.
Current status:
Potential improvements:

Principle 4: Perceptible information. The design communicates necessary information effectively to the user regardless of ambient conditions or the user's sensory abilities.
Current status:
Potential improvements:

Principle 5: Tolerance for error. The design minimizes hazards and the adverse consequences of accidental or unintended actions.
Current status:
Potential improvements:

© Copyright material from Kim Wallace (2025), Game–Changing Leadership in Action, Routledge.

Principle 6: Low physical effort. The design can be used efficiently and comfortably and with a minimum of fatigue.
Current status:
Potential improvements:

Principle 7: Size and space for approach and use. Appropriate size and space are provided for approach, reach, manipulation, and use regardless of the user's body size, posture, or mobility.
Current status:
Potential improvements:

Next Steps: Develop a timeline for which you will begin to renovate the facility to meet the threshold of each of the seven design elements.

▶ CONCLUSION

Perception is reality. Human beings' five senses of sight, hearing, taste, smell, and touch operate in the background of our daily lives, not to mention the sixth sense of gut feelings or extrasensory perceptions that guide the body and mind unconsciously as we move through time and space. Think back to the *umwelt* motif mentioned in Module 2 and how our own tiny universes exist side by side, intersecting and bouncing off of each other as we circumnavigate our mutual environments. Paying close attention to these crucial and unspoken intelligences can help leaders determine root causes beneath problems of practice they encounter on their site and address them responsively, sensitively, and effectually.

The intention behind Module 3 was to fully immerse and actively involve you in your setting in order to develop your leadership capacities as a building manager. We covered a lot of ground in this chapter (pun intended) by exploring how geographic locations, physical and virtual settings, and intentional design all influence students' and adults' experiences on your site. Though it may not be as riveting as instructional leadership topics, our settings are the foundation for learning and deserve their rightful place in the schemata. There is no story without setting, and true game–changing leadership is about imagining the spaces we want to bear into existence. Nurturing your environment is akin to nourishing the people in it. Next up: Module 4 takes us outside the school boundaries to uncover how the surroundings neighboring your site have effects and influences that need your attention as well.

▶ NOTE

1 https://explodingtopics.com/blog/edtech-stats.

References

Burgstahler, S. (2021). Universal Design in Education: Principles and Applications. Accessed on August 22, 2024 from https://www.washington.edu/doit/universal-design-education-principles-and-applications

Ertmer, P.A. (1999). Addressing first- and second-order barriers to change: Strategies for technology integration. *ETR&D*, 47, 47–61. https://doi.org/10.1007/BF02299597

Evans, I. M., Harvey, S. T., Buckley, L. & Yan, E. (2009). Differentiating classroom climate concepts: Academic, management and emotional environments. *Kōtuitui New Zealand J Soc Sci Online*, 4(2), 131–146.

Fisher, D. & Frey, N. (2022). Tending to learning environments. *ASCD* 80(4). Accessed on September 2, 2024 from https://ascd.org/el/articles/tending-to-learning-evironments

Franklin, H. & Harrington, I. (2019). A review into effective classroom management and strategies for student engagement: Teacher and student roles in today's classrooms. *Journal of Education and Training Studies*, 7(12), 1–12.

Gladwell, M. (2008). *Outliers: the story of success.* New York, Little, Brown & Co.

Hecht, M. & Crowley, K. (2019). Unpacking the learning ecosystems framework: Lessons from the adaptive management of biological ecosystems. *Journal of the Learning Sciences*, 29(2), 264–284. https://doi.org/10.1080/10508406.2019.1693381

Howarth, J. (Jan. 12, 2024). 53+ EdTech Industry Statistics. Exploding Topics blog post. Accessed on September 8, 2024 from https://explodingtopics.com/blog/edtech-stats

Johnson, E. S. (2008). Ecological systems and complexity theory: Toward an alternative model of accountability in education. *Complicity: an International Journal of Complexity and Education*, 5(1), 1–10. Alberta, Canada. https://doi.org/10.29173/cmplct8777

Khurana, A. (2022). Converting physical spaces into learning spaces: Integrating universal design and universal design for learning. *Frontiers in Education*, 7. https://doi.org/10.3389/feduc.2022.965818. Accessed on September 7, 2024 from https://www.frontiersin.org/journals/education/articles/10.3389/feduc.2022.965818/full

National Center on Safe Supportive Learning Environments (2022). Physical Environment. Accessed on September 2, 2024 from https://safesupportivelearning.ed.gov/topic-research/environment/physical-environment

National Research Council of the National Academies. (2015). *Identifying and supporting productive STEM programs in out-of-school settings*. Washington, DC: The National Academies Press. https://doi.org/10.17226/21740

Ontario Principals' Council. (2012). *The principal as leader of the equitable school*. Thousand Oaks, CA: Corwin Press.

Principles of Universal Design. (1997). *North Carolina State University*, The Center for Universal Design. Accessed on September 7, 2024 from https://design.ncsu.edu/research/center-for-universal-design/

Sasson, I., Yehuda, I. & Miedijensky, S. (2022). Innovative learning spaces: class management and universal design for learning. *Learning Environ Res*, 25, 725–739. Accessed on September 7, 2024 from https://doi.org/10.1007/s10984-021-09393-8

Singh, V. & Thurman, A. (2019). How many ways can we define online learning? A systematic literature review of definitions of online learning (1988-2018). *American Journal of Distance Education*, 33(8), 289–306. https://doi.org/10.1080/08923647.2019.1663082

Snyder, S. (2013). The simple, the complicated, and the complex: Educational reform through the lens of complexity theory. *OECD Education Working Papers*, 96, 35.

Stapleton-Corcoran, E. (2022). "Universal Design for Learning (UDL)." Center for the Advancement of Teaching Excellence at the University of Illinois Chicago. Accessed on August 22, 2024 from https://teaching.uic.edu/resources/teaching-guides/inclusive-equity-minded-teaching-practices/universal-design-for-learning-udl/

Tawfik, A.A., Shepherd, C.E., Gatewood, J. et al. (2021). First and Second Order Barriers to Teaching in K-12 Online Learning. *TechTrends*, 65, 925–938. Accessed on September 15, 2024 from https://doi.org/10.1007/s11528-021-00648-y

Wallace, K. (2021). *Leading the launch: A ten-stage process for successful district initiatives*. Bloomington, IN: Solution Tree Press.

Wang, M., Degol, J., Amemiya, J., Alyssa Parr, A., Guo, J. (2020). Classroom climate and children's academic and psychological wellbeing: A systematic review and meta-analysis. *Developmental Review*, 57, 100912, ISSN 0273-2297, https://doi.org/10.1016/j.dr.2020.100912

Yemini, M., Engel, L. & Ben Simon, A. (2023). Place-based education – a systematic review of literature. *Educational Review*, 1–21. https://doi.org/10.1080/00131911.2023.2177260

Yoon, S. A. (2011). Using social network graphs as visualization tools to influence peer selection decision-making strategies to access information about complex socioscientific issues. *Journal of the Learning Sciences*, 20(4), 549–588. https://doi.org/10.1080/10508406.2011.563655

Awareness of Surroundings

▶ INTRODUCTION

The nature-versus-nurture debate is a long-standing one. Scientists, psychologists, sociologists, anthropologists, and biologists have searched for evidence in pursuit of answers to this perennial question: what has more influence on human behavior: the way we are raised or our natural-born dispositions? Saying "both" may sound like a cop-out, but we educators know that the cumulative effects of schooling matter; otherwise, we wouldn't even bother with this business of teaching and leading for the good of individuals and our society. Nor is there such thing as a clinical environment within which to test the hypothesis, as we are products of our surroundings just as much as (if not more than) discrete parenting moves or familial relationships. Life lessons and schema creation also come from the places we traverse, explore, and frequent. It's critical, however, that we not lean solely on living conditions as pat explanations for why certain groups are thriving or barely surviving yet that, at the same time, we not negate the very real challenges that compete with students' prospects, potential, and passageways toward achievement.

Throughout Module 4, we'll explore several topics that reflect and refract various angles creating a multifaceted prism of your surroundings. This orbital composite will be framed by

- Diving back into the geographic locale introduced in Module 3 by unpacking the concentric circles encompassing your setting
- Discovering ways to incorporate place-based educational opportunities into your curriculum design and delivery
- Understanding the similarities and differences between leading in rural, urban, and suburban regions
- Seeking out expanded leadership and learning partnership opportunities in concert with your community

▶ FOUNDATIONS

Locus of Control

In the first three modules, you took inventory of yourself, supporters, and setting, and it's now time to stretch out into your surroundings. This concept of meta-leadership is defined by Leonard J. Marcus, Eric J. McNulty, Joseph M. Henderson, and Barry C. Dorn in their 2019 book *You're It: Crisis, Change, and How to Lead When It Matters Most*. The three dimensions are

1. The person you are as a leader;
2. The situation in which you lead; and
3. Connections to the people you lead.

They explicate,

> A big part of leadership is the capacity to work well with and help steer organizations beyond one's immediate circle. They start with "who are you" as a leader, the person, and how do you adjust your sights to assess the situation at hand. Then, building connectivity: How can different groups work together toward a common goal? How do they forge the coordination of effort that allows them to leverage what each knows and can do? How do they unify large groups of people to work together toward that common purpose…?
>
> (p. xxi)

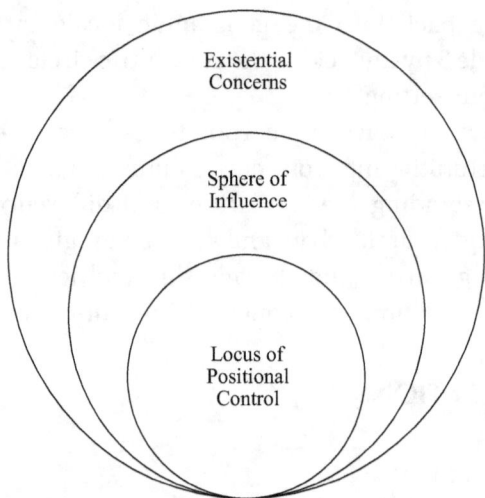

Figure 4.1 Control, influence, and concerns schematic

One of our biggest quandaries as educators is grappling with societal factors out of our control. As individual leaders, we certainly don't have the wherewithal or capacity to tackle every issue seeping from our neighborhoods into our school settings. As illustrated in Figure 4.1, spending the majority of your energy in areas where you do have a firm locus of control and sphere of influence, rather than on the existential questions regarding universal concerns, can help leaders manage overwhelm.

1. The innermost circle represents one's position or professional locus of control is squarely related to their job description, duties, and purpose. For example, if you're an assistant principal, you may have control over the standardized testing schedule, disciplinary consequences, or representing the principal at Study Support Team (SST) meetings. Alternatively, as the principal, you are responsible for instructional and operational implementations, being the lead learner at sitewide Professional Learning Community (PLC) sessions, and hosting schoolwide parent and community events. Establishing these role distinctions and staying in your lane make the organization function more smoothly. The question you need to ask

and answer is: *In my current role, what is within my positional locus of control?*
2. The middle circle is also a realm where you can affect improvements. In this sphere, you may not have direct control over a situation, but you can actively attempt to influence the direction by leveraging relationships with those whose locus of control it does reside within. Think about the power of teacher and employee associations at the bargaining table. As a unit, they are often successful at influencing contract conditions, salaries, and other benefits for their members, which individuals themselves would otherwise be unable to accomplish. Another example we commonly see is a group of parents speaking up at public meetings in the hopes of swaying the school board to make a certain decision on an agenda item they are either advocating for or deeply worried about. Depending on board culture, this can be a very effective strategy as most members are elected by their neighbors and want to keep constituents happy in order to keep their jobs on the dais. Thus, the question at hand is: *In my current role, who or what is within my sphere of influence?*
3. Like all generations before us, we live in taxing times. The proliferation of news media and incessant negative information bombards us with the woes of the planet. Climate change. Food scarcity. Natural disasters. Economic instability. Pandemics. Global wars. Political strife. You can finish the list yourself with all of the things that keep you up late at night. Now this is a vexing one because though these major dilemmas are outside of any of our direct control or influence, we shouldn't wash our hands of them. Obviously, we can vote, protest, or otherwise take action to usher in systemic change, but the crux of this domain is not to get lost or paralyzed by the state of the world at the expense of actually doing things that move the needle toward incremental progress. School funding is a solid example of this: most county offices and school districts are allocated annual funding based on various formulas dictated by state and federal legislation. We are at the mercy of tax dollars collected that year, legal mandates,

and accountability controls for how much money we get and conditions for how to spend it. However, the local governing board and leadership do decide specifically where to funnel those dollars to provide the best possible education for their students. Consider this question: *In your current role, what concerns do I hold that are beyond my ability to control but that I can do my own small part to address?*

Here is a surroundings-specific example for each realm in a real-life scenario. An elementary school located in an under-resourced part of town proposes creating a "safe routes to school" resource guide and map to better protect students from violence and crime as they walk to and from campus.

> *Positional control: The principal convenes a community task force to partner with him on developing the guide which includes shops, neighborhood watch outposts, and safety guardians along the way who are available as the eyes, ears, and hands during morning and afternoon commute routines.*
>
> *Sphere of influence: The principal personally visits each local business, organization, and individual to persuade more people to join in the efforts, successfully securing the amount and type of resources necessary to blanket the most frequent travel paths to school.*
>
> *Existential concerns: The principal is not able to independently decrease local gang activity, violence, or crime generated by high poverty and long-lived allegiance strongholds in the region. These societal and economic adversities may be ever-present, but he can minimize their power with an alternative presence.*

Practical Application

You will engage with this concept more deeply in exercise 4.1 by addressing a situation relevant to your own backyard. But keep your own scope of authority in mind throughout the next several sections to keep your sense of overwhelm at bay.

▶ GEOGRAPHIC LOCALE: DEEPER DIVE

First impressions are lasting. When someone rolls up to your campus, what do they see, smell, and hear along the way? Agricultural fields lined by dirt roads, livestock barns, and farm factory equipment? Rocky cliffsides punctuated by the sounds of crashing waves and seabirds? Homes with barred windows, chain-link fences, train tracks, or a freeway abutting the campus? Streets dotted with high-end vehicles, perfectly groomed lawns, and paved walkways? All these geographic markers clue people in to the locale. Our brains are wired to translate perceptions into meaning and then assign value. We cannot control our implicit biases, as they happen unconsciously, but we can be aware that they exist and color our reactions. Think about the words people use in reference to the schools in your district. No doubt, there is some variation on the theme of "that's the rich school" or "that's our Title I school," imbued with an implied connotation.

What they each look like and where they are located physically is pretty predictable, too. Real estate prices tell the short story: location counts. *A ton*. George Galster and Patrick Sharkey (2017) note this phenomenon:

> [Ann] Owens (2016) provides evidence suggesting that school boundaries play an important role in explaining why households with children are more segregated than those without. Segregation between school districts is higher among children than among adults, indicating that the school boundary takes on added importance for families with children. To understand neighborhood segregation, Owens argues, it is crucial to consider the way that parents use the boundaries of school districts when they make decisions about where to live.
>
> (pp. 22–23)

Depending on your experience, perhaps as a parent or as an educator, you've likely witnessed the lengths some families will go to for enrollment in the "right" school – meaning the one they perceive will provide their children the greatest opportunities for advancement. Falsifying proofs of address, doubling up with others in the neighborhood of choice, or legitimately applying for inter- or intra-district transfers are some of the tactics that people leverage to gain entry.

I once worked in a city that was carved into several unique attendance areas, and though their reputations slightly shifted over the decades, everyone knew which one was the most desirable area and which was considered the least and, not coincidentally, also perceived as most dangerous. Handling transfer requests was almost a full-time job. When residents came to the board meeting (usually to complain, explain, or demand), they undoubtedly announced which attendance area they were from as if to stake a claim in their right to be listened to. It was not uncommon for folks to share how much they paid in property taxes as if owed amenities like an Olympic-size swimming pool or a professional-quality performing arts arena. I'm not castigating folks for advocating for their children, but public education is for the public. All of us.

I've noticed an interesting distinction between living in the same area in which you lead and commuting in from somewhere nearby. Twice I've done the former and three times the latter. And there are upsides and downsides to both. Being part of the community is commonly viewed as an authentic commitment, a display of common values, and often preferred by parents, students, and your employer. Having grown up and been educated from kindergarten through high school in the same town gives you even more street cred, and many leaders have done just that. There is a certain intimacy or shorthand that living in the same school district fosters. Yet, at the same time, you may find that the lack of privacy, fuzzy demarcation lines between personal and professional life, and enmeshment in local politics or town gossip can be a bit *much*.

Likewise, there are costs and benefits to residing in an adjacent vicinity. It's certainly easier to keep your private life separate and spare yourself the awkward run-ins at the pharmacy, barber shop, or nail salon. Plus, the drive back home may proffer just the right amount of decompression time that allows you to be more present with your family each evening. But you don't have the same access to or possess the inside knowledge of interpersonal dynamics, social customs, or confidences that may be hidden or invisible to outsiders. Either way, you will need to find ways to establish your leadership persona not only as a site or central office administrator but also as a public figure who holds sway and responsibility to the community.

In addition to physical features, other geographical factors implicating economic inequality, racial and residential segregation, public facilities and transportation, proximity to toxic conditions, crime rates, and nearby access to higher education and job opportunities are critical to examine as well. Galster and Sharkey (2017) describe how *spatial inequality* occurs at the microcosmic level of groups or individuals mapped onto spaces as well as by intentional design, which results in people living just a few blocks away from each other incarnating distinctly dissimilar experiences. They state:

> Various elements of the spatial opportunity structure operate at and vary…across at least three distinct scales. Across neighborhoods, variations in safety, natural environment, peer groups, social control, institutions, social networks, and job accessibility occur. Across local political jurisdictions, health, education, recreation, and safety programs vary. Across metropolitan areas, the locations of employment of various types and associated wages, working conditions, and skill requirements vary and housing and other market conditions that affect individuals' opportunities for advancement differ.
>
> (p. 7)

Dolores Acevedo-Garcia et al. (2020) compiled a groundbreaking study called the Child Opportunity Index (COI) 2.0, which quantifies, maps, and compares "neighborhood opportunity" for children across 72,000 neighborhoods in the United States,

> Based on 29 common conditions within these domains, including: availability and quality of early education centers and schools; high school graduation rates and the number of adults with high-skills jobs; poverty and employment rates; air pollution levels; housing vacancy rates and home

ownership; and availability of green spaces and healthy food outlets. Each neighborhood receives a Child Opportunity Score and is assigned to an opportunity level: very low, low, moderate, high, or very high opportunity.

(p. 2)

In their comprehensive summary, Acevedo-Garcia et al. note four key findings:

1. Neighborhoods influence the quality of experiences that children have today.
2. Neighborhoods influence children's health and education.
3. Neighborhoods influence children's norms and expectations for the future.
4. Neighborhoods influence future outcomes.

(p. 2)

Additionally, they found that there are great variations not only across the country but within the same metropolitan area, ranging from very high- to very low-opportunity neighborhoods that provide "the very best to the very worst conditions" just miles apart. Furthermore,

> Children's race and ethnicity strongly predict whether they live in a place with access to quality early childhood education, good schools, healthy foods, parks and playgrounds, and good jobs and adequate income for the adults in their lives. The majority of black (67%) and Hispanic (58%) children live in lower opportunity neighborhoods. In contrast, the majority of white (65%) and Asian/Pacific Islander (62%) children live in higher opportunity neighborhoods.

(p. 46)

Game–Changing leadership, then, must expand beyond the campus perimeters and onto the pavement. The outer rungs of the nested circle illustrated in Figure 4.2 are highlighted in order of proximity to the campus, starting with the immediate neighborhood, town, and county in the light gray circles and followed by the macrocosmic spaces of state and country contained in the darker gray circles.

Awareness of Surroundings   169

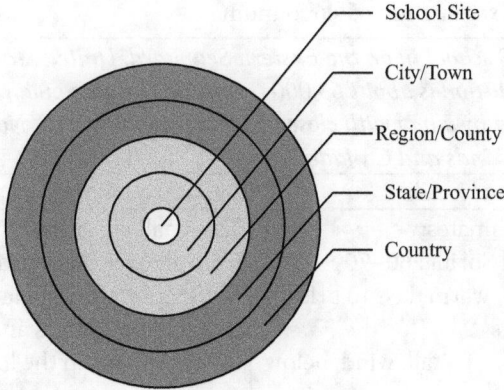

Figure 4.2 Nested layers of environmental settings

Practical Application

In Exercise 4.1, you will create a composite picture of all five rings in relationship to each other on a chosen topic of interest. Now visualize each outer ring as an orbit around your school or district and ask yourself the following questions:

1) <u>Country</u>: What are the signifying traits of my country geographically, geopolitically, and geologically?
2) <u>State/Province</u>: How is my state or province's landscape unique compared with the rest of the country, and how does that play into our collective identity?
3) <u>Region</u>: How was the natural habitat in the vicinity engineered, controlled, or eradicated through human intervention in order to settle the area?
4) <u>City/Town</u>: Name some notable landmarks, historical occurrences, natural disasters, or other events that influenced the look and feel of the community's neighborhoods.
5) <u>Site</u>: What structures and architectural design elements of the school campus were constructed to reflect or cooperate with the immediate physical geography around it?

Exercise 4.1 also offers you an opportunity to explore your setting from a bird's-eye and a bug's-eye view. This geography lesson will give you new perspectives to leverage or make better use of in your locale. Table 4.1 has been filled out as an example.

Table 4.1 Examination of surroundings

Locale: K-8 school in on the Eastern Seaboard, United States The city's population is about 63,000 people. It's located on a peninsula surrounded by a bay with close proximity to many U.S. New England islands and Canada.	
Geographical locale	Impacts on setting
Seasonal climates: • Fall and Spring: 60–70 degrees, warm days to brisk evenings • Winter: snowfall, wind, below freezing temperatures • Summer: temperate, humid days 68–82 degrees on average	The small city attracts people from all over the world and quadruples the population of up to 2 million visitors and part-time residents in the high seasons of summer and autumn. On the plus side, it benefits from economic growth from tourist dollars and support for local businesses, but alternatively suffers from environmental degradation, ecosystem destruction, traffic problems, and cultural tensions between locals and visitors.
Naturally occurring topography/landforms: • Elevation: 45 feet (~sea-level) • Mountains: 20 miles away • Rising sea level has transformed evolutionary land features, creating bays out of valleys and islands out of mountain tops.	The gulf is warming faster than 99% of the world's oceans due to climate change and fossil fuel consumption, threatening means of employment and increasing flooding.
Environmental-based industry: • One of the few working U.S. waterfronts remaining, serving as New England's largest seaport and commercial fishing port. • The local economy over time has shifted from fishing, manufacturing, and agriculture towards a service-based economy.	Overfishing and natural resource depletion has impacted many families' sense of identity and economic livelihood. Requirements for outdoors-related skill sets are diminishing and retraining must take place to support a shift in workforce needs.

(*Continued*)

Table 4.1 (Continued)

Locale: K-8 school in on the Eastern Seaboard, United States The city's population is about 63,000 people. It's located on a peninsula surrounded by a bay with close proximity to many U.S. New England islands and Canada.	
Geographical locale	Impacts on setting
Living things (flora and fauna) • Wildlife: Moose, black bear, beavers, white-tailed deer, foxes, seabirds, trout, bass, lobster • Plants: Poderosa pines, Douglas firs, potatoes, blueberries	In the Northeast, warmer spring and winter temperatures, along with increased pressure from invasive weeds and pests, may lead to large portions of the region becoming unsuitable for growing fruits, vegetables, and other crops.
Architectural/historical landmarks • Coastal lighthouses, seaports, and ferry terminals • Early Americana-style historical buildings	The locale has a wide expanse of history from indigenous settlements to early American foundations of government. Cultural clashes between long-standing families, native tribes, and stops on the Underground Railroad pepper its history.

▶ WIDE-ANGLED LENS: LEADING IN RURAL, URBAN, AND SUBURBAN SCHOOLS

We scratched the surface of geographic locale in the previous chapter as it pertains to the actual school setting. Now we're going to probe further into the subject by expanding the borders and boundaries beyond your site. As this book is meant for leaders around the globe, I will attempt to keep descriptors as universal as possible to orient everyone equitably within the practical application activities. There are many resources such as ourworldindata.org rife with statistics and reports on all aspects of human life that you can peruse to learn more about your own country. On the global education page (https://ourworldindata.org/global-education), Hannah Ritchie et al. (2023) curated decades' worth of schooling trends and propose some key insights on the state of education, including an impressive set of 87 interactive charts that show changes in time regarding literacy, completion rates, academic performance, teacher qualifications and training, gender parity, and the very granular level of percentage of primary schools with toilets. There are certainly other demographics that matter as well. These include a location's predominance of various ethnic groups, linguistic diversity, religious affiliations, political orientations, income ranges, migration and mobility patterns, residency conditions (homeowners, renters, unhoused), and employment status.

To keep things simple, I'll rely on general overarching terms of urban/city, suburban, towns, and rural/remote in the expectation that you will find elements that reflect your own terrain. Assuming that the majority of leaders picking up this book are from English-speaking North America, let's take a look at the U.S. and Canada. According to Statistics Canada (2021), the total national population was just under 37 million people, and the growth of suburban cities has outpaced that of urban and rural locations in recent years. City centers with a group size of over 100,000 constitute nearly 62% of residents, while suburban or smaller cities represent 21%, and rural the remaining 17% of citizenry. Canada's bigger southern neighbor also displays such diversity.

According to the National Center for Education Statistics (NCES 2022), in fall 2021, 49,089,640 children were attending U.S. K-12 public schools. Cities accounted for 14,647,609, or approximately 30%, of those enrolled; suburban students made up 19,091,364, or about 39%. Towns served 5,306,426 students (11%) and rural schools were at 9,801,145 (just under 20%). California and Texas lead the nation in most students enrolled at 5.8 and 5.4 million each, respectively (approximately 23% of the whole country), followed by Florida at 2.8 and New York at 2.5 million (a composite of 11%).

Furthermore, a 2018 survey by the National School Boards Association, in partnership with K12 Insight, found that

> Although school boards are becoming increasingly diverse, they do not reflect the rapidly changing demographics of the K-12 student population. National projections from the

US Department of Education for the 50.7 million students entering prekindergarten through grade 12 in 2017 were White 48%; Black 16%; Hispanic 27%; less than 1% each Asian/Pacific Islander and American Indian/Alaska Native students, and nearly 3% identifying as two or more races. Most board members in the 2018 survey were White (78%) followed by African American/Black (10%), Hispanic or Latino(a) (3%) and American Indian/Alaskan Native (1%). Board members who self-describe as Multiracial comprised 1% of survey respondents with an additional 7% who preferred not to answer.

(p. 4)

These stats are strikingly similar to the racial composition of site administrators. According to an NCES (2023) report, in 2020–21, 77% of all public school principals were White, 10% were Black, 9% were Hispanic, and 1% or less each were of two or more races, Asian, American Indian/Alaska Native, and Pacific Islander. The teaching workforce is incongruent with the race/ethnicity demographics of students as well. This is not a judgment statement but a fact to be aware of. While we can govern, lead, and teach across difference, we must do so consciously to avoid letting stereotypes and biases creep in, which is game–changing leadership at its core.

Rural/Remote Surroundings

Though provincial schools account for just one in five U.S. students and 20% of the total national population, rural land spans over 97% of the country; contrast this with the fact that urban and large suburban regions make up 3% of the nation's real estate and amass more than 80% of its residents (U.S. Census Bureau, 2017). Every state has significant amounts of sparsely occupied landscape, largely invisible to the rest of the populace unless they happen to be driving through on their way to another destination. Rural contexts have their own unique history, economic circumstances, demographics, politics, and culture. Assets include a strong sense of community, respect for nature, coexistence with the elements, and high levels of resourcefulness. These attributes are important as high poverty, unemployment or underemployment, and distance from material supply chains increase interdependence and reliance upon one another (Hayes, Flowers & Williams, 2021).

As far as school leadership goes, administrators in remote locales play a plethora of roles. I once met a 27-year-old school superintendent/principal/7th-grade teacher at a conference and was intrigued to learn how his southern Louisiana school enrolled just 56 K-8 students coming from within a 35-mile range. He was also the de facto transportation director and groundskeeper on site, which he termed "bustodian," a witty portmanteau of bus driver and custodian. My lengthy conversation with him comports with what Sonya Hayes, Jamon Flowers, and Shameka Williams (2021) conclude in an article on rural leadership during the pandemic:

> Rural school leaders understand what it means to lead schools that are geographically isolated, and they understand the challenges of (a) retaining and supporting quality teachers; (b) working with students and families who live in poverty; and (c) providing a quality education with a lack of resources. In essence, rural school principals lead in crisis every day. Their unique context has empowered them to become self-reliant and resilient so that they can be caretakers of their school communities.
>
> (p. 9)

Unfortunately, in our country's narrative, ruralism has often been misdiagnosed as a persistent and unsolvable problem as opposed to a setting to appreciate and understand (Burton, Brown & Johnson, 2013). Rural folks, likewise, have been characterized as "hillbillies," "backwater," "rednecks," "country bumpkins," or "poor white trash," slurs that have few real equivalents for those who live in bigger towns and cities, other than perhaps "ghetto." These epithets only foment the divide between people. No one chooses where and when to be born. It is our collective responsibility to educate all kids. And that means supporting rural leaders in authentic and environmentally responsive ways.

In a research brief titled "Equity-Driven Leadership in Rural Education," Annie Bae, Joy Esboldt, and Alison Munzer (2024) note,

> In response to one-size-fits-all policy mandates that often overlook rural education, place-conscious leadership theory emphasizes cultural and ecological contexts to encourage contextually responsive leadership in rural communities. Critical place-conscious leadership, a revisionist model of place-conscious leadership, emphasizes social and ecological justice, inextricably linking schools and local communities to address external forces that may threaten the wellbeing of the community. This form of leadership recognizes that each school and community's ability to thrive depends upon the other. As critical leaders of place, rural superintendents collaborate with staff and the community to pose key questions about how certain policies, curricula, or school structures reproduce power dynamics.
>
> (p. 4)

Relegating rural schools to the fringes as neglected entities presents educators with equity dilemmas that extend beyond racial segregation and discrimination. In conversations with rural leaders, extreme poverty and mere survival in sometimes ecologically unforgiving conditions are often at the forefront of their equity-centered problems of practice. While providing strong instructional leadership is the ultimate goal, they have to perpetually attend to the community's basic needs first.

In a piece on challenges facing schools in rural America, Mara Casey Tieken and M.K. Montgomery (2021) observe,

> Policymakers must spend time in rural communities and schools, getting to know their unique obstacles and opportunities and, importantly, their most pressing equity issues. They should partner with rural leaders – school administrators but also community leaders like pastors and organizers – to design policies. These policies must account for the local context, such as a town's brutal racial history or the

effects of a recently closed mill or long and mountainous bus routes. These details will dramatically shape a policy's effectiveness.

(p. 10)

If you are a rural leader or someone who supports those in remote locales, consider the following environmentally responsive approaches to generating leadership capacity in service of collective teacher efficacy and student learning outcomes:

1. Check your assumptions about the region's politics, values, and cultures. Rural communities are not a monolith, and there is a continuum of beliefs and orientations that exist alongside one another, both harmoniously and otherwise. (Just like anywhere else!)
2. Embed curriculum, instruction, and learning activities in the vast spaces surrounding the school as well as on campus. (For example, hold science classes at the local pond, create physical education assignments that include hikes or canoeing, or take a field study trip to a working farm.)
3. Adapt state-approved and adopted materials for core subject areas to reflect the demographics and characteristics of the region to engage students authentically in place-based education (e.g., math lessons based on seasonal climate trends, literacy skills connected to trail map navigation, or tap local artisans, craftspeople, or musicians to make local history come alive).
4. Connect students and adults in reciprocal learning events such as adults teaching kids country life and survival skills and kids showing adults how to access global perspectives via virtual reality gaming platforms.
5. Co-construct public service learning opportunities that benefit the community, build career skills, and tackle shared local issues (e.g., repairing facilities or infrastructure impacted by a recent storm, developing fundraising or grant writing campaigns to secure additional town resources, or training students to manage a peer social emotional support or crisis hotline).

Rural leaders reading this book know much better than I about the circumstances they find themselves in on a daily basis. We have much to learn as legislators, researchers, and educational experts about understanding, approaching, and responding to the many and varied demands and urgencies facing rural regions. And we must do so in ways that respect the dignity of the families who take up residence in the mountains, woods, prairies, pastures, scrublands, deserts, and coastlines that dot the map.

Suburban Surroundings

Though suburban schools serve a much greater population than their rural brethren, John Diamond, Linn Posey-Maddox, and Maria Velázquez (2021), in "Reframing Suburbs: Race, Place, and Opportunity in Suburban Educational Spaces," write about the dearth of attention on suburbia as well.

> Most students in the United States attend suburban schools, yet the vast majority of education scholarship focuses on urban schools rather than suburban ones. For example, between 2000 and 2018, of the articles published in the top five American Educational Research Association Journals, 80% explicitly focused on urban schools, 11.7% focused on suburban schools, and 8% focused on rural schools.
> (Diamond & Posey-Maddox, 2020) (p. 249)

Suburban schools are a complicated lot. Though racially and socio-economically integrated at unprecedented rates at this point in the 21st century, many contend their very existence was engineered as a "white flight" phenomenon. That is, the more a zone becomes democratized, thus diversified, a critical mass of white middle class folk seek out exclusivity and separation elsewhere. In some places, it means sending your children to elite private schools while the rest of their peers attend local schools while still living side by side. In other cases, it looks like packing up the moving truck and moving into a posher zip code.

John L. Rury's (2020) book, *Creating the Suburban School Advantage: Race, Localism, and Inequality in an American Metropolis*, provides this brief but elucidating historical account:

> A revolution of sorts also occurred in American education during the long postwar era, stretching roughly from 1945 through the 1970's. It entailed consolidation of resources and deliberate creation of locally defined boundaries, representing a departure from the past. In geographic terms, America's educational center of gravity started in the countryside, moved to the cities after the Civil War, and shifted dramatically to the suburbs during the latter half of the twentieth century. At the beginning of the twentieth century, most people believed city schools to be an improvement over rural institutions, but eventually, suburban schools came to be seen as superior to both. There were certainly exceptions to these tendencies, but the direction of historical transformation was unmistakable. By 1980 more students attended suburban schools than either rural or urban institutions.
>
> (p. 2)

While this trajectory may be isolated to the American experience, other national education systems may reveal similar patterns in that parents with means either migrate and follow along the enrollment of others of their social class, religious, or racial make-up or purposely put roots down in premier communities that serve a more homogenized population that mirrors their own. Rury continues,

> This seismic shift reflected the creation of a decisive suburban educational advantage. The legacy of these developments remains readily evident today, as the superiority of suburban schools became more or less normalized...The suburbs, after all, represent and American dream, at least for many families.
>
> (p. 2)

Rury unpacks this suburban reality related to "localism," a sentiment representing

> a foreshortening of interests and concern to exclude matters that did not directly benefit a particular community. When considering a proposed policy or public expenditure, individuals with this perspective would focus resolutely on how it could affect their immediate neighbors and themselves. Consequently, sharing resources was not high on the agenda and neither was relinquishing control of institutions that served them.
>
> (p. 12)

You might know it as the [insert town/neighborhood name] "bubble" or "the way." And it's usually said with an insider's distinct sense of pride.

Ann Owens and Peter Rich's (2023) article "Little Boxes All the Same?" also underscores that

> Boundary lines are often drawn to preserve advantaged groups' advantages, such as majority-White school district secession or political district gerrymandering. Boundaries create real inequalities in the types and affordability of housing that is built, the funding regimes for public goods, and the political appetite for integration.
>
> (pp. 46–7)

I know this well from experience. Most of my 30 years as an educator have been in mid-sized (8,000–10,000 students) to large (35,000–65,000 students) suburban districts adjacent to very large California cities (Oakland, San Francisco, Los Angeles, and Sacramento). In each setting, there was an undercurrent of superiority mindsets related to their neighboring districts as well as the schools abutting less wealthy enclaves. A whistle call to desirability, areas are often described directionally, such as the district's north-end or eastside schools (which means something to the people who live there but not necessarily anyone from the outside unless universally recognized like Chicago's Southside or East LA).

Deirdra Preis's (2020) article on preparing suburban school leaders to recognize everyday narratives that promote opportunity gaps suggests that

> A characteristic common to equity-minded school leaders is the ability to create what Johnson & Uline (2005) refer to as a "collective relentlessness" in their schools around interrogating operational beliefs, structures and practices for their impact on historically underserved student populations. As some of the exclusionary beliefs and attitudes that sit at the foundation of unhealthy school cultures might be overlooked or underestimated in terms of their contributions to sustaining opportunity gaps, it is critical that school leaders enter their roles able to identify marginalizing, exclusionary narratives in their buildings and to critically examine how they are tied to operational and relational practices that promote inequitable outcomes for some students. (Marx & Larson, 2012; Shields, 2004)
>
> (p. 3)

Some may think that leading in suburbia is an easier gig than the polar extremes of rural and urban settings, but it is not without its sincere and serious challenges. In a 2023 article titled "Political Battles in Suburbia," Rachel S. White, Michael P. Evans, and Joel R. Malin report findings from a national survey of superintendents that, when compared with urban and rural superintendents:

- Suburban superintendents reported the most contentious political environments
- The more political battles superintendents engage in, the less time they have to lead on educational issues
- Political tensions affect superintendents' mental health and well-being. (p. 7)

Though this study's focus was on superintendents, the same can be applied to other site and district leaders as well. The stressors unique to suburban locales can be thorny territory as they tend to skew less obviously to the right or left politically. Battleground states in particular are aptly named – and as residents migrate in and out, so do political agendas. It's not uncommon for a school board to vote on an issue one way only to overturn their own decision just weeks later due to public pressures, especially on controversial topics like sexual health and education, race and social justice, or course pathways (aka tracking) in math and science. I've personally been involved in marathon board meetings into the wee hours of the morning as each "side" lined up in queues outside the building to make sure their voices were heard and agendas advanced.

Since there is a rather insufficient amount of research on the topic, supporting suburban leaders is fertile ground for conducting research practice partnerships, including future directions suggested by Diamond, Posey-Maddox, and Velázquez (2021):

> Moreover, suburban schools do not exist in a vacuum, and education and learning also occur outside of school walls. Future education research could more closely attend to links between schools and their contexts. That includes students' experiences outside schools in neighborhoods, community spaces, homes, families' economic realities, and the infrastructure that supports education in communities. Therefore, we argue that more work on suburban education needs to examine what happens outside of schools, and particularly in the community-based education spaces (Baldridge et al., 2017; Park, 2020) that play a crucial role in students' learning beyond the school day. While a growing body of scholarship has identified the vast inequities that exist within and across suburban schools and communities, few studies attend to how students, families, and community members navigate, organize, and resist these unequal terrains and policy contexts.
>
> (p. 253)

In addition to these new research frontiers, there are practical approaches that suburban leaders and their advocates can implement in the meantime:

1. Capitalize on the vast resources at your disposal as there are often limitless partnership opportunities with businesses and community organizations that can enrich outside of school learning experiences.
2. Nimbyism is a historical feature of suburbia and remains alive and well today. Look for cloaked language that *others* newcomers or people who don't look, sound, or act in mainstream ways. Even in the most liberal of places, you can uncover "not-in-my-backyard" mentalities that implicitly (or explicitly) seek to keep certain groups marginalized. Call it out when you see it.
3. Combat the concept of normal. Suburban kids, despite their middle-class status, are not always all right. Mental health, peer relations, achievement competition, and keeping up with the Joneses (or Kardashians) pressures can result in unproductive coping skills that may evolve into substance abuse, depression, anxiety, suicidal ideation, shaming, and other problems that compromise growth and well-being. Develop prevention, intervention, and postvention plans to help youth navigate these uncharted waters.
4. Provide your instructional and support staff talking points, strategies, and approaches that (re)channel individual parental involvement into collectively productive volunteerism that benefits the whole site.
5. Get into the mindset behind why people choose to live in the suburbs in the first place and assume positive intent: more space, fewer crowds, less traffic, larger homes, safety, affordability – and, most importantly, excellent public schools which offer a wide array of curriculum, arts and music, athletics, clubs, and enrichment activities. Think about how these motivators (and additional resources) can contribute to the development of programs that enhance educational experiences for all kids.

Urban Surroundings

Like their rural counterparts, we have to be cognizant of the language we use to describe urban settings in asset-based ways.

Our society holds stereotypical portrayals of city life that obviously have kernels of truth but that run rampant in our imaginations. When I meet folks from both near and far and reveal that I live in Oakland, California, the reaction is visceral. The immediate images conjured of Oakland – otherwise known as *Oaktown* or simply *The Town* (as distinguished from San Francisco, *The City*) – tend to be of a gang-infested, poverty-stricken, trash-filled, drugged-up, violent, lawless, and generally desperate metropolitan area. I'm not saying these things aren't true, but Oakland is also a charming, foodie heaven, and strikingly beautiful natural environment where diversity thrives in highly integrated neighborhoods and arts and culture abounds. Like every place, it's complicated and complex.

In a conceptual review and empirical exploration of redefining urban education, Richard O. Welsh and Walker A. Swain (2020) contend that, as a remedy to pre-existing negative-leaning constructs,

> A sociological oriented definition of urban education is, in some ways, antideficit, antigeneralization, and antiessentialization. This broader conceptualization of urban education focuses on the causes (the inside and outside of school factors shaping learning) rather than the outcomes associated with urban schools. Such a conceptualization shifts the conversation from a deficient perspective (blaming the challenges and context of urban schools on the characteristics of people living in urban environments) to a sociological perspective rooted in education, economic, health, and social policy and reform over time. The crisis in public schools is not simply due to reckless individual choices but rather systemic institutional failures.
>
> (p. 95)

When did blame ever get us anywhere? It's wholly unconstructive, as well as unfair, to assign fault *especially to children* for what they bring with them into the classroom. Trying to tease out whether certain behaviors stem from this, that, or the other type of living situation (e.g., single-parent home, doubled-up families in a small apartment, residency at the local trailer park,

Section 8 housing, and myriad other configurations) matters less than dispensing the right kinds of resources along with a sincere dosage of respect to families under our care. The uneven distribution of resources underpinning the concept behind the "haves" and "have nots" results in stark realities. Christopher J. Schell et al. (2020) researched this dynamic in a study of the ecological and evolutionary consequences of systemic racism in urban environments:

> Because structural inequalities form the foundation of city infrastructure, urban development, governance, management, and landscape heterogeneity, inequality among humans defines the ecological setting and evolutionary trajectories for all urban organisms. Urban areas are dynamic ecological systems defined by interdependent biological, physical, and social components. The emergent structure and heterogeneity of urban landscapes drives biotic outcomes in these areas, and such spatial patterns are often attributed to the unequal stratification of wealth and power in human societies.
>
> (p. 1)

Simply put, these human-made, densely populated ecosystems are rife with injustice and inequality. But I contend, since they are humanly constructed, we also hold the capacity and agency to deconstruct and reconstruct our surroundings to advance equitable solutions and conditions. Vanderbilt University scholars Maury Nation, Brian D. Christens, Kimberly D. Bess, Marybeth Shinn, Douglas D. Perkins, and Paul W. Speer (2020) concur. In their study, "Addressing the Problems of Urban Education: An Ecological Systems Perspective," they also

> Believe there is value in having urban education interventions become integrated multi-sectoral interventions (focusing not just on schools but also housing and urban planning, public health, juvenile justice, and violence prevention, and the civic voluntary sector) rather than focusing on an isolated piece (e.g., changing superintendents) of a complex, connected, and interdependent system. The

challenges inherent in ecological analyses and interventions require not only more resources and more interventions, but also critical long-term commitment to building and exercising power to challenge and transform the status quo.
(p. 725)

The often-revolving door of leaders through urban systems adds complexity to this section. Comparatively, the tenure of principals and superintendents in large city schools is shorter than that of their peers in rural and suburban districts. According to a Broad Institute study's (2018) findings recounted in a 2018 *Education Week* article by Denisa Superville:

- Tenure was half as long for superintendents serving districts with the highest percentages of students of color. In districts where 76% to 100% of the student enrollment were students of color, superintendents stayed on the job for less than five years. In districts where 25% or fewer of the students were students of color, the average completed tenure was nearly 12 years.
- Tenure was nearly 3.5 years shorter for superintendents in districts with the highest poverty levels. As the percentage of students in poverty increased, so did superintendent turnover. The average tenure in districts where 76% to 100% of students was low-income was 5.13 years. In districts with 25% or fewer low-income students, the average superintendent tenure was 8.59 years.
- Tenures for women are 15 months shorter. On average, women stayed on the job for about 5.18 years whereas men stayed on the job for 6.42 years.
- Tenure was also shorter in larger districts. In districts with more than 100,000 students, superintendents stayed on the job for 5 years on average, compared with 6.62 years in districts with fewer than 100,000 students.

There are myriad reasons for the statistics listed above and too many directions to delve into sufficiently here (such as racial dynamics, gender disparities, funding inequities, governance models, politics, and personalities). I will say this: educational leadership is really hard, no matter where you serve. And just as we should refrain from blaming students and families for difficulties they face, that same grace must be extended to our leaders. The general public cannot even begin to imagine the pressures and stressors that school and systems leaders face on the daily (if not hourly).

Thus, in lieu of longevity, urban leadership truly requires a collective approach so that when a top-level administrator departs, they don't take all of the good work they did with them. This leads to the following considerations for leaders in and of urban constructs:

1. Communicate, elevate, and activate the concept of locus of control and influence among colleagues, associations, support providers, community groups, and other institutions in the surrounding area to collaborate on the right grain size to generate change.
2. Mobilize resources. Cities have the benefit of scale in supporting families. Even when provisions and services such as banks, grocery stores, health clinics, dentist offices, or family planning organizations are not close by, think about ways to put them on wheels. It's much easier to get care when centralized in one place where most community members are already connected, such as our schools.
3. Now do the opposite and transport your school's resources into the surroundings. Do what schools do best: educate! Host events, workshops, and series that support adults and caregivers, such as parenting classes, literacy programs, technology training, budgeting basics, or other life skills that promote family health and well-being.
4. Living in concentrated spaces can breed both familiarity and contempt. It's naïve to think that external issues will resolve themselves between rival gangs, religious factions, or political adversaries or that they won't spill onto your campus. While fixing societal problems is not your exact charge, maintaining a safe space for learning is. Establishing norms, expectations, and consequences for breaching those terms while on your watch should be done upfront. But you have to be willing to follow through,

so make sure your broadcasted criteria are both reasonable and feasible.
5. Urban life is immensely rich in culture, arts, and entertainment. There are limitless opportunities to educate students outside of the classroom via theatre, museums, exhibitions, events, athletics, volunteer activities, service learning, and exposure to diverse cultures. Take walking trips, subway rides, or even virtual tours that teach students about where they live, the history of their forebears, and conduct action-research to solve neighborhood problems of practice that matter to them.

▶ PLACE-BASED EDUCATIONAL OPPORTUNITIES

Regardless of whether you are a leader in the hills, the hood, or a hamlet, your geographic locale has much to offer as an instructional tool. As Mira Yemini, Laura Engel, and Adi Ben Simon (2023) explain in their literature review, place-based education (PBE) is "an umbrella term for pedagogical practices that prioritise experiential, community-based, and contextual/ecological learning to cultivate greater connectivity to local contexts, cultures, and environments (Gruenewald, 2003; Smith, 2002; Sobel, 2004; Orr, 2013)" (p. 1). While the term is meant to be applied to students, the adults in our organizations could benefit from PBE as well. Taking a fresh look at your stomping grounds from top to bottom may reveal prospects and potential for optimizing the spaces we inhabit in order to draw from the natural and human-developed resources for in situ teaching and learning.

With the advancement of AI technology and geo-mapping applications, we have tools at our disposal that previously didn't exist. Yuhao Kang, Fan Zhang, Song Gao, Hui Lin, and Yu Liu (2020) conducted a fascinating review of urban physical environment sensing. In public health studies in China, they used internet-based street view imagery that presents an expanded perspective on our surroundings:

> Street view images represent real-world scenery including natural scenes and man-made landscapes from a pedestrian

> perspective and allow users to navigate the realistic streetscape remotely. The emergence of such a big data source provides unprecedented opportunities in digitalizing the world, which enables researchers to investigate the physical urban environment and human activities on a large scale. By sensing the elements and scenes captured by street view images, the urban physical environment can be modelled more accurately and comprehensively, and the connection between the built environment and various health outcomes can be established.
>
> (p. 262)

Since health and well-being are foundational components for readiness to learn, this study can inform our understanding of how where families reside can affect both opportunity and access to education. Individual leaders have begun to employ community asset mapping around their sites to locate wraparound services that mitigate the effects of environmental circumstances.

Practical Application

In Exercise 4.4, we'll apply your own geographical details to create a place-based curriculum plan. Here is an example of a high school–level course of study in Figure 4.3.

▶ EXPANDED LEADING AND LEARNING PARTNERSHIP WITH COMMUNITY

Collaborative, shared, or distributive leadership has almost exclusively been studied as it pertains to instructional staff and site administrators operating under models in which they perform their distinct roles on equal footing instead of hierarchically. In an article on distributive leadership and innovative teaching practices, Cailen O'Shea (2021) defines the approach as follows:

> Distributed leadership as a practice is one where educators in formal and non-formal leadership positions are allowed

 **English Composition/ Literature**: Compare and contrast regional authors and compose your own piece of writing on the environment within which you live.

 **Social Sciences**: Attend a city council meeting and create a poster or infographic on an environmental issue of concern to the community.

 **Mathematics**: Choose a quantifiable regional subject such as birth rates, racial composition, or migration trends over the past three decades and create a mathematical formula.

 **Science**: Select a location to explore; gather data on the natural elements; then develop a recommendation for future scientific research based on your inquiry project.

 **Physical Education**: Learn an indoor or outdoor activity elemental to your region and report back your discoveries about the environment and yourself as a result.

 **Electives**: Check out a new area, interview locals, take photos or draw pictures, and create a storyboard, film, song, play, or podcast about what you learned about local culture.

 **Career & Technical Education (CTE):** Connect with nearby institutions and research employment pathways. Design a slide deck and present it at the career fair.

 **Field Study Trips:** Explore the great outdoors (and indoors) of landmarks, natural phenomena, museums, or exhibits such as a zoo, aquarium, planetarium, or botanical garden.

Figure 4.3 Place-based education course of study

more autonomy through decision-making. Distributed leadership has been linked to innovation in teaching practices by empowering teachers to make decisions regardless of their status.

(p. 1)

All of this takes place on campus and in the module 3 domain of setting rather than this one, but as community schools have become more prevalent and popular, especially in under-resourced areas, the berth has widened into our surroundings.

While there are at least 31 flavors of design, community schools, in general, are characterized by "four pillars", as identified by Learning Policy Institute researchers Anna Maier, Julia Daniel, Jeannie Oakes, and Livia Lam (2017) in their comprehensive review on the subject:

1) **Integrated student supports** address out-of-school barriers to learning through partnerships with social and health service agencies and providers, ideally coordinated by a dedicated professional staff member. Some employ social-emotional learning, conflict resolution training, trauma-informed care, and restorative justice practices to support mental health and lessen conflict, bullying, and punitive disciplinary actions, such as suspensions.
2) **Expanded learning time and opportunities**, including after-school, weekend, and summer programs, provide additional academic instruction, individualized academic support, enrichment activities, and learning opportunities that emphasize real-world learning and community problem-solving.
3) **Family and community engagement** brings parents and other community members into the school as partners with shared decision-making power in children's education. Such engagement also makes the school a neighborhood hub providing adults with educational opportunities, such as ESL [or English Language Development] classes, green card or citizenship preparation, computer skills, art, and STEM (Science, Technology, Engineering, and Mathematics).
4) **Collaborative leadership and practice** build a culture of professional learning, collective trust, and shared responsibility using such strategies as site-based leadership/governance teams, teacher learning communities, and a community school coordinator who manages the complex joint work of multiple school and community organizations. (p. 16)

In this section, we'll focus primarily on pillar #3 in correlation with this module's cornerstone.

In a 2020 article, Noel E. Kelty and Tomoko Wakabayashi cite the following theoretical perspective:

> Ecological systems theory demonstrated how child development is supported and embedded within a set of nested structures, from immediate microsystems, such as the home and school, to more remote systems such as policies, neighborhoods, laws, and social archetypes. The theory holds that these models are concretely established in children's immediate experiences (i.e., microsystems). Thus, the priority for engaged partnerships between families and schools in the surrounding social, cultural, and political context (i.e., macrosystem) is manifested in everyday support that children's microsystems can provide for their learning and development.
>
> (p. 4)

Consider this construct as a three-legged stool held up by two microsystems – home and school – and one macrosystemic composed of an aggregate of elements found in one's neighborhood, town, or region. Children are products of all three, so all three must be adequately supported to prevent wobbles or, worse, collapse. The days of believing our schools are protected islands seem to be waning. There is no sanctity of the space as an isolated variable; rather, it's a beehive of activity in and out and around. How's that for three mixed metaphors in one paragraph to illustrate the complexity of our game–changing leadership charge?

A word to the wise: Doing things the way we've always done them is a pitfall to avoid, especially when it comes to partnering with the surrounding community. Unless, that is, you've already found the secret recipe for high attendance, active participation, abundant volunteerism, and enthusiastic engagement that proportionately represents all student groups in your enrollment area. But if you, like me, have always grappled with full inclusion, we might want to figure out some novel outreach strategies to legitimately build collective agency effecting change. Here are some familiar quandaries:

- The same few people apply for and serve on every committee at your site.
- Parents of marginalized student populations are either tokenized or significantly underrepresented at school events.
- Surveys and input polls consistently garner low response rates; when disaggregated, they are found to disproportionately trend toward groups that already hold power.
- Even when events are repeatedly publicized through multiple media channels, there are still many who seem unaware of invitations to join in the experience.
- Teachers and administrators find themselves employing external motivators (or flat-out bribes) like giving extra credit for attending back-to-school night in exchange for parental presence, which can penalize our most marginalized students whose family conditions or commitments may prevent them from coming.
- Lack of resources such as transportation, child care, and internet create barriers to extensive engagement.
- Educators make erroneous assumptions that other grown-ups feel as positively about school as we do, and do little to build trust, especially with those who may have been damaged by our system themselves as young people or again as parents.

Consider this: How might school look differently if educators imagined, designed, and implemented school programming *with* those involved instead of *to* them? Figure 4.4 presents three levels of interaction that encourage leaders to discern to what degree they are including parents, caregivers, community members, local businesses, and nonprofit agencies in their schools. Occasionally, the lowest level of participation suffices, but we should challenge ourselves to reach into the engagement and involvement gradations as much as possible to bring people off the sidelines and onto the starting line.

Assessing how outreach efforts look in your school, district, or county office is a good first step to taking action to increase involvement. Do you regularly

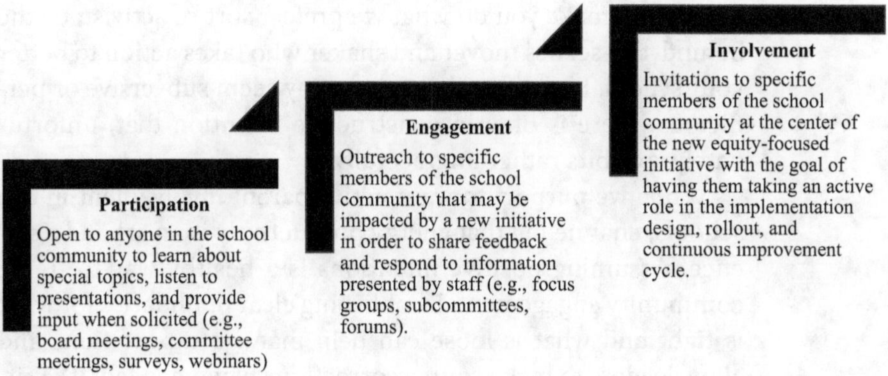

Participation
Open to anyone in the school community to learn about special topics, listen to presentations, and provide input when solicited (e.g., board meetings, committee meetings, surveys, webinars)

Engagement
Outreach to specific members of the school community that may be impacted by a new initiative in order to share feedback and respond to information presented by staff (e.g., focus groups, subcommittees, forums).

Involvement
Invitations to specific members of the school community at the center of the new equity-focused initiative with the goal of having them taking an active role in the implementation design, rollout, and continuous improvement cycle.

Figure 4.4 Levels of interaction

- ☐ Consciously partner with underrepresented students and families?
- ☐ Take into consideration special needs when choosing settings?
- ☐ Offer multiple options for attendance (repeat sessions, recordings, or virtual or hybrid participation)?
- ☐ Invite an equitable representation of the community impacted by the issue?
- ☐ Monitor voices in the space to balance and elicit participation from a variety of participants?
- ☐ Provide for accommodations that show respect for diversity (translators, accessible locations, neutral/friendly settings)?
- ☐ Communicate in jargon-free, understandable language?
- ☐ Authentically involve participants in decision-making and recommendations?
- ☐ Show sincere appreciation for being involved?
- ☐ Follow up with the results, actions, or next steps?

Community relations can be tricky territory. I'm guessing that in your career as an educator, you have likely encountered a variety of personalities that represent certain types: the person who volunteers, helps coordinate, and shows up to everything you invite them to; the self-appointed social-media commentator who narrates every move you make; the "let's make an online petition to make you do what we prefer" sort of activist; or the behind-the-scenes mover and shaker who takes action to better your school. Even when behaviors may seem subversive or pernicious, there is often a constructive intention that, unfortunately, exhibits rather ungracefully.

While we purport to want active parent involvement in our schools, channeling that energy productively is an art and a science. Assuming positive intentions is a healthy way to frame community engagement. Establishing clear boundaries for what is tight and what is loose can help manage expectations and allow leaders to make course corrections when needed. It's critical that we articulate these expectations as behaviors we do want to see rather than a list of don'ts. We want to pose opportunities and outlets for involvement that produce the results we desire to see. The parent letter in Box 4.1 exemplifies this mental model.

BOX 4.1 SAMPLE BACK-TO-SCHOOL LETTER

Dear Community Caregivers,   *[date]*

On behalf of the staff at Aspen Middle School, we welcome your partnership throughout the school year as we work together to create the best learning environment for our children. We are so fortunate to have such a diverse community that possesses such a wide variety of skills, talents, and backgrounds that continually enrich student experiences here at Aspen. As such, we want to celebrate some of the contributions that made an enormous impact on some schoolwide goals last year:

- ✓ *Neighbors envisioned and then constructed a community garden on campus so that we have fresh fruits and vegetables year-round for kids and families to harvest and bring home.*
- ✓ *A group of parents coordinated an "adulting day" where people from all over the city volunteered their time to teach students practical skills such as car maintenance, basic sewing techniques, healthy meal prep, and financial literacy, to name just a few.*
- ✓ *Believe it or not, some of you actually enjoy chaperoning dances, operating carnival activities, and supervising field trips. We're eternally grateful (and need to clone people like you)!*

We know you are incredibly busy with work, life, and engaging in the important business of bringing up happy and healthy tweens and teens, so we've developed and attached a yearlong calendar with all major events and activities on deck for this coming year. Please fill out this online form, or grab a hard copy from our front office, to indicate any that you are interested in and check off which roles you might want to play. Speaking of roles, we've learned over time that providing clear guidelines and parameters is key to successful collaborations. We value your volunteerism and want to ensure that we're not asking you to do work that is under the purview of our staff. The table below contains some of those distinctions to help us all work together productively and harmoniously.

Volunteer partner roles	*School staff roles*
1. Suggesting age-appropriate activities that might benefit student learning	1. Designing, planning, and executing age-appropriate activities
2. Volunteering for any open assignment specifically connected to each event	2. Establishing volunteer opportunities and outlining specific needs to fill
3. Reporting student behavior issues or safety concerns to staff	3. Addressing student discipline and ensuring safety measures
4. Collaborating and cooperating with other volunteers and staff	4. Coordinating adult responsibilities and managing interactions
5. Jobs distinct from employees that are voluntarily accepted and committed to your own degree of comfort and availability	5. All duties included in staff job descriptions, for which they are compensated, accountable for, and trained to professionally execute

Thank you for your continued support and invaluable gift of time, energy, and enthusiasm for our middle schoolers. You are making a real difference in their lives! Please reach out to me or any school staff member if you have any questions about upcoming opportunities for involvement. Here's to a great new year!

Sincerely, Principal _____
Contact information: _____

You probably already noted the carefully chosen language and tone the principal attempts to strike in the memo: friendly, inclusive, appreciative, specific, and actionable. Here are some additional components to point out as well:

- ✓ Leader communicates for the organization, not as an individual, to emphasize group agreement on the involvement protocols.
- ✓ Recognitions include diverse ways people can contribute.
- ✓ Use of nouns and verbs foster inclusion and respect, with a positive tone throughout.
- ✓ Examples of involvement from the previous year offer exemplars to inspire innovation.
- ✓ Inclusion of annual calendar of events for pre-planning purposes respectful of time donated.
- ✓ Online and hard copy form translated to all major languages increases accessibility.
- ✓ Options included on the form are limited to specific roles to manage expectations.
- ✓ Concrete responsibilities are outlined for appropriate staff and non-staff roles to set clear boundaries.

Practical Application

Using the blueprints in this section as a starting point, exercise 4.5 is a five-part set of activities that prompt leaders to devise outreach mechanisms to invite and encourage community involvement on campus via a variety of tools and strategies. You'll start by assessing what outreach efforts look like in your school, district, or county office, then compose a back-to-school letter like the one in Box 4.1. Then you'll create an annual calendar of events to share with the community and send out a poll or survey to gauge interest in volunteer opportunities.

▶ MODULE 4 EXERCISES

The exercises in module 4 correspond to the four primary areas of study in this chapter: (1) dissecting your own geographic region to uncover clues that unlock the potential of your students; (2) discerning how rural, suburban, and urban surroundings present both obstacles and opportunities for game–changing leadership; (3) coming up with creative approaches to curricular redesign that capitalize on the pedagogy of PBE; and (4) forging strong connections with your community to amplify leadership influence and impact. The exercises include

- 4.1. Control, Influence, and Concerns Schematic
- 4.2. Nested Layers of Environmental Surroundings
- 4.3. Rural, Suburban, and Urban Launching Pads
- 4.4. Place-Based Education Curriculum Design
- 4.5. Reciprocal Leading and Learning Partnerships

Exercise 4.1 Control, Influence, and Concerns Schematic

Environmental Issue:

Select an environmental issue you'd like to examine concerning surroundings adjacent to your school. It could be anything from rebuilding after a recent natural disaster or toxic waste accident, to blight from illegal dumping or freeway air and noise pollution, to loss of biodiversity or food and clean water insecurity. Applying the control, influence, and concerns model to the topic of interest, document what is under your direct authority, who you might be able to prompt action from or collaboration with, and what is outside of your scope within each circle on the schematic.

Environmental Issue:

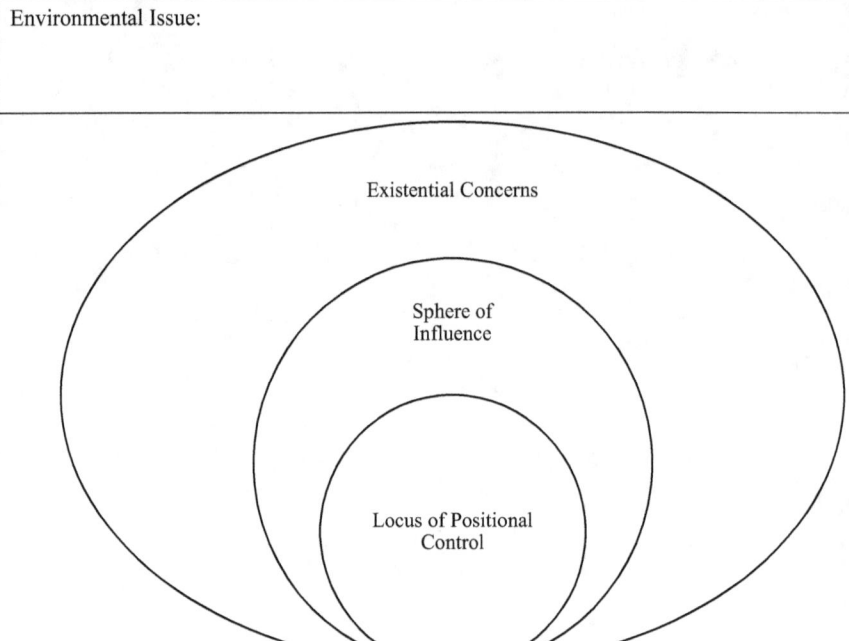

© Copyright material from Kim Wallace (2025), Game–Changing Leadership in Action, Routledge.

Exercise 4.2 Nested Layers of Environmental Surroundings

Part I: This activity combines what you learned in Modules 3 and 4. Starting at the center (your school site) and working your way outward to the final outer ring (your country), decide on a single attribute that you want to delve into to create a composite picture of the setting and surroundings your students, staff, and families experience related to that domain. Pick any one topic that interests you most from the ideas listed below, or color outside of the lines and develop your own area of inquiry.

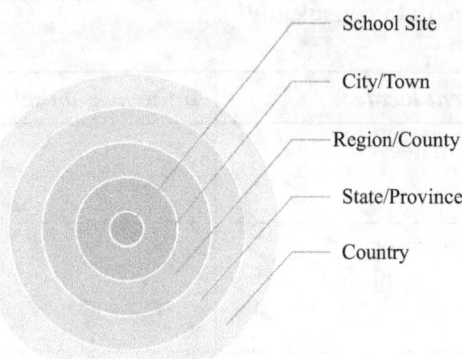

Demographics: e.g., racial/ethnic diversity, range of political affiliations, socioeconomic conditions, income distribution, birth/death rates, migration trends, educational attainment levels, employment data, predictive models
Human history: e.g., individuals or groups that impacted or influenced the culture, language, and social structures for each location; current impacts of past events; unresolved or lingering conflicts; progress and achievements; religious or cultural factors at play
Natural history: e.g., physical features that characterize the location's geography; patterns or evolutionary changes over time; indigenous animals, vegetables, and minerals; pivotal events such as disease, famine, disasters, climate change, human interventions

Part II: If you are in a country that collects routine demographics on its citizens, you can learn a lot about how your own

geographic locale is nested within surrounding contexts. In this activity, you will use online resources to learn more about your area and then write down possible impacts of the setting's features on students, staff, and families. I've listed three United States' governmental websites to get you started. After exploring them and/or other sources you discover on your own, you can start connecting the dots between how your setting is influenced by your geography.

- https://apps.nationalmap.gov/viewer/
- https://nces.ed.gov/programs/maped
- https://data.census.gov/

Geographical locale	*Influences on setting*
Seasonal climates	
Naturally occurring Topography/Landforms	
Environmental-based industry	
Living things (flora and fauna)	
Architectural and historical landmarks	

© Copyright material from Kim Wallace (2025), Game–Changing Leadership in Action, Routledge.

Exercise 4.3 Rural, Suburban, and Urban Launching Pads

Review the recommendations at the end of each segment on rural, suburban, and urban surroundings and identify which one fits your current leadership situation most closely. Feel free to mix and match suggestions from the different environs that apply to your own circumstances. The lefthand column contains the three sets of five recommendations from pages 176, 182 and 187. In the righthand column, collaborate with your community to devise specific strategies to pilot or implement in the coming year.

Suggestions	Our plan
Rural settings: 1. Check your assumptions about the region's politics, values, and cultures. 2. Embed curriculum, instruction, and learning activities in naturally occurring surroundings. 3. Customize adopted curricular materials to reflect the demographics and characteristics of the region. 4. Connect students and adults in reciprocal learning events. 5. Co-construct public service learning opportunities that benefit the community and tackle shared issues.	

(Continued)

Suggestions	Our plan
Suburban settings: 6. Seek out and capitalize on the vast resources at your disposal. 7. Publicly commit to advancing educational equity and celebrating diversity. 8. Develop prevention, intervention and postvention plans to help youth navigate social-emotional health. 9. Provide talking points for communicating effectively; find ways to channel individual parental involvement into collectively productive volunteerism. 10. Tap into suburban living motivators that contribute to the development of programs that enhance educational experiences for all kids.	
Urban settings: 11. Activate your locus of control and influence in the surrounding area to elicit productive change. 12. Think about ways to get mobile resources on your campus to serve a variety of family needs. 13. Host events, workshops, and series that support adults and caregivers and promote family health and well-being. 14. Establish clear norms, expectations, and consequences for when neighborhood issues breach your campus. 15. Take field study trips that teach students about where they live and conduct action-research to solve neighborhood problems of practice that matter to them.	

© Copyright material from Kim Wallace (2025), Game–Changing Leadership in Action, Routledge.

Exercise 4.4 Place-Based Education

Just like the examples presented on page 189, work with your curriculum council or instructional leadership team to brainstorm age-appropriate and progressively rigorous place-based learning activities and lessons that seek to embed student learning in typical spatial contexts surrounding them.

Primary (Gr. TK–3)	Intermediate (Gr. 4–6)	Middle school (Gr. 6–8)	High school (Gr. 9–12)
Language and Literacy	Reading/ Language Arts	Reading/ Language Arts	English Literature/ Composition
Social Sciences	Social Sciences	Social Sciences	Social Sciences
Mathematics	Mathematics	Mathematics	Mathematics
Science	Science	Science	Science
Social Emotional Learning (SEL)	Social Emotional Learning (SEL)	Civics/Electives	Civics/Electives
English Language Development (ELD)	English Language Development (ELD)	English Language Development (ELD) & World Languages	English Language Development (ELD) & World Languages
Play-Based Education	Visual & Performing Arts	Visual & Performing Arts	Visual & Performing Arts
Special Services: English Language Development (ELD), Special Education, Extended Day	Special Services: ELD, Special Education, Extended Day	Special Services: ELD, Special Education, Extended Day	Special Services: ELD, Special Education, Extra-Curriculars
Physical Education/ (PE), Recess	Physical Education, Recess	Physical Education	Career & Technical Education

(Continued)

Primary (Gr. TK–3)	Intermediate (Gr. 4–6)	Middle school (Gr. 6–8)	High school (Gr. 9–12)
Field Study Trips	Field Study Trips	Field Study Trips	Field Study Trips
Additional Topics:	Additional Topics:	Additional Topics:	Additional Topics:

Exercise 4.5 Reciprocal Leading and Learning Partnerships

Capturing the central elements contained in the principal letter posed in Figure 4.4, create your own volunteer toolkit including any of the features below:

1) Start by assessing how outreach efforts look like in your school, district, or county office. Rate your organization on a scale from (1) low, (2) medium, or (3) high regarding each of the sentence stems.

Impactful involvement indicators	*Scale(1) low(2) medium(3) high*
We consciously partner with underrepresented students and families.	
We take into consideration special needs when choosing settings.	
We offer multiple options for attendance (repeat sessions, recordings, virtual or hybrid participation).	
We invite an equitable representation of the community impacted by the issue.	
We monitor voices in the space to balance and elicit participation.	
We provide accommodations that show respect for diversity (translators, accessible locations, neutral/friendly settings).	
We communicate in jargon-free, understandable language.	
We authentically involve participants in decision-making and recommendations.	
We show appreciation for being involved.	
We follow up with the results, actions, or next steps.	

© Copyright material from Kim Wallace (2025), Game–Changing Leadership in Action, Routledge.

2) Write a welcome volunteer memo outlining the range of school events for which you're seeking external helpers.
3) Fill out an annual calendar with your staff that includes schoolwide and grade level/subject area specific events, study trips, or activities that would benefit from community involvement, prior to the first day of school. Then work with staff to spell out what is needed or required for each occasion to run successfully.

School year 20___ - 20___				
August/ September	*October*	*November*	*December*	*January*
February	March	April	May	June

4) Draft up poll or survey prompts for information-gathering purposes. Employing a single strategic mechanism to collect high-level participation interest, skill sets, and availability produces a comprehensive pool of talent to draw from throughout the year (as opposed to sending out individual requests for every unique event). You might include variations of these particulars on your form.
   a) Basic info: Name, contact information, and role (parent, community member, nonprofit organization, business entity, etc.)
   b) Availability: a.m./p.m. weekdays; weekends; range of hours per month (up to 5, 6–10, greater than 10)
   c) Skills/Knowledge: General proficiencies or talents to offer (e.g., music, storytelling, cooking, visual design,

event planning, carpentry, organizing, tutoring, website development, guest speaking) as well as a blank field for volunteers to insert other aptitudes not otherwise listed.

d) Areas of interest: These can be content-related, like working in a specific grade level classroom or subject area (writing, math, science), and/or functionally explicit, such as organizing, setting/cleaning up, phone banking, mentoring, and newsletter design.

e) Pre-planned opportunities: Since you're already sending out a yearly calendar that contains a significant quantity of anticipated activities, take this opportunity to get signups right away by itemizing them on the form. Then respondents can volunteer right away by simply checking the boxes next to each they are free to participate in. Note that you will have to send follow-up reminders at least 3 to 4 weeks in advance so people remember what they have already committed to, and again a few days prior to the event with any updated details.

f) Open-ended response: The final question on your survey should be a free-form narrative space to elicit any other ideas for your team to consider. (But phrase the prompt carefully so that people don't automatically think that their suggestions will be incorporated or acted upon. Your team will have to vet them for appropriateness.)

5) Create a shared digital folder periodically updated by staff in order to maintain the integrity of the data collected. Consider also having one or two individuals who regularly match volunteers to assignments and coordinate communications and instructions.

▶ CONCLUSION

One main goal of module 4 was to get you out of your office and into the streets by continually zooming in and out on the site in relationship to what orbits it. On the journey into your surroundings, we gained a deeper understanding of rural, suburban, and urban leadership contexts and the similarities and differences between them. We also delved into the practice of PBE to spark ideas and creative outlets you might pursue for both student and staff learning experiences. Finding and operating in your locus of control and sphere of influence were key focus areas as well, with the hopes that holding this paradigm in mind will keep your leadership focal points steady. Finally, we sought out ways to expand reciprocity with your community by sharing leading and learning in community-centric ways.

I recommend starting small if much of this is new to you. We are all on a continuum of connecting with our surroundings, especially as they are ever-changing. For some, these concepts are already embedded in your leadership practice and mindsets. For others, it might be more of dipping a toe in the water situation. Either way, you are donning a game-changing learning-leader hat with an attitude, lens, asnd awareness that rich, edifying, and delightfully unexpected adventures await. This chapter concludes the pair of modules 3 and 4 in Domain 2: Educational environment and ecosystems. Module 5 introduces the final domain of study regarding institutional structures and organizational systems.

References

Acevedo-Garcia, D., Noelke, C., McArdle, N., Sofer, N., Huntington, N., Hardy, E., Huber, R. Baek, M. & Reece, J. (2020). The geography of child opportunity: Why neighborhoods matter for equity. *Diversity Data Kids*.

Bae, A., Esboldt, J. & Munzer, A. (Spring 2024). *Equity-driven leadership in rural education*. 21CSLA Brief, University of California Regents. Accessed on September 19, 2024 from https://21cslacenter.berkeley.edu/publications/equity-driven-leadership-rural-education

Baldridge, B. J., Beck, N., Medina, J. C., Reeves, M. A. (2017). Toward a new understanding of community-based education: The role of community-based educational spaces in disrupting inequality for minoritized youth. *Review of Research in Education*, 41(1), 381–402. https://doi.org/10.3102/0091732X16688622

Burton, M., Brown, K & Johnson, A. (2013). Storylines about rural teachers in the United States: A narrative analysis of the literature. *Journal of Research in Rural Education*, 28(12), 1–18. Accessed on September 22, 2024 from http://jrre.psu.edu/articles/28-12.pdf

Diamond, J. B. & Posey-Maddox, L. (2020). The changing terrain of the suburbs: Examining race, class, and place in suburban schools and communities. *Equity & Excellence in Education*, 53(1–2), 7–13. https://doi.org/10.1080/10665684.2020.1758975

Diamond, J. B., Posey-Maddox, L. & Velázquez, M. D. (2021). Reframing suburbs: Race, place, and opportunity in suburban educational spaces. *Educational Researcher*, 50(4), 249–255. https://doi.org/10.3102/0013189X20972676

Galster, G. & Sharkey, P. (2017). Spatial foundations of inequality: A conceptual model and empirical overview. *RSF: The Russell Sage Foundation Journal of the Social Sciences*, 3(2), 1–33. Accessed on September 1, 2024 from https://doi.org/10.7758/rsf.2017.3.2.01

Gruenewald, D. A. (2003). Foundations of place: A multidisciplinary framework for place-conscious education. *American Educational Research Journal*, 40(3), 619–654. https://doi.org/10.3102/00028312040003619

Hayes, S., Flowers, J. Williams, S. (2021) Constant communication: Rural principals' leadership practices during a global pandemic.

Frontiers in Education, 5. Accessed on September 21, 2024 from https://doi.org/10.3389/feduc.2020.618067

Johnson, Jr, J. F. & Uline, C. L. (2005). Preparing educational leaders to close achievement gaps. *Theory Into Practice*, 44(1), 45–52. https://doi.org/10.1207/s15430421tip4401_7

Kang, Y., Zhang, F., Gao, S., Lin, H. & Liu, Y. (2020). A review of urban physical environment sensing using street view imagery in public health studies. *Annals of GIS*, 26(3), 261–275. https://doi.org/10.1080/19475683.2020.1791954

Kelty, N. E. & Wakabayashi, T. (2020). Family engagement in schools: Parent, educator, and community perspectives. *Sage Open*, 10(4). https://doi.org/10.1177/2158244020973024

Maier, A., Daniel, J., Oakes, J. & Lam, L. (2017). Community schools as an effective school improvement strategy: A review of the evidence. Palo Alto, CA: Learning Policy Institute. Accessed on November 3, 2024 from https://learningpolicyinstitute.org/product/community-schools-effective-school-improvement-report

Marcus, L. J., McNulty, E. J., Henderson, J. M. & Dorn, B. C. (2019). *You're it: Crisis, change, and how to lead when it matters most.* New York: PublicAffairs.

Marx, S. & Larson, L. L. (2012). Taking off the color-blind glasses: Recognizing and supporting Latina/o students in a predominantly white school. *Educational Administration Quarterly*, 48(2), 259–303. https://doi.org/10.1177/0013161X11421923

Nation, M., Christens, B. D., Bess, K. D., Shinn, M., Perkins, D. D. & Speer, P. W. (2020). Addressing the problems of urban education: An ecological systems perspective. *Journal of Urban Affairs*, 42(5), 715–730. https://doi.org/10.1080/07352166.2019.1705847

National Center for Education Statistics (2022). Table 203.72 Public elementary and secondary enrollment, by locale and state: Fall 2021. *Digest of Education Statistics*. Accessed on September 1, 2024 from https://nces.ed.gov/programs/digest/d22/tables/dt22_203.72.asp

National Center for Education Statistics. (2023). *Characteristics of Public and Private School Principals. Condition of Education.* U.S. Department of Education, Institute of Education Sciences. Accessed on September 25, 2024 from https://nces.ed.gov/programs/coe/indicator/cls/public-school-principals

National School Boards Association. (2018). Today's school boards & their priorities for tomorrow: 2018 survey conducted by the National School Boards Association in partnership with K12 Insight.

Accessed on September 25, 2024 from https://cdn-files.nsba.org/s3fs-public/reports/K12_National_Survey.pdf

O'Shea, C. (2021). Distributed leadership and innovative teaching practices. *International Journal of Educational Research Open*, 2, 100088, ISSN 2666-3740, https://doi.org/10.1016/j.ijedro.2021.100088. Accessed on November 3, 2024 from https://www.sciencedirect.com/science/article/pii/S2666374021000583

Orr, D. (2013). Place and pedagogy. *NAMTA Journal*, 38(1), 183–188.

Owens, A. (2016). Inequality in children's contexts: The economic segregation of households with and without children. *American Sociological Review* 81(3): 549–574.

Owens, A. & Rich, P. (2023). Little boxes all the same? Racial-ethnic segregation and educational inequality across the urban-suburban divide. *RSF: The Russell Sage Foundation Journal of the Social Sciences*, 9(2), 26–54.

Park, E. (2020). Asian Americans in the suburbs: Race, class, and Korean immigrant parental engagement. *Equity & Excellence in Education*, 53(1–2), 30–49. Accessed on September 17, 2024 from https://doi.org/10.1080/10665684.2020.1758974

Preis, D. (2020). Preparing suburban school leaders to recognize everyday narratives that promote opportunity gaps. *Journal of Educational Leadership and Policy Studies*, 4(1). Retrieved from https://go.southernct.edu/jelps/#issues

Ritchie, H., Samborska, V., Ahuja, N., Ortiz-Ospina, E. & Roser, M. (2023). *Global Education*. Published online at OurWorldinData.org. Retrieved on September 17, 2024 from: https://ourworldindata.org/global-education

Rury, J. L. (2020). *Creating the suburban school advantage: Race, localism, and inequality in an American metropolis.* Ithaca, NY: Cornell University Press. Accessed on September 22, 2024 from https://books.google.com/books?id=1PuzDwAAQBAJ&lpg=PR5&ots=NwnAq62AGI&dq=suburban%20schools%20leadership&lr&pg=PA2#v=onepage&q=suburban%20schools%20leadership&f=false

Schell, C.J., Dyson, K., Fuentes, T.L., Des Roches, S., Harris, N.C., Miller, D.S., Woelfle-Erskine, C.A., Lambert, M.R. (2020 Sep 18). The ecological and evolutionary consequences of systemic racism in urban environments. *Science*, 369(6510): eaay4497. doi: 10.1126/science.aay4497. Epub 2020 Aug 13. PMID: 32792461.

Shields, C. M. (2004). Dialogic leadership for social justice: Overcoming pathologies of silence. *Educational Administration Quarterly*, 40(1), 109–132. https://doi.org/10.1177/0013161X03258963

Smith, G. A. (2002). Place-based education: Learning to be where we are. *Phi Delta Kappan*, 83(8), 584–594. https://doi.org/10.1177/003172170208300806

Sobel, D. (2004). Place-based education: Connecting classroom and community. *Nature & Listening*, 4(1), 1–7.

Statistics Canada. (February 9, 2021). Population counts, population centre size groups and rural areas. Accessed on September 17, 2024 from https://www150.statcan.gc.ca/t1/tbl1/en/tv.action?pid=9810000801&geocode=A000011124

Superville, D. (May 8, 2018). How long do big-city superintendents typically stick around? *Education Week*. Accessed on March 28, 2025 from https://www.edweek.org/leadership/how-long-do-big-city-superintendents-typically-stick-around/2018/05

Tieken, M. C. & Montgomery, M. K. (2021). Challenges facing schools in rural America. *State Education Standard*, 21(1), 6–11. Accessed on September 22, 2024 from https://files.eric.ed.gov/fulltext/EJ1286832.pdf

U.S. Census Bureau: America Counts Staff, (August 9, 2017). One in Five Americans Live in Rural Areas. Accessed on September 22, 2024 from https://www.census.gov/library/stories/2017/08/rural-america.html

Welsh, R. O. & Swain, W. A. (2020). (Re)Defining urban education: A conceptual review and empirical exploration of the definition of urban education. *Educational Researcher*, 49(2), 90–100. https://doi.org/10.3102/0013189X20902822

White, R. S., Evans, M. P. & Malin, J. R. (2023). Political battles in suburbia. *Phi Delta Kappan*, 104(5), 6–10. https://doi.org/10.1177/00317217231156223

Yemini, M., Engel, L. & Ben Simon, A.(2023). Place-based education–a systematic review of literature. *Educational Review*, 1–21. https://doi.org/10.1080/00131911.2023.2177260

Module 5

Leveraging Structures & Navigating Systems

▶ **INTRODUCTION**

The field of navigation has gotten a lot easier since the days of using a handheld compass, sun and star positioning, or a foldable atlas to plot out where you're going. With GPS, online maps, and Siri and Alexa to help us out, the universe of possibilities is wide open. Society has made enormous technological progress in recent generations: self-driving cars, voice-activated programming, automated machinery, smart thermostats, virtual reality simulators, and likely even newer technologies on the horizon before I even finish this paragraph. How we get from point A to point B is largely a result of the creation of systems bred by innovations responding to life's conundrums. When we get lost, find ourselves at dead ends, or go off course, it's human nature to develop methods to unstick ourselves. And those methods, when combined with tactical moves, can result in replicable and reliable approaches to address future situations.

Social systems are also developed and utilized for myriad purposes – to improve quality of life, fix common problems, fulfill basic needs, and itch creative scratches. Humans have forever been trying to invent a better mousetrap, not just for the sake of catching mice but for the thrill of the catch itself. There is much to be said for why systems and structures are necessary and desired in a shared culture. In the best of cases, frameworks, guidelines, rulebooks, policies, organizational models, and other mechanisms serve to convey messages about the kind of behaviors we collectively rely on to keep ourselves and each other safe and secure. When those codes of conduct are broken, ideally the system works to correct the crossed boundary, rehabilitate the transgressor, and restore equilibrium to the community. If systems and structures are not in place, chaos, dysfunction, and anarchy sweep in – as in the aphorism, nature abhors a vacuum. That's one theory, at least.

Systems exist for good reason, but in reality, they can also operate in controlling, suppressive, and domineering ways if we're not careful. Being in the business of school systems leadership is a mighty responsibility to bear. If the structures we inherit, uphold, or concoct aren't squarely helping students learn and grow in humanistic ways, the damage we cause may not be undone, individually or societally. No one entered this occupation to do harm; it's simply not who we are as a profession. We, ourselves, experienced school in a certain way and entered a field that still looks a lot like it did when we were kids. Paddling against that powerful current is not only exhausting but overpowering, especially when going at it alone (which is why I don't recommend it). I do and still want to believe that people just want what they think is right for children, even when it manifests in unsavory ways. Gen X rap icon Ice-T famously proclaimed in his 1999 hit: "Don't Hate the Playa (Hate the Game)". As in, don't blame an individual for finding a way to beat the system, blame the system for being gameable. That's why continually upgrading our systems and structures is important.

▶ FOUNDATIONS

You've probably heard the decades-old refrain and oft-repeated stories in the media that our education system is broken. It doesn't work anymore. It needs fixing. The headlines clamor: Schools are failing... unions striking... parents petitioning... superintendents discredited... school boards clashing...

teachers quitting in droves... students running amok... and many more variations on the theme. Instead of blaming teachers, administrators, parents, children, or any other player that participates in, shapes, or reflects the system, consider this: *The System* is doing *exactly* what it was commissioned to do. It's actually not broken at all.

The system we currently have is man-made or rather, Mann-made, à la Horace Mann's (1796–1859) development of the Common School in the 1830s. Prescient at the time, it has operated for nearly 200 years to successfully rank, sort, stratify, categorize, discard, and spit out workers and citizens equipped for earning a 19th- and 20th-century living. It's a bureaucratic machine, kept well fed by the observance of strict rules, compliance, and conformity with the stated objective of acquiring literacy, content knowledge, and basic skills. William Treseder's (July 4, 2017) blog post in *Medium* declares,

> Mann was a founder. He sacrificed the perfect at the altar of the good. You enter the system one way, and are crammed through an extended molding process. The result? A 'good enough' cog to jam into an industrial machine. Dependable. Interchangeable. Replaceable. But today, that system delivers us into a digital economy that has no need of our outdated skills.
>
> (no p. #)

Couldn't have stated it better myself.

That said, this anachronistic model does still work surprisingly well for those whom it was designed: white, middle-/upper-class, English-speaking young people who maintain traditional aspirations to earn degrees from reputable-enough post-secondary institutions before entering the white-collar workforce. The news headlines and Treseder's admonition, however, directly point to the albatross around the system's neck: that already a quarter into the 21st century, it does not work so advantageously for anyone else.

Game–Changing leadership in this institutional domain means steering your site, department, or central office toward the goals and outcomes schools are supposed to be designed for: cultivating an educated populace who function and contribute in healthy and constructive ways to advance the good of the whole. As we traverse through this unit, we'll critically assess your systems and structures and determine whether each is aligned to the primary goals described in this introduction by

- Applying systems thinking to envision schools of and for the future
- Making invisible tensions visible, tempering their ramifications
- Teasing apart the web of systems operating in your organization and assessing existing structures for efficacy
- Developing continuous improvement approaches as a systems leader

Before we delve into the educational leadership domain, what follows is a general definition explaining how systems and structures interface.

A. A system encompasses a variety of processes, approaches, and protocols that work in concert to create coherence and consistency in an organization.
B. Structures are arranged and constructed within that system to help the institution functionally reach its goals.

Simply put, structure is the underlying framework that supports the operation of a system. Let's begin with a few familiar examples from other disciplines to orient you to the forthcoming content via Table 5.1.

In education, systems refer to an interconnected network of components within an institution and structures represent the established framework or organizational layout of that system, as demonstrated in Table 5.2.

Table 5.1 Systems and structures general examples

Mechanism/ Organism	Structure	System
Aircraft wings	Physical design and interaction between flaps, propellers, tips, and ribs	Wing systems work together for the purpose of taking off, flying, and landing
Forest ecosystem	Different species of plants, animals, and minerals coexisting interdependently in nature	A variety of indigenous wildlife provides checks and balances to support a sustainable and productive environment
Human skeleton	Bones with joints, cartilage, ligaments, and muscles to coordinate ambulation	Gives a body its shape, allows movement, and provides protection for organs

Table 5.2 Systems and structures educational examples

Mechanism	Structure	System
Curricular	Curriculum mapping, vertical and horizontal articulation between and within grade levels, course pathways, matriculation standards, grades, graduation requirements	Provides progressively rigorous learning experiences as students advance between grade levels to ultimately reach completion of a course of study
Disciplinary	Code of conduct, progressive behavioral consequences, adopted board policy and administrative regulations, interventions/restorative practices	Creates a safe and secure environment for students and staff while on campus

(*Continued*)

Table 5.2 (Continued)

Mechanism	Structure	System
Accountability	State and federal legislation or mandates, standardized assessments, data dashboards, school rankings, district report cards	Establishes criteria for determining whether schools and districts are meeting expectations or requirements for educating their students

▶ SYSTEMS THINKING FOR SCHOOLS OF THE FUTURE

Now that you have a general sense of the interplay between systems and structures, we're going to delve into more complex material on systems leadership. Haim Shaked and Chen Schechter (2020), in an article on exploring systems thinking leadership for school improvement, write:

> Systems thinking [as] a holistic approach that focuses on how the parts function together in networks of interaction, not on breaking down systems into parts in order to understand them separately. Thus, to improve the whole, systems thinkers optimize the interactions among the parts. Interaction management may result in improved performance, reduced conflicts, expanded delegation of responsibility and overcoming resistance (Boardman and Sauser, 2008).
>
> (p. 108)

Furthermore, underscoring why this module conjoins structures and systems holistically, they warn,

> by focusing on the parts rather than on the whole, school leaders do not adequately consider the complex interactions among various parts in the system, thus may find it difficult to face the contemporary growing complexity, change and diversity characterizing school organizations.
>
> (p. 112)

It is not dissimilar to the challenges inherent in the environmental domain; as people continually interact and engage in a physical place or virtual space, their human impacts affect the very nature of it. We see evidence of this in the wear and tear on our school buildings and adjustments to technological advancements. The two worlds collide when either is anachronistically out of sync with the other. Most of the time, it's the structural aspects of school that are way behind the times of everything outside of it. It's a constant push and pull between chasing modernity and upholding tradition. The most obvious example is the fact that we are walking around with high-tech computers in our pockets or on our wrists, in the face of school policies that forbid cell phones or other digital devices as tools for learning.

As Jamie P. Monat and Thomas Gannon (2023), in "The Meaning of 'Structure' in Systems Thinking," observe,

> The description of component interrelationships must be more than just spatial, hierarchical, temporal, sequential, or reporting, because those relationships do not fully explain the impact of one system component on another. To explain the impact of one component on another, one must understand the *cause-and-effect relationships* among the components...."structure" is the cause-and-effect manner in which the system components interrelate to yield the system behavior; and the rules, laws, protocols, procedures, policies, and incentives/rewards that govern those interactions.
>
> (pp. 6–7)

To concretize this theory, think about before and after school traffic operations. The system is meant to allow caregivers to drop off and pick up their children in a timely, safe, and orderly manner. The physical structures include the parking lot or roundabout, speed bumps, directional signage, orange cones, and posted speed limits on the adjacent streets. They also include a detailed schedule, assigned personnel such as crossing guards, and potential consequences for unwelcome behaviors (e.g., double parking, driving the wrong way, verbal or physical aggression). In the best-case scenario, everyone gets to and from school without incident. In reality, there will inevitably be fender benders, rule breakers, absentee or lax monitors, inclement weather, or other underlying structural elements that cause the system to glitch. Systems thinking, therefore, is not a cure-all for solving for every x-factor but rather a mindset that takes into consideration the variables at play in any given situation that can be refined or adjusted to build that better mousetrap. Flexibility, agility, and responsiveness are key.

Any good leader is responsible for attending to the basic needs of students, staff, and families, but game–changing leaders strive for higher aspirations. Georgia Ketikidou and Anna Saiti (2022) state, in their article on the promotion of inclusive education through sustainable and systemic leadership, that

> Decisions and initiatives for policy-making and daily practices should be taken on the basis of sustainable and systemic values, values such as solidarity, justice, meritocracy, trust, honesty, and a collaborative culture. A sense of community involvement is a critical foundation for deepening and sustaining the changes and improvements coveted by those in the school.
>
> (p. 6)

How do we create this sense of community in our schools so that young people and adults alike are motivated to do the right thing not solely in avoidance of punishment but as a sense of personal and communal duty to their peers and colleagues?

We might start by dismantling the structures that enforce systems devoid of human dignity. Shame, for example, has long been part of our educational history – spanking and paddling behinds, forcing to wear a dunce cap, standing in the corner, writing "I will exercise self-discipline" on the chalk board fifty times, rapping a ruler on the fingers of a lefthander, plugging a bar of soap into a foul mouth, banging dusty erasers together, or scraping gum from under desks are a few of the obviously archaic tools of control based on humiliation as a form of correction. You may be thinking, but those old school techniques are rarely, if ever, used anymore. Well, what about suspending kids for cutting class (an oxymoron if I ever saw one), or holding the whole class in for recess because someone sharpened their pencil without asking, or fashioning hall passes out of a toilet seat lid to deter requests to use the restroom? All of which I've witnessed in the not-so-distant past. Educators everywhere may unknowingly perpetuate such degrading customs unless game–changing leaders provide them with true alternatives that work.

Esteemed scholar on educational progress (or rather lack thereof), Larry Cuban has been beating this drum for decades. In his 2020 article, "Reforming the Grammar of Schooling Again and Again," Cuban proclaims,

> For each generation of progressive educators since the early twentieth century, the history of attempted classroom, school, and district reforms to alter the 'grammar of schooling' has been a dismal tale of disappointment and failure. The structures of the age-graded school and the district bureaucracy, both of which tilt pedagogy toward teacher-centered instruction, have seemingly forged cage-like steel bars to hold the 'grammar of schooling' in place.
>
> (p. 665)

I get why Cuban is frustrated. But I also share his relentless conviction to keep on banging those cymbals as a call to action. So, let's keep at it.

The I's of Impact iterative flowchart (Figure 5.1) is a simple conceptual model for educators to work on undoing the grammar of schooling. First take a critical look at your most persistent problems of practice woven into the fabric of your organization's systems and structures, then imagine the ideal

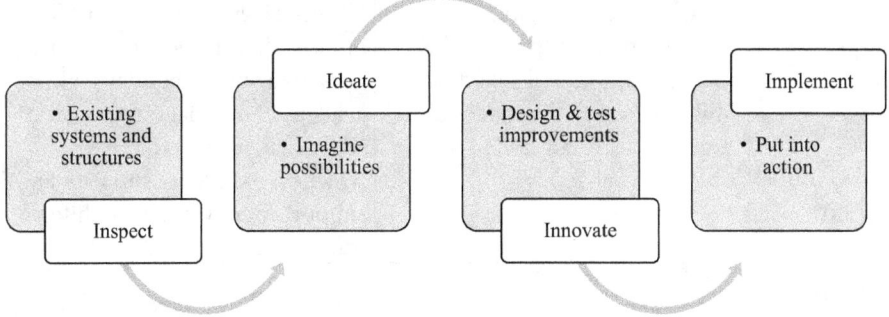

Figure 5.1 I's of impact

educational experiences you want your students, staff, and families to have. Try some of those ideas in practice, see what differences or outcomes are evident (and if they are worth pursuing), and take action.

One caution though: determine readiness levels before jumping right in. It's important to be aware of resistance or 'third rail' topics (hot button issues that elicit extreme reactions from constituents) in your community before pursuing systemic change. Tina Wang, Diane Olivier, and Peying Chen (2020) propose that

> A high level of individual readiness for change and a high level of organizational readiness for change will enable a high level of system readiness for change…The organization enacts the change in a sustainable ecosystem and has the capacity and resilience to deal with the issues and challenges in a dynamic changing environment.
>
> (p. 1052)

One way to actualize this triad of readiness is by applying systems thinking to our practices to generate solutions that heighten both external expectations and intrinsic motivation. Table 5.3 demonstrates how we might transform customary structures that enforce existing paradigms into innovative approaches that actually improve hoped-for cause and effect outcomes.

Table 5.3 From conventional to innovative

Conventional	*Innovative*
Tutorial program: Middle school students with D's and F's are assigned extra time in a subject area with their teacher on a predetermined schedule, while the rest of the students go to quiet study hall staffed by a long-term sub.	**"Go where you need" support model**: All students are allowed to self-select from a menu of options that support an area they personally need that day from academic to social emotional. All staff are equipped to meet whichever students show up and support them via whole-child frameworks.

(*Continued*)

Table 5.3 (Continued)

Conventional	Innovative
Academic counseling assignments: Students are evenly divided between high school counselors by objective criteria such as first letter of their last name or grade level so that each counselor has the same number on their caseload, regardless of urgency or priority.	**Needs-based counseling assignments**: Students are assigned to counselors based on specific demographics and/or proportionate to academic and social emotional needs (e.g., English learners paired with multilingual counselors or students on Individual Education Plans [IEPs] with one counselor with a 60% reduced total caseload).
Elementary school library: Staffed with a classified position library tech. Populated with hard copy books, computers, and other materials for children to access or check out. Quiet, independent working environment.	**Multimedia learning center**: Led by a credentialed teacher-librarian overseeing volunteer staff that work with children individually or in groups using digitally mediated learning tools. Buzz of excitement in the air.

Practical Application

Exercise 5.1 prompts you to connect your structures and their systems in instructional, operational, and administrative realms to condition your systems thinking muscles and mindsets. Once you understand how the architecture influences implementation, you can begin to identify where unseen barriers may be thwarting your improvement efforts and interrupt unproductive cycles.

▶ TENACIOUS TENSIONS

Just as we cannot separate structure from systems, it's likewise ambitious to discern what a policy is actually meant to do from what comes out of its implementation. Many institutions pair federal, state, and Board Policy (BP) with Administrative Regulations (ARs) to fill the gaps between knowing and doing.

The policy states the *what* (and arguably the *why*), and the ARs offer the *how*. Even the *how* is subject to individual interpretation within one district, much less between how administrators in a single school may apply the same principle into practice differently. There is the letter of the law and the spirit of it. Even dictates titled as "zero tolerance" or "three strikes" have their loopholes as applied by stereotypically "good cops" and "bad cops."

Tobey Greany and Peter Earley (2021), editors of *School Leadership and Education System Reform*, believe this paradox

> is a set of contradictions that sit at the heart of education policy in many school systems. Policymakers in these systems want things that, if not inherently at odd, are nevertheless in tension – freedom *and* control; tightly defined national standards *and* a broad and balanced curriculum; choice *and* diversity and equity; academic stretch for the most able children *and* a closing of the gap between high and low performers; competition *and* collaboration. In other words, these policymakers want their educational cake, but they also want to eat it.
>
> (p. 3)

Look no further than the volumes produced on the subject matter ruling public schooling. The 2023 edition of the Illinois Administrative Code[1] Table of Contents alone is 68 pages long; the latest version of Texas Education code[2] is a whopping 162 chapters; Maryland's State Code[3] is 1,894 pages; and California's Ed Code[4], containing 1,264 distinct articles, is denser than a three-layer cake. When the Common Core State Standards (CCSS) were adopted in 2010, a common mythology surrounding them was that it would take 23 years for a K-12 student to master each and every one as intended (all within their approximately 13-year school career), inciting states and localities to establish "power" or "essential" standards of their own determination. Again, illustrating the incongruence between policy and implementation.

County and central office administrators are commonly divided into topical departments like student services, special education, curriculum and instruction, secondary and elementary education, and assessment and accountability to name a few.

These middle managers act as a conduit between policymakers and implementers and play a strategic role in the delivery of information about how to put procedures into action. Non-site-based administrators, unfortunately, are rarely the focal point of research conducted on educational leadership, much to the detriment of our site implementers. But Tania Leach's 2024 study on Australian system middle leaders (known as district or central office directors and managers stateside) found that

> Lack of role clarity hinders achieving policy coherence, stemming from the inconsistent interpretation and translation of policy into system strategy documentation and a deficiency in formal policy interpretation and role induction practices. As a result, individual system leaders often turn to informal policy interpretations and interactions with peers to clarify roles, leading to role tensions, accountability ambiguity and partial policy implementation.
>
> (p. 1)

Maxwell Yurkofsky (2022) noted a phenomenon associated with the cake-and-eat-it-too paradox in his work from compliance to improvement, positing that when organizations face competing and seemingly unachievable expectations, they "engage in avoidance by disguising non-conformity" and "maintain legitimacy by ceremonially complying" (p. 303).

> In these situations, leaders sometimes respond in ways that appear purposeful and strategic. They might *avoid* such expectations (which involves *buffering* teachers from unhelpful policies or partially implementing policies to avoid potential negative consequences), develop *compromises* (e.g., constructing hybrid versions of competing policies), or make substantive *adaptations* to policies so that they are more in line with local constraints (Carraway & Young, 2015; Donaldson & Woulfin, 2018; Ganon-Shilon & Schechter, 2019; Ganon-Shilon et al., 2020; Gu et al., 2018; Kraft & Gilmour, 2017; LeChasseur et al., 2018; Marsh et al., 2017).
>
> (p. 314)

While this can be construed as gaming the system, it's not necessarily a bad thing but rather a strategic and purposeful approach to unraveling the mysteries of policy intent in relation to what makes sense to a leader's own context. When faced with hundreds, if not thousands, of dictates coming down from on high, you don't really have any other option than to pick and choose what gets implemented and how. The reality is: the checks and balances in place that determine whether you're in compliance are feeble at best. The system itself cannot handle the volume, so it's typically an exercise in checking off the right boxes to show you "did the thing" that was asked, even if minimally or to little substantive impact. This alone is demoralizing and reduces skilled and able leaders to paper-pushing bureaucrats.

I don't have a pat solution to offer, but I can recommend two approaches: (1) quickly check those boxes and move on to do the real work of leadership and/or (2) finagle and finesse the compliance mechanisms into meaningful plans for transformation. The policies in and of themselves are usually well intended and come from a place of concern and care for our students, but the politics behind them make for an incoherent mishmash of stuff to do in the form of structure instead of a coordinated medium for substantial progress.

There are probably many things that come to mind when thinking about your systemic "sticky wickets." Unspooling the tangled webs we weave takes persistence paired with ingenuity, undergirded by conclusive research. The next scenario is based on tenets from the root-cause analysis approach in which practitioners look for the primary causes of a problem of practice rather than treating its conspicuous symptoms in order to course-correct. This meta-analysis process leaves no stone unturned in exploring the existing tensions in an attempt to uncover them. Using a fishbone diagram, an instructional leadership team decides to confront escalating barriers for specific groups accessing advanced course pathways at the secondary level. English learners and under-resourced students are decreasing in representation in higher tiers of math, English, and science instruction, including Gifted and Talented Education (GATE), honors, and Advanced Placement (AP) classes. While there has been an overall expansion of these types of courses in the district, the corresponding opportunities seem to be shrinking for marginalized students.

In a 2024 systematic review of research on equity in advanced education, Melanie S. Meyer, Yuyang Shen, and Jonathan A. Plucker call out Plucker and Scott J. Peters' (2016)

> seven key research-based strategies for reducing excellence gaps, including (a) addressing advanced performance in school accountability systems, (b) improving teacher preparation and professional development, (c) providing accessible advanced learning opportunities, (d) frontloading to prepare students for those opportunities, (e) equitable screening and placement in advanced learning contexts, (f) grouping students so they can move flexibly through content, and (g) using psychosocial interventions in postsecondary settings (see also Plucker & Peters, 2018; Plucker, Peters & Schmalensee, 2017).
>
> (p. 36)

The team keeps these factors in mind as they fill out the fishbone diagram in Figure 5.2 to see which root causes might be addressed by the recommended strategies.

The diagram illustrates several core issues related to the low incidence rates of certain subgroups in advanced pathways. The system appears to be rife with (1) faulty identification and support mechanisms for pursuing and being admitted into advanced learning opportunities; (2) obsolete adult beliefs, biases, and mindsets about teaching and learning; (3) inflexible scheduling protocols, and (4) reinforcement of social emotional conditions that play into students' personal choices and relational behaviors. The structures under each main category are problematic as well. As you can see, there are physical, pedagogical, and institutional obstacles that must be addressed and overcome to open up access and opportunity for underrepresented students. These first-order (physical), second-order (pedagogical), and third-order (institutional) barriers combined pose hurdles which deter even the most motivated individuals' ambitions. Unsurprisingly, the Instructional Leadership Team (ILT) learns that all seven conditions for reducing excellence

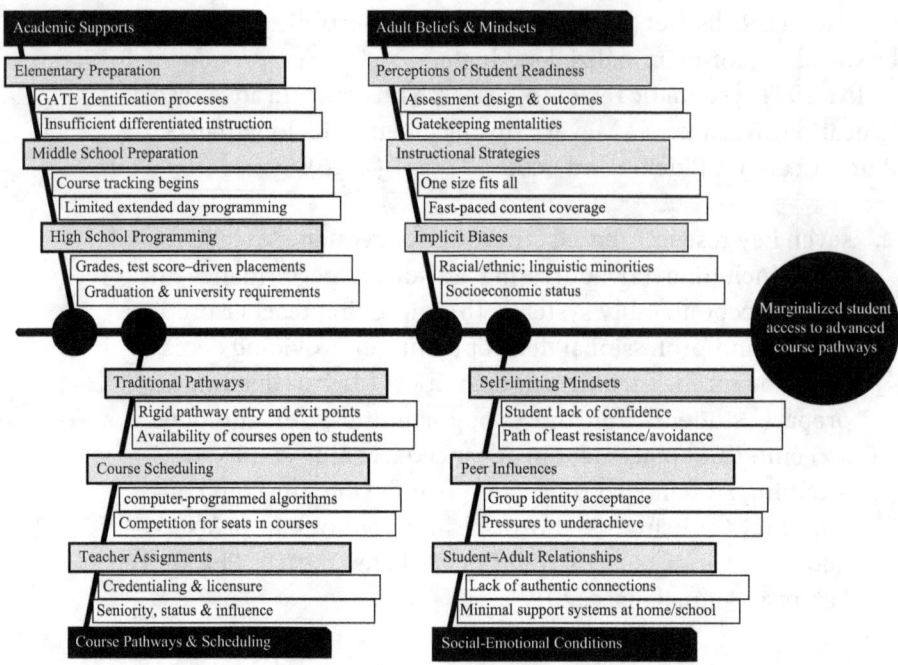

Figure 5.2 Fishbone diagram root-cause analysis

gaps will need to be implemented at varying degrees to reduce or eventually eliminate the inherent tensions. They cluster them into categories in their multipronged approach to remedy the structures limiting systemic progress.

<u>Adult learning</u>:
(b) improving teacher preparation and professional development

<u>Student learning</u>:
(d) frontloading to prepare students for those opportunities
(g) using psychosocial interventions in postsecondary settings

<u>Processes and protocols</u>:
(a) addressing advanced performance in school accountability systems
(c) providing accessible advanced learning opportunities
(e) equitable screening and placement in advanced learning contexts
(f) grouping students so they can move flexibly through content

Referencing the study by Meyer et al. (2024), the team focuses on the following promising approaches:

> Prepare students for advanced learning opportunities, place them in supportive environments in which their current academic needs can be met, and use ongoing formative assessment to evaluate progress and adjust grouping configurations, in-class supports, or course placements as student needs change.
>
> (p. 63)

Practical Application

It's time to take a good hard look at your own stated policies and procedures to see where tensions are causing weak links in their application. Settle on a subject you suspect is causing strain on your structures and systems and unpeel the layers of the onion (or pick the bones from the fish) to determine areas to strengthen or bring into alignment in Exercise 5.2.

▶ MAKING THE INVISIBLE VISIBLE

Lest it seem like a simplistic "a + b = c" equation, I'm not suggesting that any of this is easy. It's incredibly challenging to navigate the unspoken mores underpinning organizational conventions that Richard Karash (n.d.), "The Systems Thinker," alludes to in this explanation:

> Structure is the network of relationships that creates behavior. The essence of structure is not in the things themselves but in the relationships of things. By its very nature, structure is difficult to see. As opposed to events and patterns, which are usually more observable, much of what we think of as structure is often hidden.
>
> (no p. #)

Discernment is the leadership challenge in these cases. Developing keen intuitive powers – otherwise known as your "Spidey sense" or that niggling feeling of "Hey, what's *really* going on here?" – takes both time and experience, as in you might have to touch a hot stove or two to anticipate and recognize imminent perils.

The maxim of not being able to "see the forest for the trees" is an apt metaphor to describe the complexities of how structures and systems produce certain outcomes. Each individual tree has components such as leaves, roots, a trunk, flowers, or fruit, and they coexist alongside other trees, representing a multitude of systems containing their own unique structures. Together, they create a forest or an orchard, which we call our educational system. This metaphor is symbolically illustrated in Figure 5.3.

Now think about the sorts of systemic or structural dilemmas that students, families, or staff have been expressing, exhibiting, or feeling about your school or district that may point to a particular problem of practice related to any of these focal areas:

- Classroom rules and behavior expectations
- Attendance/Absenteeism
- Course periods/bell scheduling
- Instructional delivery and practices
- Well-being and social-emotional health
- School enrollment; teacher assignments
- School climate and culture
- Student achievement and performance
- Discipline and safety

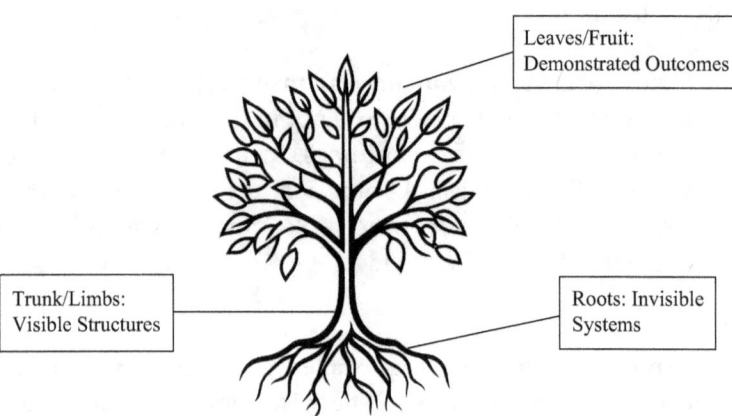

Figure 5.3 Educational ecology

- Engagement, inclusion, and belonging
- Operations (transportation, human resources, nutrition services)
- Extracurricular activities, clubs, and athletics

It is up to us as leaders to ensure that the structures and systems that we uphold or establish are not reactionary, punitive, or vindictive. One way to accomplish this is to sit down with your leadership team during the summer or preservice days and reflect on the kinds of issues that cropped up during the year that warrant attention and pick your top three to tackle. Outside the heat of the moment, you'll make sounder decisions as illustrated in Table 5.4. The left column is a short description of recurring incidents or repetitive infractions that have risen to the surface as primary concerns. The middle column is the

Table 5.4 Top three trials

Infraction	Consequence	Intervention
Student using AI to write papers or complete their homework	Zero tolerance for cheating; automatic failure on assignment or course	Embed digital literacy tutorials into curriculum; teach students how to use AI ethically
Families taking extended vacations or traveling outside of sanctioned district holidays	Policy on unexcused absences disallows makeup work or test retakes; students being misdesignated as chronically truant	Look at whole school absentee patterns adjacent to times of year and develop high-quality independent study assignments for students to complete while away
Interpersonal student misconduct such as bullying, teasing, ostracizing, gossip/rumors, intimidation	Detention, suspension or, in severe harassment cases, expulsion	Take a varied approach including lessons on empathy; increased supervision in campus hotspots or at certain times of day; developing simulations to build capacity for responding in healthy ways

current set of disciplinary consequences that are in use but may not be achieving results or changed behaviors. And the right column is a brainstorm of ways to intervene that focus on growth rather than punishment.

The Harwood Institute for Public Innovation (2023) is an organization designed to co-construct solutions to community problems and speaks to the power of exposing unseen dynamics through

> "the practice of naming, telling and spreading stories of change and progress as they emerge – in essence, making "visible" what is often "invisible." Making the invisible visible is a critical part of creating a "can-do" narrative […]. People must be able to see where they are, what came before, and hope for the future. A new narrative only takes form when people can see and make sense of the connections between and among different stories."
>
> (website landing page)

In Harwood's making-the-invisible-visible tool, following questions are posed for group consideration:

1. What are we trying to achieve in our efforts together?
2. What are we building together?
3. Why is this important to our community?
4. What "wins" are we already seeing?
5. What are some of the ripple effects we're seeing from our efforts? (These are positive things that are happening as a result of our actions.)
6. What challenges have we faced in doing this work?
7. What are important next steps for us?
8. Again, what are we trying to achieve, and why?

Translating this from the community organizing space for which it was intended and into the institutional domain, I've listed some variations on the theme below:

1. What systemic and structural changes may help our school or organization function better?

2. What might we build together in place of or on top of what currently exists?
3. Why is this issue this important to our school community?
4. What do we hope to see as a result of these changes? What does success look like?
5. What are some positive ripple effects that may also result from our efforts?
6. What challenges do we anticipate by taking on this systemic change? How will we proactively address them?
7. Who and what resources are available and needed to accomplish our shared goals?
8. What are some important first and next steps to move our plans forward?

The Harwood tool includes a story frame that creates a narrative of the situation you are attempting to realize in reality and then identifying which audiences need to hear the story. This messaging should be differentiated depending on whom you're telling it to. The student version, staff rendition, and parent incarnation contain language that evokes and elicits desired responses. For example, using the first example from Table 5.4 on the AI cheating scenario, here are short blurbs that might resonate with each clientele:

> <u>To Students</u>: We recognize you are living in a digital world that most adults are simply less familiar with. That advantage is one that our staff has struggled to react to effectively, by shutting down rather than seeing artificial intelligence (AI) as a constructive tool. While using AI to entirely complete your homework for you is still a no-go, the staff here want to support your use of AI programming as a learning resource. So, we are looking at reversing our total ban on AI and need your help to establish a new school policy and guidelines for ethically appropriate use related to schoolwork. You know the tech; we know teaching and learning. Let's figure it out together.
>
> <u>To Staff</u>: It's been tough fighting the "AI battle" this year. We can't ignore the fact that platforms like ChatGPT are only

going to get smarter as people engage with them. It's not a war we can win, so we need to figure out how to adjust our expectations. Our total ban on AI has caused daily headaches for instructors and administrators, and we're spending way too much valuable time on maintaining our zero-tolerance policy to no tangible impact. The leadership team proposes convening a joint task force with students and families to develop a reasonable plan going forward – one that embodies our collective belief that school is first and foremost a learning institution, and since AI is here to stay, why not harness it to everyone's advantage?

<u>To Families</u>: *Raising children in today's technologically advanced society is a hard job. We adults know that our kids are way more in tune with the latest apps and platforms than most of us are. Parenting in this environment is unknown territory. Like you, we have been grappling with the widespread and rapid expansion of artificial intelligence (AI) programs online while keeping our students safe and responsible in digital spaces. While we've done some informational campaigns this year, we recognize that our complete ban on AI usage has not accomplished our educational mission to prepare students for the world they are living in and for the future they will inherit. We invite you to partner with us on a task force that will inform policy revisions for next fall. We could really use your expertise!*

Practical Application

Later on in Exercise 5.3, there's a blank version of Table 5.4 and critical reflection questions to use with your lead team to identify and address the hot topics that need strategic reflection. As always, you are highly encouraged to involve the individuals and groups at the center of the issue to partner with you on devising solutions to the problems of practice at hand. Don't forget about the immense power of storytelling that will inspire collaboration and commitment to transforming outmoded policies and practices that may be causing more harm than help.

▶ PRACTICES PROMOTING INCLUSION

Teasing apart the web of systems operating in our organizations and assessing existing structures for efficacy to recommend improvements requires us to dig into the roots of past practices that may marginalize or thwart student growth, inclusion, and belonging. There is usually some stated or silent reasoning behind the convention that may have just overstayed its welcome. Have you seen any of the practices outlined in Table 5.5 before? What are some others that you can think of perhaps borne out an objective that no longer serves us in the schools of today?

Table 5.5 Marginalizing practices

Practice	Intent/Purpose	Assumptions
Sorting students by blue and pink cards to assign classes/activities by gender	Balance out the number of boys and girls in a learning environment, often for behavioral management purposes	There are only two genders; all males and all females share the same group characteristics; one gender is better behaved or easier to manage than the other.
Using the term parent or mom/dad exclusively in communications	Easy-to-use generic terms or templates for all communications purposes	All nuclear families contain two biological parents of different genders.
Saying Christmas/Easter break instead of winter/spring break	Signifies a time of year for extended time off	Everyone celebrates or recognizes Christian-centric holidays.
Banning dress, foods, or customs considered ethnic, political, religious, or cultural	Maintains and promotes a certain look and conformity that is "American"	Reinforces misconceptions that certain races/ethnicities have "foreign" (or lesser) values from the mainstream

(*Continued*)

Table 5.5 (Continued)

Practice	Intent/Purpose	Assumptions
Projects based on autobiographical information, ancestry, genetics, or family history tracking	Attempts to connect students to their history, culture, and family origins via classroom assignments	Everyone has a family tree they can trace, ancestry they know, or positive life experiences to share.
Extracurricular activities, field trips, assemblies, or other events that require caregiver support	Fulfill the chaperone requirements in board policy; balance student to adult ratios; involve families in school activities	Exclusion due financial hardship, physical accessibility, language fluency, availability, or other constraints
Opt-out forms for children to be excused from "controversial" material	Allows a blanket excuse to avoid learning about uncomfortable topics (e.g., sex ed, racism, minoritized cultures' history)	Perceptions that what is age-inappropriate is better decided by caregivers rather than professional educators; or "it's not worth the fight"

Conducting a Systemic Audit

Taking a clinical look from time to time at your school's or department's programming, much like the data equity walk described in Module 3, can revitalize and sharpen your lens on lingering problems of practice. What follows is a district-based scenario where a student support services leadership team continues to wrestle with widespread chronic absenteeism and realizes that they need to re-evaluate the attendance platform and processes currently in place to examine whether they need more robust structures to improve student attendance, especially at a handful of sites. They wonder if their legacy attendance accounting system is not fulfilling the school district's needs or if the adopted platform isn't being used to its full capability or capacity. First, they create an attendance system rubric and ask five targeted sites' attendance teams to complete the self-assessment to evaluate the existing attendance framework on a scale from 1 (low effectiveness) to 5 (high effectiveness), as illustrated in Table 5.6. Once the data is submitted, the director of student support services interprets the findings with her team and makes a set of initial recommendations.

Table 5.6 Self-assessment tool

District Attendance System Structural Elements	Rating scale	Notes/ Comments
Accurately reports attendance data with minimal computer or human error	1 2 3 4 5	
Uploads new data on a timely schedule (within 24 hours)	1 2 3 4 5	
Communicates frequently and in multiple ways with families (e.g., phone, text, emails, social media, and newsletters)	1 2 3 4 5	
Collects diverse data on individual students, accessible to attendance support teams	1 2 3 4 5	
Provides a variety of prevention resources	1 2 3 4 5	
Provides a variety of intervention resources as soon as interventions become applicable	1 2 3 4 5	
Is compatible and interfaces well with other school systems and technologies	1 2 3 4 5	
Attendance data, interventions and related documentation is centralized	1 2 3 4 5	
Recognizes and rewards improvement and positive attendance behaviors	1 2 3 4 5	
Customizes and automates interventions for each student	1 2 3 4 5	
Provides alerts, trends, and updates to school staff to act upon	1 2 3 4 5	

(Continued)

Table 5.6 (Continued)

District Attendance System Structural Elements	Rating scale	Notes/Comments
Contains detailed absence definitions that reflect a multitude of reasons/sources	1 2 3 4 5	
Offers robust professional development and training for staff	1 2 3 4 5	
Provides timely tech support and is responsive to feedback or suggestions for better functionality	1 2 3 4 5	
Total High Effectiveness: 50–70 Medium Effectiveness: 30–49 Low Effectiveness: 29 or less	____/70	

1) Summarize the top three strengths your team has come to consensus on below.
2) Based on your responses, what are some unmet needs in your district's attendance system?
3) Check the statement below that describes your situation most accurately:
   ☐ Our current system is working effectively and provides the majority of what we need to support staff, students, and families to meet attendance goals. We are using most of the tools and strategies to a high degree.
   ☐ Our current system is working sufficiently to support staff, students, and families to meet attendance goals. We are using some of the tools and strategies but not everything the platform/system has to offer.
   ☐ Our current system is insufficient in supporting staff, students, and families to meet attendance goals. We don't have access to or training to use the tools effectively to impact student attendance.
   ☐ Other:

4) As a team, we recommend:
   ☐ Continuing with our current system as is or with a few adjustments.

- ☐ Continuing with our current system but focusing more on filling identified gaps (additional training, increased use of components, awareness, technical support, etc.)
- ☐ Investigating a new system that may better meet our district's needs.
- ☐ Other: _____

Practical Application

Exercise 5.4 offers a skeletal framework for composing your own self-assessment on a persistent problem of practice with the goal of discovering to what degree the structural elements are supporting the system's functions as designed. Once you've drilled down into the responses, you'll be able to identify the weakest structures reducing effectiveness and reboot the system with superior architecture.

▶ CULTIVATING SUCCESSFUL SYSTEMS

Continuous improvement methodology is composed of a series of steps that generally consist of some variation on the plan-do-study-act (PDSA) cycle as W. Edwards Deming designed it for the Japanese marketplace in 1951 and updated in 1993 for other industries. The original cycle attempted to answer three basic questions:

a) What are we trying to accomplish?
b) How will we know that a change is an improvement?
c) What change can we make that will result in improvement?

The version you see most in our field includes these descriptors that David P. Langford offers in his 2015 book *Tool Time for Education*:

1. *Plan.* Consider your initial opportunity for improvement, or your problem. Study the surrounding details and likely causes and collect data as needed.
2. *Do.* Develop a theory for improvement. Strategize about the best way to implement the theory and then do so. This is the change, and we're hoping it will lead to improvement.

3. *Study*. Look at the results of the change and determine if it worked to solve the problem or improve the situation.
4. *Act*. Make more improvements as needed. Decide how the new momentum can be maintained.

(pp. 4–5)

While the PDSA format meets many needs and attends to a variety of circumstances, the reason I've selected the following alternative framework, however, is that its more inclusive of the interpersonal domain, with a more intense focus on coalition and capacity building to elevate impacts. McKinsey & Company's executive summary of their February 2024 extended report titled *Spark and Sustain: How School Systems Can Improve Learning at Scale* found in their global analysis that

> Successful systems, at every level of spending and national development, use reinforcing strategies to create a virtuous cycle (n.d.), enabling significant, long-term gains in student learning including seven levers nested within three broader categories:

Build a durable coalition for change:
1. Set fewer priorities to get more done
2. Cultivate leadership beyond a single leader
3. Engage educators and families authentically

Create delivery capacity to scale:
4. Create coordination and cadence for change
5. Build implementation structures and skills

Drive and adapt with data:
6. Measure student outcomes and make them transparent
7. Roll out what works, but create space for innovation

(p. 9)

Module 2 provided you a blueprint for building a durable coalition for change; modules 3 and 4 emphasized how driving and adapting with data positively improves your setting and maximizes your surroundings; and this module tackles the middle domain: Create delivery capacity to scale.

But first, let's unpack some of the terminology used in the study. A virtuous cycle is commonly known in other fields such as business, economics, and health care as "a chain of events in which one desirable occurrence leads to another which further promotes the first occurrence and so on resulting in a continuous process of improvement" (Merriam-Webster online dictionary). An example of this in our world may be something like college and career frameworks to

> Create a progression of career education activities for young people where one activity builds on the past activity and creates a sequence of continuous learning about jobs and careers. This virtuous cycle ensures that by the end of high school, young people acquire knowledge, skills, relationships, and aspirations, the foundation for developing their individual and social identity and agency. It prepares them to take the next step in life, whether that be a job, further education and training, or a combination of both.
>
> (Bruno V. Manno, *Forbes*, Dec. 10, 2024)

Here is how it might look in a visual format in Figure 5.4.

The term lever, used in the management context, is an operational component or scaffold within a complex system that has higher potential to make an impression than lesser interventions. The McKinsey study's seven levers, when approached

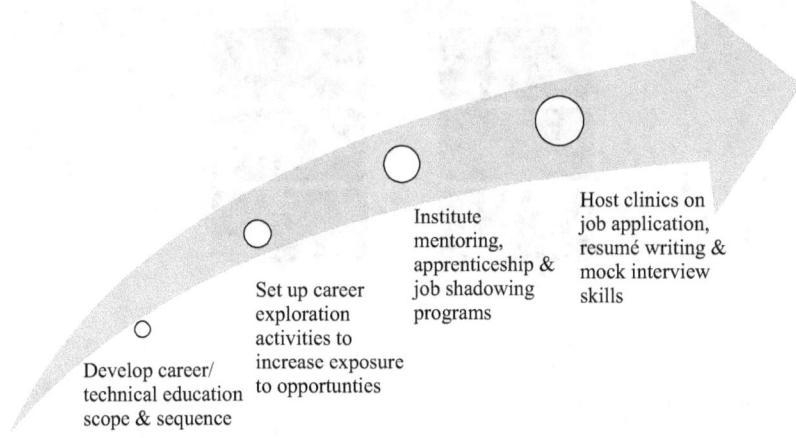

Figure 5.4 Virtuous cycle

systematically, have proven to elevate the educational outcomes for students in countries or regions that hit each and every mark. Leaders don't need to reinvent the wheel when we already have ample evidence for making the right moves. Figure 5.5 is a rudimentary layout of the seven structural levers, including some brief descriptions continuing on the thread of the career technical education progression example.

College and career readiness levers:

1) Set fewer priorities related to college and career readiness. Eliminate programs and activities producing minimal effects on student outcomes and expand those that are making significant impacts.
2) Compose a leading coalition with principals, the director of secondary education, high school and middle school counselors, and teachers to expand collective capacity.
3) Involve students and caregivers in structural design to support the systemic college and career readiness goals.
4) Coordinate a vertically and horizontally aligned instructional and experiential learning program of study from middle school through high school.
5) Build skills and structures that sustain the implementation process based on continuous improvement practices.

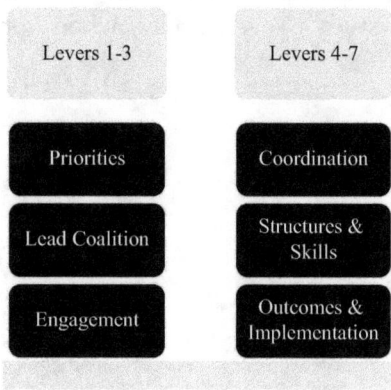

Figure 5.5 Reinforcing levers

6) Create an online dashboard to track student outcomes and present quarterly updates at public board meetings.
7) Continue to implement promising practices in the spirit of the virtuous cycle as they both organically and organizationally arise.

Practical Application

Assembling the parts into the whole reinforces the approach discussed in the "Systems Thinking for Schools of the Future" section. In Exercise 5.5, you'll employ a visual model to enact a virtuous cycle based on the seven levers for change.

Leveling Up

This closing section of module 5 centers on what makes systems leaders, well, actual leaders of systems. Lisa Drier, Sir Davis Nabarro, and Jane Nelson, of the World Economic Forum (2019), define it as such:

> Systems leadership is a set of skills and capacities that any individual or organization can use to catalyze, enable and support the process of systems-level change. It combines collaborative leadership, coalition-building, and systems insight to mobilize innovation and action across a large, decentralized network.
>
> (no p. #)

To break it down further, scholars Alma Harris, Michelle Jones, and Nashwa Hashim (2021) provided four concluding observations in their 2021 article on systems leadership:

1) Seniority or years of experience as an educator should not be the main criterion for promoting site leaders to systems leadership roles. They must have the status, recognition, and skills to positively influence others, at all levels, in the system.

2) Leaders within a system are not automatically system leaders. System leaders need to be carefully selected to ensure they have the relevant skill set and expertise.
3) System leaders need to be thought leaders as well as practical leaders that understand how change is successfully led and managed outside their own context or setting and be able to push the boundaries of professional practice.
4) System leaders need a clear theory of action and the ability to refine and extend the practice of others through modelling 'next practice' not simply sharing 'existing or best practice.' They should be able to add value to the system by building the professional capacity, capital, and capability of others, in ways that are tangible and demonstrate a clear impact.

(pp. 401–402)

These qualities exemplify the idea that *being* a systems leader is different from *doing* systems leadership. The first tenet pits tradition against talent. As in many other behemoth institutions such as state and federal governments or the military, "earning your stripes" is ingrained in the fabric of public education, and seniority is held in the highest esteem. This belief has an elder-bias or experience favoritism based on total years on the job. That in and of itself is not a bad thing – dedicated service and longevity are noteworthy attributes. Inside candidates may feel they are *owed* advancement or a hiring manager may think someone is *overdue* a promotion when the person actually hasn't displayed the requisite chops to be successful at next-level leadership. Conversely, there are many other folks who possess a natural disposition for systems thinking and corresponding behaviors and have demonstrated their prowess in a smaller pond – it's clear they are ready to jump into deeper waters no matter their age or tenure. It's not hard to recognize the influencers, shot callers, and those with social capital to steer a larger ship. They may just not look like your conventional conception of a chief executive. And that's a great thing! We need diverse representation in our ranks.

This dovetails with the second tenet that just because one has risen to a district, county, state, or federal role, and maneuvers within it, does not translate automatically to being a game–changing systems leader. Perhaps you've heard of the axiom of "failing upward" or that "mediocrity rises to the top"? Unfortunately, there's a fair amount of accuracy in that. I'm sure we've all scratched our heads in puzzlement over how some clearly less-than-competent people are running departments to the detriment of everyone else. Mitigating liability means providing ample support, holding people accountable and/or reassigning them for underperformance. That alone takes fortitude, but it's not enough to separate the wheat from the chaff. Highly functioning organizations require a vetting process focused on recognizing competencies and qualities that propel the system to change. Otherwise, we'll keep on getting what we get (but not what our students deserve).

The third truism pairs the Wonder Twin powers of thought leadership with hands-on action to "push the boundaries of professional practice." Though Gen X readers may immediately get this reference, for everyone else the Wonder Twins are alien brother-and-sister superhero cartoon characters from the late 1970s, named Zan and Jayna, who can, respectively, shape-shift into any form of water or animal when they bump fists. Their catch phrase – "Wonder twin powers, activate!" – was a staple of many childhood make-believe games. All this is to say, thinking is good. But not enough. Action is also good but also not enough if there's lack of forethought behind it. Game–Changing leaders harness their own alongside others' superpowers to push the perimeters of our systems.

The fourth point from Harris et al. suggests that, by broadening our scope, we can realize rippling impacts by modeling 'next practice' rather than relying on the 'best practice' clichés common in our industry. Knowing past practice, understanding existing practice, and researching better practices are all well and good. But don't stop there. The Higher Education Summit website explains:

> We are all familiar with the term 'best practice': sharing what is working well in one institution so that it might be implemented in another. A 'next practice' is about critically reflecting on how our current practices could work differently,

> more efficiently, more powerfully, thinking about failures, and considering future contexts and scenarios. It is about the process and not the final output.
>
> (no p. #)

By doing so, you are laying the groundwork for those in your circle of influence as well as in the line of succession. Training up those who will step into our places someday builds system-wide capacity and a sustainable legacy. Some of the key qualities embedded in this finding include

- Exhibiting behaviors you want to last
- Controlling less and sharing power more
- Modeling vulnerability in the face of trial and error
- Investing time, energy, and resources for the long term
- Inspiring commitment to the work as opposed to a "cult of personality" individual
- Displaying humility, grace, and service
- Leaving concrete hand-offs to trusted successors

Practical Application

Exercise 5.6 gives you an opportunity to deepen your systems leadership dispositions as you consciously develop your Wonder Twin powers of thinking connected to action to challenge the status quo and lead people from 'best practice' to 'next practice' mindsets and methodologies in your organization. You'll examine ways to help yourself and your team build professional capacity, capital, and capability in tangible and impactful ways. Table 5.7 presents a few examples to spark your own ideas.

Table 5.7 From best practices to next practices

Systems leadership focal area	Best practices research	Promising next practices
Gifted and Talented Education (GATE) placement, scheduling and programming	- Book: *Best Practices in Gifted Education: An Evidence-Based Guide* (2021, 2nd ed.) - Article: "Maximizing the Potential of Twice-Exceptional Learners: Creating a Framework of Stakeholder Supports" (2023)	Select and adapt 10 of 29 suggested best practices (p. 2) for task force review and recommendations that meet the needs of "twice-exceptional" students (who exhibit both exceptional intellectual abilities and significant learning differences or disabilities, such as attention-deficit/hyperactivity disorder, autism, or dyslexia)
Implementation of Literacy for 21st Century Learners systemwide initiative	- Book: *Best Practices in Literacy Instruction* (2023); focus on • Chapter 8: Equitable Literacy Instruction • Chapter 15: Digital Literacy • Chapter 20: Linking Professional Learning, Literacy Coaching and Equity	Conduct a staff-wide book study on three chapters to inform the direction of the site's implementation of the district literacy initiative. Each grade level will adopt one strategy a month with their Professional Learning Community teams and report back at whole staff meetings

(*Continued*)

Table 5.7 (Continued)

Systems leadership focal area	Best practices research	Promising next practices
Design a distributive leadership model at each district school	- Book: *School Effectiveness and School-Based Management* (2022) - Article: "School leaders as change agents: Do principals have the tools they need?" (2020) - PBS Video Series: School Leadership in Action (n.d.)	Create a 10-month apprenticeship series for assistant principals and principals on finance, policy, and site-based management led by central office administrators in each specialty area prior to transitioning fully to a school-based management model

▶ MODULE 5 EXERCISES

This final set of exercises for module 5 is a blend of activities for building and integrating game–changing mental models at an institutional level to generate authentic breakthroughs. The various theoretical frameworks introduced are meant to be not prescriptive but rather demonstrative of ways of being, thinking, and acting in this leadership domain. Navigating systems and leveraging structures result in increased agency. And increased agency leads to confidence, optimism, and possibility, which are the end goals of this set of exercises:

5.1. Systems Thinking Conditioning
5.2. Root-Cause Analysis Fishbone Diagram
5.3. Making the Invisible Visible
5.4. Infrastructure Investigation
5.5. Leveraging Virtuous Cycles
5.6. Empowering Systems Leadership

Exercise 5.1 Systems Thinking Conditioning

With your leadership team, choose one system and some of their corresponding structures under each of the three categories of curricular (anything pertaining to teaching and learning activities), administrative (supervisory, managerial, coordination, or leadership functions), and operational (procedures, logistics, infrastructure, etc.). Then scrutinize one traditional structural element from each area that may be ripe for change and pose some innovative alternatives for consideration.

Mechanism	Structures	System
Curricular		
Administrative		
Operational		
Conventional Practice	**Innovative Alternative**	

© Copyright material from Kim Wallace (2025), Game–Changing Leadership in Action, Routledge.

Exercise 5.2 Root-Cause Analysis Fishbone Diagram

Conducting a root-cause analysis exercise helps teams unfurl the underlying structures contributing to the tensions within their systems. If you purport to serve all students but there is misalignment between words and deeds, inequities will only be exacerbated. Select a system that may be ripe for re-evaluation at your school or central office. Be sure to confirm your assumptions with solid research to ensure that you're on the right track in developing solutions.

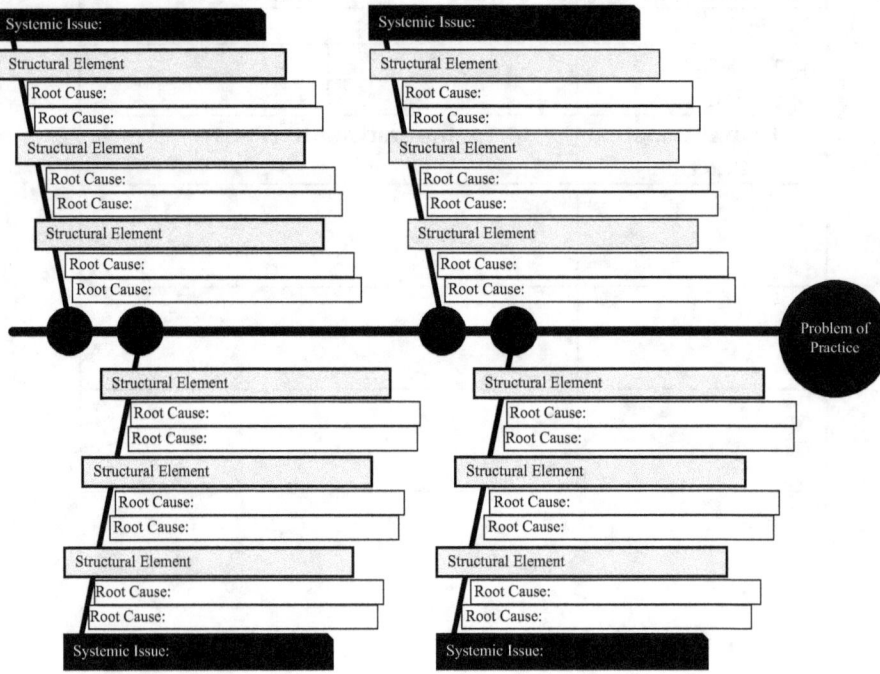

Exercise 5.3 Making the Invisible Visible

In the spirit of the Harwood Institute, game–changing leaders help our systems and structures evolve by exposing invisible or hidden processes to the light of day. In the first part of the exercise, you'll spend time whittling down some key concerns on campus and then picking one to air out through a re-envisioning conversation with stakeholders. Finally, you'll draft a few elevator speech messages that appeal to different groups involved in partnering on solutions.

Infraction	Current consequence	Intervention

Re-envisioning Conversation:
1. What systemic and structural changes may help our school or organization function better?
2. What might we build together in place of what currently exists?
3. Why is this issue this important to our school community?
4. What do we hope to see as a result of these changes? What does success look like?
5. What are some positive ripple effects that may also result from our efforts?
6. What challenges do we anticipate facing by taking on this systemic change? How will we proactively address them?
7. Who and what resources are available and needed to accomplish our shared goals?
8. What are some important first and next steps for us to move our plans forward?

Messaging:
To Students:
To Staff:
To Families:

Exercise 5.4 Infrastructure Investigation

Create a self-assessment to evaluate an existing set of structures associated with a current system you want to reappraise on a scale from 1 (low effectiveness) to 5 (high effectiveness). Feel free to borrow any of the phrasing from Table 5.6 to compose your own criteria or build off of the topics offered in the left column.

System structural elements	Rating scale	Notes/Comments
Resources	1 2 3 4 5	
Training	1 2 3 4 5	
Functionality	1 2 3 4 5	
Customization	1 2 3 4 5	
Compatibility	1 2 3 4 5	
Cost/impact ratio	1 2 3 4 5	
Equitable/unbiased	1 2 3 4 5	
Reliability/Consistency	1 2 3 4 5	
Productive	1 2 3 4 5	
Supportive	1 2 3 4 5	
Responsive to inputs/feedback	1 2 3 4 5	
Alignment to goals	1 2 3 4 5	
Security/Safety	1 2 3 4 5	
Sustainability	1 2 3 4 5	
Total High effectiveness 50–70 Medium effectiveness 30–50 Low effectiveness 29	____/70	

1) Summarize the top three strengths your team has come to consensus on:
   a)
   b)
   c)
2) Based on your responses, what are some unmet needs in the system under evaluation?
3) Check the statement below that describes your situation most accurately:

- ☐ Our current system is working effectively and provides the majority of what we need to support staff, students, and families to meet goals. We are using most of the tools and strategies to a high degree.
- ☐ Our current system is working sufficiently to support staff, students, and families to meet goals. We are using some of the tools and strategies but not everything the system has to offer.
- ☐ Our current system is insufficient in supporting staff, students, and families to meet goals. We don't have access to or training to use the tools in impactful ways.
- ☐ Other: _____

4) As a team, we recommend
   - ☐ Continuing with our current system as is or with a few adjustments.
   - ☐ Continuing with our current system but focusing more on filling identified gaps (additional training, increased use of components, awareness, technical support, etc.)
   - ☐ Investigating a new system that may better meet our school's needs.
   - ☐ Other: _____

© Copyright material from Kim Wallace (2025), Game–Changing Leadership in Action, Routledge.

254 Game–Changing Leadership in Action

Exercise 5.5 Leveraging Virtuous Cycles

Select a system and the discrete structures therein you are interested in exploring for gaps and opportunities. If you don't currently have a system for something you'd like to probe into, you can use this framework to plan out a new project through the virtuous cycle mindset: "a chain of events in which one desirable occurrence leads to another which further promotes the first occurrence and so on resulting in a continuous process of improvement" (Bryant, McKinsey & Co., 2024, p. 9). Then plot out the seven structural levers to employ in your launch.

System Under Consideration: _____
_____

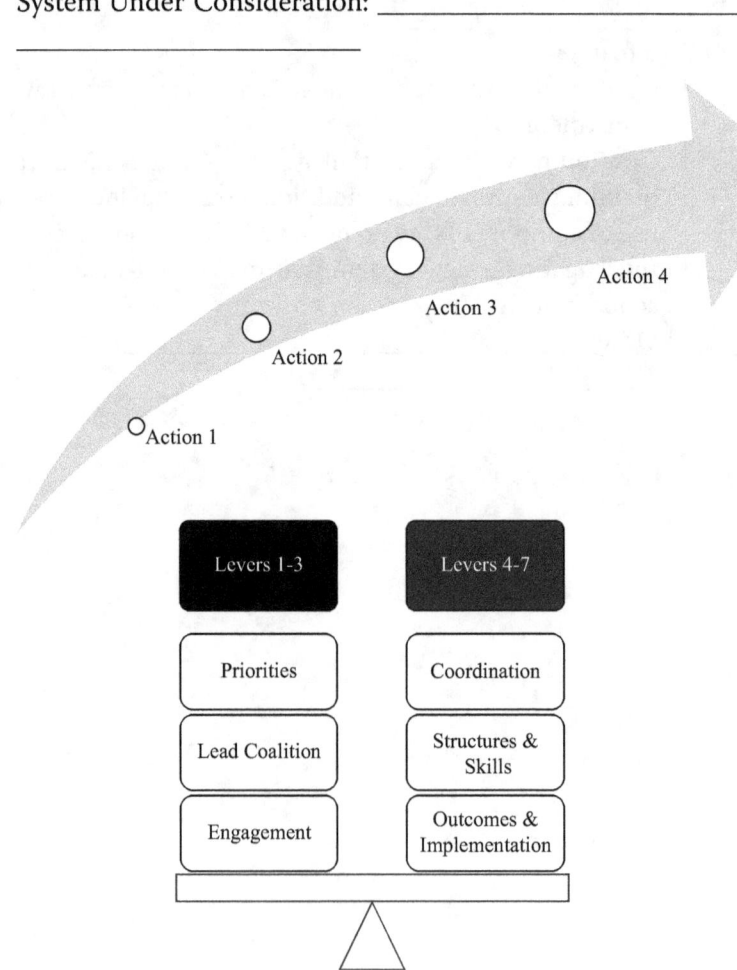

Exercise 5.6 Empowering Systems Leadership

Wonder Twin powers, activate! Taking your game–changing leadership to the next level includes self-education through research, observations, thought partnership, and reflection. Going from best practice to next practice means understanding what works according to the greatest minds in the field and customizing it to fit into your own structures and systems. This action-learning template prompts you to research educational experts' findings around a subject you're interested in, digest the content, and then reframe it to meet the needs of your local context.

Systems leadership focal area	Best practices research	Promising next practices

▶ CONCLUSION

I am a jigsaw puzzle junkie. Opening a fresh box of 1,000 unconnected pieces, figuring out the frame, and discerning the objects to come fill me with eager anticipation. I first separate by color, organize by quadrant, and select images one by one to concentrate on. When I get overwhelmed, bored, or frustrated, I take a break and come back to it with fresh eyes later on. It's astonishing how the one piece you've been searching for suddenly appears like a spotlight shining down on it. I liken this to illuminating the structures in place that stimulate your systems into a fully formed portrayal of the organization. You may not know what the picture is supposed to be. You will get stuck. Forcing odd pieces to fit doesn't work. You will have a-ha's. You will want to quit and throw everything back into the box. You will plug away, unplug, and redouble your efforts. Systems change is playing the long game. And each step, no matter how small it feels, contributes to a manifestation of your game–changing leadership in action.

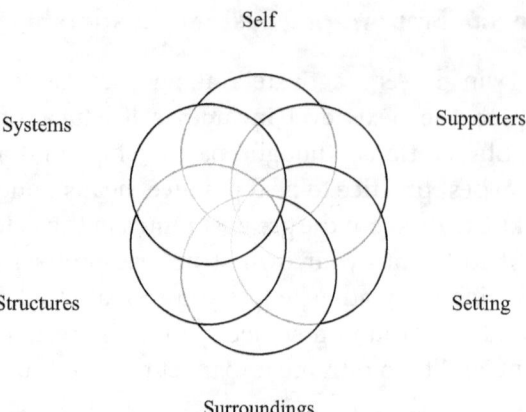

Figure 5.6 Intersectional game–changing leadership zones

The final module to come consolidates the three domains and five modules you've engaged with so far into strategies for sustenance. Though each previous chapter has had a central focus on a particular topic (exploration of self; mobilizing supporters; analysis of setting; awareness of surroundings; leveraging structures and navigating systems), we all know that those categories look more like Figure 5.6 and naturally flow between and within one another. As we finish up our course of study, you will integrate the knowledge, capabilities, and methods you've gained and put them into strategic practice.

▶ NOTES

1. chrome-extension://efaidnbmnnnibpcajpcglclefindmkaj/https://www.isbe.net/documents/25ark.pdf.
2. https://statutes.capitol.texas.gov/?link=ED.
3. chrome-extension://efaidnbmnnnibpcajpcglclefindmkaj/https://marylandpublicschools.org/programs/Documents/Charter-Schools/MD-CODE-Ed-Art-9-101-2024-A.pdf.
4. https://leginfo.legislature.ca.gov/faces/codesTOCSelected.xhtml?tocCode=EDC&tocTitle=+Education+Code+-+EDC.

References

Best Practices in Literacy Instruction. (2023). Editors: *Ernest Morrell, Heather Kenyon Casey, Lesley Mandel Morrow.* New York: Guilford Publications.

Boardman, J.T., Sauser, B.J. (2008) *Systems thinking: Coping with 21st century problems.* Boca Raton, FL: CRC.

Bryant, J., et al., (Feb. 2024) *Spark and sustain: How school systems can improve learning at scale.* Boulder, CO: McKinsey & Company. Accessed on December 16, 2024 from https://www.mckinsey.com/industries/education/our-insights/spark-and-sustain-how-school-systems-can-improve-learning-at-scale

Carraway, J. H., Young, T. (2015). Implementation of a districtwide policy to improve principals' instructional leadership: Principals' sensemaking of the skillful observation and coaching laboratory. *Educational Policy,* 29(1), 230–256.

Cuban, L. (2020). Reforming the grammar of schooling again and again. *American Journal of Education,* 126(4), 665–671. Accessed on December 1, 2024 from https://doi.org/10.1086/709959

Donaldson, M. L., Woulfin, S. (2018). From tinkering to going "rogue": How principals use agency when enacting new teacher evaluation systems. *Educational Evaluation and Policy Analysis,* 40(4), 531–556.

Drier, L., Nabarro, D., Nelson, J. (Sept. 14, 2019). Systems leadership can change the world but what does it mean? Accessed on December 22, 2024 from https://www.weforum.org/stories/2019/09/systems-leadership-can-change-the-world-but-what-does-it-mean/#:~:text=Systems%20leadership%20is%20a%20set,process%20of%20systems%2Dlevel%20change

Ganon-Shilon, S., Schechter, C. (2019). School principals' sense-making of their leadership role during reform implementation. *International Journal of Leadership in Education,* 22(3), 279–300.

Ganon-Shilon, S., Shaked, H., Schechter, C. (2020). Principals' voices pertaining to shared sense-making processes within a generally-outlined pedagogical reform implementation. *International Journal of Leadership in Education,* 22, 1–25.

Greany, T. & Earley, P. (Eds.). (2021). *School leadership and education system reform.* New York: Bloomsbury Publishing.

Gu, Q., Sammons, P., Chen, J. (2018). How principals of successful schools enact education policy: Perceptions and accounts from senior and middle leaders. *Leadership and Policy in Schools,* 17(3), 373–390.

Harris, A., Jones, M. & Hashim, N. (2021). System leaders and system leadership: Exploring the contemporary evidence base. *School Leadership & Management,* 41(4–5), 387–408.

Harwood Institute for Public Innovation. (2023). Making the invisible visible tool. Accessed on December 15, 2024 from https://static1.squarespace.com/static/5602cde4e4b04430b90a97fd/t/654e3f14fcff9136b688036c/1699626772153/Making+the+Invisible+Visible+-Tool+.pdf

Karash, R. (n.d.). How to see "structure" Innovation Associates, Inc., Arthur D. Little Company. Accessed on December 14, 2024 from https://thesystemsthinker.com/how-to-see-structure/

Ketikidou, G. & Saiti, A. (2022). The promotion of inclusive education through sustainable and systemic leadership. *International Journal of Leadership in Education,* 1–16. https://doi.org/10.1080/13603124.2022.2032368

Kraft, M.A. & Gilmour, A.F. (2017). Revisiting the widget effect: Teacher evaluation reforms and the distribution of teacher effectiveness. *Educational Researcher,* 46(5), 234–249.

Langford, D. P. (2015). *Tool time for education: Choosing and implementing quality improvement tools.* Molt, MT: Langford International, Inc. Accessed on December 22, 2024 from https://deming.org/the-power-of-pdsa-in-education/

Leach, T. (2024). System reform: The ever-elusive quest – an Australian study of how system middle leaders' role enactment influences the attainment of policy coherence. *Education Sciences,* 14(6), 596. https://doi.org/10.3390/educsci14060596

LeChasseur, K., Donaldson, M., Fernandez, E., Femc-Bagwell, M. (2018). Brokering, buffering, and the rationalities of principal work. *Journal of Educational Administration,* 56(3), 262–276.

Manno, B.V. (Dec. 10, 2024). A virtuous cycle of career education for young people. *Forbes.* Accessed on December 16, 2024 from https://www.forbes.com/sites/brunomanno/2024/12/10/a-virtuous-cycle-of-career-education-for-young-people/

Marsh, J. A., Bush-Mecenas, S., Strunk, K. O., Lincove, J. A. & Huguet, A. (2017). Evaluating teachers in the big easy: How organizational context shapes policy responses in New Orleans. *Educational Evaluation and Policy Analysis*, 39(4), 539–570.

Meyer, M. S., Shen, Y. & Plucker, J. A. (2024). Reducing excellence gaps: A systematic review of research on equity in advanced education. *Review of Educational Research*, 94(1), 33–72. https://doi.org/10.3102/00346543221148461

Monat, J. P. & Gannon, T. F. (2023). The meaning of "structure" in systems thinking. *Systems*, *11*(2), 92. https://doi.org/10.3390/systems11020092

Moving from best practices to next practices. (n.d.). Accessed on December 22, 2024 from https://www.higher-education-summit.com/next-practices

Plucker, J. A., Glynn, J., Healey, G. & Dettmer, A. (2018). *Equal talents, unequal opportunities: A report card on state support for academically talented low-income students.* (2nd ed.) Lansdowne, VA: Jack Kent Cooke Foundation.

Plucker, J. A. & Peters, S. J. (2018). Closing poverty-based excellence gaps: Conceptual, measurement, and educational issues. *Gifted Child Quarterly*. 62(1), 56–67. https://doi.org/10.1177/0016986217738566

Plucker, Jonathan, Peters, Scott & Schmalensee, Stephanie. (2017). Reducing Excellence Gaps: A Research-Based Model. *Gifted Child Today*, *40*, 245–250. https://doi.org/10.1177/1076217517723949

School Leadership in Action. (n.d.). PBS Learning Media. Accessed on March 21, 2025 from https://thinktv.pbslearningmedia.org/collection/leadership-in-action/

Shaked, H. & Schechter, C. (2020). Systems thinking leadership: New explorations for school improvement. *Management in Education*, 34(3), 107–114. https://doi.org/10.1177/0892020620907327

Speirs Neumeister, K. L. (2023). Maximizing the potential of twice-exceptional learners: Creating a framework of stakeholder supports. *Gifted Child Quarterly*, 68(1), 19–33. https://doi.org/10.1177/00169862231193699 (Original work published 2024).

Treseder, W. (July 4, 2017). One man created the education system holding you back. *Medium*. Accessed on December 22, 2024 from: https://medium.com/the-mission/one-man-created-the-education-system-holding-you-back-c50c39496023

Virtuous Cycle. (n.d.). Definition. Merriam-Webster online dictionary. Accessed on December 16, 2024 from https://www.merriam-webster.com/dictionary/virtuous%20circle

Wang, T., Olivier, D. F. & Chen, P. (2020). Creating individual and organizational readiness for change: Conceptualization of system readiness for change in school education. *International Journal of Leadership in Education*, 26(6), 1037–1061. https://doi.org/10.1080/13603124.2020.1818131

Yurkofsky, M. (2022). From compliance to improvement: How school leaders make sense of institutional and technical demands when implementing a continuous improvement process. *Educational Administration Quarterly*, 58(2), 300–346. https://doi.org/10.1177/0013161X211053597

Conclusion

Strategies for Sustenance

▶ INTRODUCTION

The closing chapter of the game–changers framework blends the three domains and six modules into a comprehensive leadership strategy to sustain your longevity. The word sustenance is used intentionally to indicate the need to feed, nourish, and provide a source of strength to leaders in the field physically, mentally, and emotionally. We are people first, leaders second. But we operate on so many levels simultaneously that it's hard to tease out whether the interpersonal, environmental, or institutional realms dominate a space and need your immediate attention. Truthfully, it's likely all of them do to some degree, which is why we all need help along the way. Since we've covered each topic – exploration of self, mobilizing support, analysis of setting, awareness of surroundings, leveraging structures, and navigating systems – in depth already, we'll close with a few final ingredients to add to your personalized recipe for game–changing leadership.

To get started, let's take a look at what it means to be both a giver and receiver of support. Having developed a good sense of yourself throughout this series, it won't be a stretch for you to recognize that just because you like something doesn't mean everyone else enjoys it, too. When it comes to support, some people want a shoulder to cry on, others a venting session, and others still, coaching or consultancy. Assuming that a hug is welcomed, advice is warranted, or knowledge is desired can turn what you think is a supportive condition into just the opposite. Box 6.1 lists a number of different ways to customize your approach based on what you and the other person need. If you don't know, just ask.

Early into my superintendency, I joined a cohort of six other women superintendents in the area. Each month, we met at one of our district offices for a half day under the auspices of following an agenda prepared by the organization sponsoring us. Early into each meeting, the agenda was all but abandoned as we riffed on our particular challenges, told stories, and offered advice or support. After the formal relationship concluded, we decided to keep meeting on our own, both socially and professionally. Now almost a decade later, even with half of us no longer in the position, our text chain is going strong, and we meet as much as we can, now lasting friends and chosen family for life.

BOX 6.1 SUPPORTIVE OUTREACH

- Display empathy and kindness
- Help others work as a team
- Model and encourage vulnerability
- Reach out, check in, touch base
- Authentically listen
- Provide (solicited) advice
- Reframe/contextualize problems
- Refrain from judgment
- Ask open-ended questions
- Celebrate incremental wins
- Acknowledge barriers/obstacles
- Recognize, appreciate, and celebrate
- Respect boundaries (stay in your lane)
- Recognize their challenges
- Be available to answer questions
- Prioritize together
- Coach, consult, mentor
- Simply ask – how can I help?
- Connect them to resources
- Give them your full attention
- Redirect (if off track)
- Mirror and identify emotions

Practical Application

After noting what types of support that you personally respond to best, you'll be asked in Exercise C.1 to identify a variety of folks who can serve different purposes in your cadre of confidantes. Keep an open mind and you may even add some unlikely allies into the mix.

▶ CARE AND FEEDING

Self-care is important. Yet educators are notoriously bad at it. The systems we work under may advocate health and wellness in words while not so much in practice. We know that taking even one day off equals at least two days of catch up, so it doesn't always feel worth it to rest or take a break. However, burnout is a real possibility if you don't find ways to restore your personal equilibrium. Amanda McKay, Katrina MacDonald, and Fiona Longmuir (2022), in a study on the emotional intensity of educational leadership, explain:

> Principals are experiencing emotionally intense work both at an individual level, and collectively across the principalship. This is not an issue faced only by a small number of individuals. However, the proffered solutions often responsibilize principals themselves, expecting them to address or manage their own care and health rather than attending to the systems and practices that no longer work. There are direct consequences of the lack of understanding of the emotional intensity of principals' work.
>
> (pp. 1–2)

This is otherwise known as emotional labor. When compounded by the physical labor of being on site for upwards of 10 to 12 hours a day, constant high-alert activity paired with prolonged periods at one's desk, and the lack of proper nutrition that comes with the territory, it's grueling work. And, yes, it appears to be incumbent upon the leader to manage it all without showing a crack in the façade. Not fair, but factual.

The crack in my own wall materialized in early 2020 after serving three years as assistant superintendent of instruction and another three as superintendent in the same district. The more strained I felt, the more I thought that "more" was the answer. If I could just stay longer at work, if I could just go to one more event, if I could just please everyone, if I could solve all of the problems… yet the more I tried, the less effective I became. No longer were people calling me a 'breath of fresh air' as they once had, and I felt like I could barely breathe myself. At the beginning of March that year, I informed my school board that I didn't want my contract renewed. Two weeks later, the pandemic hit. There's a lot more to that story, but I'll leave the rest up to your imagination and just share the ending: it took a long time to resurface and recover my spirit, but I got myself back.

I'm sure there are similar tales out there, as corroborated by the data regarding superintendent turnover in the U.S. in a *District Administration* brief by Micah Ward (January 9, 2024):

> Between 2019-20 and 2023-24, more than 40% of districts witnessed one superintendent departure, according to data visualizations created by Rachel White, founder/PI of The Superintendent Lab. Some 7.9% of districts had two superintendents leave and 1.5% saw three or more depart. Overall, more than half of districts across 37 states had at least one superintendent departure since 2019-20.
>
> (no p. #)

That's a lot of folks leaving unnecessary years of service still on the table.

A piece (2021) aptly titled "Burning Passion, Burning Out," by Marcus Horwood, Herbert W. Marsh, Philip D. Parker, Philip Riley, Jiesi Guol, and Theresa Dicke, sheds light on the dual reality of being a devoted servant leader.

> Paradoxically, school leaders as a group report high levels of burnout but also high job satisfaction and passion for their work. School principals are passionate about their job, but this passion can be a double-edged sword leading to good (job satisfaction) and bad (burnout) outcomes.
>
> (p. 1668)

They distinguish between the harmoniously passionate leader who is in "control of the activity and is free to choose when to engage or disengage with the activity, so it does not conflict with other aspects of their life (e.g., relationships with friends and family)" and the obsessively passionate individual "contingently motivated to pursue an activity to gain valued outcomes, such as tangible reward, social acceptance, or self-esteem. This manifestation of passion can have destructive effects on the individual, how they perform the activity itself, and other life domains" (p. 1670). This is reminiscent of Module 1 regarding intrinsic and extrinsic motivators. Once you've crossed firmly into the camp of external incentives, marked by a notedly absent sense of joy, it's time to reassess.

Stressor and Stress Management

It's a tragedy for everyone when a formerly exuberant and energetic leader bites the dust. An ounce of prevention might be found through fortifying leaders' stressor management (changing exposure) or stress management (coping with exposure) (Allison, 1997). Changing exposure is a little trickier because just going to work each day automatically exposes leaders to a host of challenges. Responding to those urgencies, however, is up to the leader. *Will I pause and take a deep breath, will I seek counsel, will I invite others in to problem-solve, will I take one small step instead of leaping in*? All of these mental decision-making moments offer options, which naturally release the pressure valve a notch or two. Sebrina L. Doyle Fosco's (2022) piece on educational leader well-being contends that

> Attending to the health of educational leaders is vital, especially for those with more experience. While one can argue about how stress affects emotional health, physical health checks can be more straightforward. Stress has cumulative effects on the body; as much as it can be okay in the short run, in the long run, it can be damaging. Attending to health behaviors such as sleeping, exercising, and eating can support wellbeing.
>
> (p. 11)

Fosco cites eight key domains that contribute to long-term site or district administrator success: accomplishment, health, spirituality, autonomy, emotions, engagement, relationships, and meaning and purpose (p. 9). In short, these are the things that, research has found, keep us going. While a few are tangible, most of them are more ethereal. I've cooked up my own list of fifteen fundamentals for working through your tenure on the job melding the interpersonal, environment, and institutional domains:

1. **Go slow to go fast**. When in a new role, don't change anything for at least six months unless there is a groundswell of voices asking for intervention or there are dangerous conditions demanding it. It's enough change to merely have a new person at the helm. Let that reality settle in for a bit.
2. **Be patient with yourself**. There's a big learning curve ahead. You cannot and will not know everything you need to know from the get-go. Set a personal goal that your first days, weeks, and months will be mostly as a learner to help you (and others) manage expectations.
3. **Focus on small wins**. Very few grand moments or accolades are awaiting you in the educational leadership wings. The true rewards are found in the daily satisfaction of helping a struggling student, lending a hand to your office staff, or receiving a message of gratitude from a parent. Small things add up big. Capture them and hold them dear.
4. **Learn the lay of the land**. Explore every inch of your new setting. Become familiar with the subcultures, the territories, and the hotspots to formulate a better understanding of how things work and the ways people interact within their terrain.
5. **Figure out who the influencers are**. It won't be hard; they're the folks whom everyone quiets down to listen to in a staff meeting, the ones who act as spokesperson, those who nudge certain decisions. Don't make the mistake of thinking that titles matter. Influencers can be the school secretary, custodian, or crossing guard. Power is merely a mental construct that plays out in physical spaces.

6. **Build relationships equitably**. This one can be in direct opposition to what the influencers in the item prior want to see happen. But paying attention to the loudest voices will only limit your own ability to eventually make large-scale changes when the time comes. The power brokers do need and often command attention, so ignoring them is ill advised. However, that doesn't mean you allow them disproportionate engagement opportunities. Others are watching and will appreciate your spreading out your time and focus in a balanced manner, sending a message that you are fair, consistent, dependable, and not easily swayed.
7. **Communicate clearly, in multiple ways, and check for understanding**. Yes, there are some who still don't read and respond to email. Even worse, there are those who purposely or inadvertently contribute to rumors and misinformation. It's imperative that you find every conceivable way to get your messages out: email, newsletter, one-on-one conversations, meetings, input sessions, videos, websites, and so on. Use all of them. As much as humanly possible.
8. **Be present, visible, and active**. The work piling up on your desk is important. So is sitting with kids at lunchtime, attending performances, visiting classrooms, frequenting parent events, and managing parking lot duty. Organize your day to maximize the time you have on the right priorities. Carve out time for emails, paperwork, and other independent activities before and after the hustle and bustle of the school day. You are an important figure on site, and seeing you in action goes a long way toward building rapport.
9. **Get a coach or mentor**. Bouncing ideas off and problem-solving with peers or experts in the field make leadership seem a lot less isolating. It's morale-boosting to confirm that "no, you're not crazy"; "yes, this is super hard"; and "I've been there before, and you will get through this too." And you'll be able to pay it forward for others later in your career.
10. **Model humility**. You will make mistakes or execute poor judgment at times. One of my favorite mentors said

to me early on in my first principalship when I was lamenting over an error I made: "Kim, I wouldn't have been to work if I hadn't made a mistake by the end of the day," and laughed as she proclaimed it. That changed my whole perspective. She taught me the importance of apologizing after making a mistake, owning it, and finding a way to correct it. And then to move on!

11. **Be decisive**. Decision-making in a vacuum is rarely a clever idea. The best decisions are arrived at in collaboration, communication, and consultation with those involved in the process or hoped-for outcome. Take in ample input before issuing a final decision. But once a decision is made, stick to it. Going back on it will teach people that making a fuss gets results and push that call button every time thereafter.

12. **Don't do it all yourself**. Everyone on campus or in your department has a job to do. New leaders often forget to let go of the work they used to do in the previous position while tacking on additional duties. Delegate tasks appropriately and refrain from micromanaging. Being a strong project manager and a people supervisor and satisfaction in a job well done will be mutually shared.

13. **Make Meetings Meaningful**. This triple-M cannot be overemphasized. We have all been in countless hours of meeting purgatory over the years that were a waste of time and only served to diminish morale. I tend to go by the 3Rs to ensure that all meetings make sense: rigor, relevance, and relationships. Tend to each of these in your agenda planning and you will have a happier and more productive staff in the end game.

14. **Monitor Morale**. Both your own and those whom you serve. Educating can be exhausting. For kids, parents, teachers, supporters, and leaders. There are some predictable ebbs and flows through the school year when energy is high or low. You can probably intuitively name those months. When you notice flagging momentum, spirit, or stamina, recognitions, celebrations, and fun go a long way to boost morale. Put yourself at the center of it, too. Sit on the dunking booth platform, bring in the

petting zoo during finals week, or surprise your community with a special event. Laughter is cost-free stress release.

15. **TAKE CARE OF YOURSELF.** All caps for a reason. We need to stop taking pride in being burned out, impossibly busy, and overburdened. It's a tiring old trope and the sad part is, we're all replaceable. I vividly remember one of my professors in grad school telling me, "If you continue on at this pace and intensity, someone is going to find you dead at your desk – and you do no good to anyone being dead." That was a bit of a rude wake-up call, but I needed to hear it. So, eat, hydrate, take breaks, breathe, and leave work at work as much as you can manage. Compromising your personal well-being is off the table if you want to flourish.

Practical Application

In Exercise C.2, you'll consider the fifteen fundamentals and identify where you might incorporate some of this advice into your own work life. It truly takes practice to embrace and embed sustaining ways of being, especially when they often run counter to how others want us to be. But as the saying goes, we teach people how we want them to treat us. So don't be a martyr for the cause. We need you alive and well for the long run.

▶ GAME-CHANGING LEADERSHIP IN ACTION

This final bit explicitly fits all of the modules as one under the umbrella of strategy. Strategic planning is common to many entities from large corporations to nonprofit organizations to educational institutions. The "five year plan," "theory of change model," "objectives and key results (OKRs)," "balanced scorecard," and so on are various methods of analytical approaches. I love a good plan! I'm neutral on which is the best, for the best option is the one you will actually use and consistently apply in your leadership setting. I am against, however, doing tons of work for naught. Too often, dollars, energy, and time are committed on the front end only to have the resulting product lay dormant on your website or in a 4-inch binder on the bookshelf. If you stick around long enough, you can play a pretty decent game of Jenga with the multiple volumes and iterations generated over decades. So, what are our alternatives?

Adopting a tried-and-true research-based strategy is one option. Nothing wrong with that. But being willing to push the boundaries into game–changing territory requires greater speculation and prognostication. Berkeley School of Business (formerly known as Haas) scholars Paul J. H. Schoemaker, Sohvi Heaton, and David Teece published an article (2018) in which they borrowed a concept from the U.S. Military Academy called VUCA (volatility, uncertainty, complexity, and ambiguity) (Whiteman, 1998) to explain conditions that business leaders may encounter in unpredictable dynamically shifting markets. They explain:

> Few managers in business, public administration, education, and so on deal with VUCA environments daily, and neither does the military – except during times of combat and other crisis situations. But top managers must take a longer view that includes VUCA awareness, or else they may not be prepared when surprising events call for change. Leaders who came of age during more stable times may struggle with how to handle the turbulent or unpredictable markets in our digital age. They will likely cling to extrapolative planning, which limits their line of sight to linear projections emanating from standard planning and budgeting systems. They may continue to manage for risk (quantifiable) when they should manage for deep uncertainty (unfathomable).
>
> (p. 16)

Covid-19 is the perfect example of such unfathomable historical times worldwide. It put almost every institution back on its heels, trying to figure out how to function or even persist under catastrophic conditions. It was truly an existential crisis for the educational system, which had a snowball effect (or rather avalanche) on the rest of business-as-usual operations. We weren't prepared. Will we be next time? There is no failsafe way to predict the future, but we can take into consideration the triad of people, places, and things in our midst and try to leave no stone unturned. What follows in Box 6.2 includes the five module topics you've engaged with throughout this learning series along with prompts that encourage foresight and projection:

> ### BOX 6.2 STRATEGIC PLANNING PROMPTS
>
> 1) Self
>   a) What do I need to learn about or research in more depth? What new skills or capacities do I need to develop?
>   b) What leadership dispositions, mindsets, and actions do I need to model for others?
> 2) Supporters
>   a) Who might serve as contributors who represent diverse and divergent perspectives?
>   b) Who should be invited to participate on strategic evaluation or implementation teams?
> 3) Setting
>   a) What specific strategies might we employ to gather more intel about our campus/workspace experiences from multiple points of view?
>   b) What elements of our setting feel counterproductive or archaic?
> 4) Surroundings
>   a) Which parts of the community may need mapping or exploration to enhance our understanding? What community resources or partnerships can we tap into?
>   b) What existing and emerging social, political, or local dynamics do we need to be keenly aware of?
> 5) Structures & Systems
>   a) How will we identify, leverage and/or reconstitute operational, functional, or architectural elements to meet future needs?
>   b) Which structures are upholding the status quo to the detriment of those we serve?
> 6) Systems
>   a) Which rules, customs, traditions, or practices in the school, department, or district directly support our goals?
>   b) What systemic changes are needed to align our mission with our practices?

To do this well, you must simply define your reason for being and use that as your filter for developing strategy. For example, if we say that our number one mission is for "all learners to be equipped for college and career readiness," make that the benchmark to meet. If your vision says that we want to "create citizens of the world," everything you do must serve that purpose. Let's take a look at how this might manifest in Box 6.3 for a leader in a hypothetical district.

Practical Application

Starting with your school or district mission or vision statement and breaking it down into the most critical pieces if it's your quintessential everything-but-the-kitchen-sink varietal,

---

BOX 6.3   STRATEGIC APPLICATION

District Mission Statement: *To provide culturally and linguistically diverse learners with equitable access to cohesive learning opportunities.*
Domain 1: Personal/Interpersonal
   a) I need to research and learn more about each of the racial, cultural, and linguistic groups' backgrounds enrolled in my school.
   b) I need to model open mindedness, acceptance, and a spirit of inclusion in all of my communications, interactions, and involvement with the school community.
   c) I need to identify influential people from diverse populations that are willing to serve as thought partners, cultural brokers, and leaders on the strategic planning team.
Domain 2: Setting/Surroundings
   a) We need to reach out to and attend events and activities that are important to people in the surrounding areas.
   b) We need to ensure that the physical environment respects, values, and is reflective of all groups on campus equitably.
Domain 3: Structures/Systems
   a) We need to assess the curricular pathways and course progression and remove any barriers that prevent English learners from reaching optimal outcomes.
   b) We need to focus on multilingualism as a core value and align all structures accordingly.

Exercise C.3 is designed to get your game–changing leadership juices flowing.

Parting Words

To conclude this segment, I'll leave you with one of my favorite quotes. It's from President Teddy Roosevelt's April 23, 1910 speech at the Sorbonne, Paris:

> It is not the critic who counts; not the man who points out how the strong man stumbles, or where the doer of deeds could have done them better. The credit belongs to the man who is actually in the arena, whose face is marred by dust and sweat and blood; who strives valiantly; who errs, who comes short again and again, because there is no effort without error and shortcoming; but who does actually strive to do the deeds; who knows great enthusiasms, the great devotions; who spends himself in a worthy cause; who at the best knows in the end the triumph of high achievement, and who at the worst, if he fails, at least fails while daring greatly, so that his place shall never be with those cold and timid souls who neither know victory nor defeat.

Practical Application

Channeling the spirit of Roosevelt and embodying the four findings in the systems leadership report, exercise 5.6 encourages you to write your own theme or thesis statement about who you are "in the arena" and why. Here's mine:

> As a game–changing systems leader, I believe that the greatest power we can harness to elevate both individuals and our society is a laser-focused commitment to a high-quality education for every single one of us, at all ages and life stages. I am also certain that we collectively already possess the limitless and requisite intellect, talent, drive, passion, and creativity needed to help our institutions better reflect the 21st-century realities within which especially our most marginalized students can flourish. I'm here to dislodge

outdated mindsets about what public education is (and has been) as the only way forward and then align action to intention, changing our systems from the inside out.

▶ CONCLUDING EXERCISES

These exercises concern maintaining your health and well-being as a site or systems leader and integrating your learning into a game–changing performance out on the field. It's about melding mindsets, behaviors, and stances that illustrate your values, purpose, and aims. While you may have interests, a calling, or passion that differs from others around you, that's good. We need leaders in all niches of our educational ecosystem to mosaically constitute the whole. Drawing upon the activities from earlier material, apply your acquired knowledge to these closing exercises:

C.1 Roll Call
C.2 Fifteen Fundamentals
C.3 Game–Changing Leadership in Action
C.4 In the Arena

Exercise C.1 Roll Call

Let's start by taking inventory. Looking back at the distinct types of support and adding your own ideas to the list, write down some approaches that make you feel most cared for or relieved when under stress or anxious about a workplace situation. Consider sharing it with your frequently tapped resources identified in the next part of the exercise. Pick any of the sentence frames that speak to you and complete them with your own responses.

1) Someone I know, work with, and look up to is [name]: _____. They [said/did] _____ [to/for] me in a moment of need, and I keep [these words/actions] _____ at the forefront when I'm struggling.
2) The most impactful [author/researcher/scholar] I've come across in my studies on educational leadership [is/are]: _____. These are the key learnings I lean on regularly: _____.
3) A time when I received unexpected or unwarranted feedback that actually turned out to be sage advice came from _____. When they told me _____ _____, I took it to heart and changed my [behavior/actions/perspective] by _____ _____.
4) Students can be a major source of support or inspiration as well. I will always remember [name] _____ from [point in career] because _____.
5) Someone who thanked me or showed me appreciation at work recently was [name] _____ for _____.
6) Another person who leads very differently than I do has these assets that I admire: _____ _____. I will intentionally see how I can adopt some of those traits into my own leadership repertoire.

© Copyright material from Kim Wallace (2025), Game–Changing Leadership in Action, Routledge.

Exercise C.2 Fifteen Fundamentals

Review the items from the Fifteen Fundamentals to set yourself some goals for the near future to sustain your potential for leadership longevity.

List the number of the items that you have a natural tendency or affinity towards	List the number of the items that you find difficult or have yet to develop a strategy for	Which ones might you want to try out or establish as a long-term leadership practice?

© Copyright material from Kim Wallace (2025), Game–Changing Leadership in Action, Routledge.

Exercise C.3 Game-Changing Leadership in Action

You may want to begin with your district or school mission statement, select an overarching goal you've established for the year, or pick a large-scale implementation you're embarking on. What matters most is that it matters. To you and to your school community. Write down the key elements and expected outcomes and then what you and your team need to strategically put in place regarding game–changing actions that make an impact.

Mission/Value/Goal Statement: _____
_____
_____

Domain 1: Personal/Interpersonal
    a) I need to
    b) I need to

Domain 2: Setting/Surroundings
    a) We need to
    b) We need to

Domain 3: Structures/Systems
    a) We need to
    b) We need to

Exercise C.4 In the Arena

Much like the material you engaged with in Module 1, this is an opportunity to remind yourself who you are when you need re-energizing, inspiration, or a tune-up. Compose your own version, copy it down onto a large index card or sticky note, and put it in your desk drawer, attach it to your computer monitor, or stash it in some other place you will come across it to remind you who you are, where you came from, and where you want to go as a game–changing systems leader. The sentence starters below are merely suggestions – feel free to add your own statements or adjust these as you see fit to uplift you when you need a boost.

As a game–changing leader…

- *I am*
- *I come from*
- *I know I am here right now to*
- *I feel passionate about*
- *I am preparing for*
- *I am championing*
- *I want to*
- *I will persist until*
- *I am uniquely qualified to*
- *I envision*

▶ CONCLUSION

Domains: 3. Modules: 5. Exercises: 32. Learning Opportunities: limitless. You've not only passed "Go" on the gameboard, but you're more than on your way to accomplishing the incredible feat of mastering leadership game play. Recalling the various definitions of game–changers in the introduction, reflect on how you've stretched and grown into those uncomfortable spaces that make you different today from when you picked up this personalized learning series. As we move into the next three quarters of the 21st century, your game–changing leadership is going to be what alters the trajectory of our education system for generations to come. While the road will be anything but smooth, you are paving the way for a future of hope and possibility for all of us. Roll those dice, and let's go!

References

Allison, D. G. (1997). Coping with stress in the principalship. *Journal of Educational Administration*, 35(1), 39–55. https://doi.org/10.1108/09578239710156971

Fosco, S. L. D. (2022). Educational leader wellbeing: A systematic review. *Educational Research Review*, 37, 100487. Accessed on December 30, 2024 from https://doi.org/10.1016/j.edurev.2022.100487

Horwood, M., Marsh, H. W., Parker, P. D., Riley, P., Guo, J. & Dicke, T. (2021). Burning passion, burning out: The passionate school principal, burnout, job satisfaction, and extending the dualistic model of passion. *Journal of Educational Psychology*, 113(8), 1668–1688. https://doi.org/10.1037/edu0000664

McKay, A., MacDonald, K. & Longmuir, F. (2022). The emotional intensity of educational leadership: a scoping review. *International Journal of Leadership in Education*, 1–23. https://doi.org/10.1080/13603124.2022.2042856

Roosevelt, T. (April 23, 1910). *Speech at the Sorbonne*, Paris. Accessed on December 22, 2024 from https://www.trcp.org/2011/01/18/it-is-not-the-critic-who-counts/

Schoemaker, P. J. H., Heaton, S. & Teece, D. (2018). Innovation, dynamic capabilities, and leadership. *California Management Review*, 61(1), 15–42. https://doi.org/10.1177/0008125618790246

Ward, M. (January 9, 2024). What the data says about superintendent turnover in 2023-24. *District Administration*. Accessed on December 30, 2024 from https://districtadministration.com/briefing/what-the-data-says-about-superintendent-turnover-in-2023-24/

Whiteman, W. E. (1998). *Training and educating army officers for the 21st century: Implications for the United States Military Academy*. Fort Belvoir, VA: Defense Technical Information Center.

For Product Safety Concerns and Information please contact our EU representative GPSR@taylorandfrancis.com
Taylor & Francis Verlag GmbH, Kaufingerstraße 24, 80331 München, Germany